Federalism and Constitutional Law: The Italian Contribution to Comparative Regionalism

This volume examines the relationship between central government and local institutions, taking Italy as a case study to present a comparative perspective on how the Italian experience has influenced the global developments of federal and regional states.

As the country with the longest standing regional system, Italy has a lot to tell countries that are dealing with similar issues in present times. Adopting a theoretical/analytical approach coupled with comparative analysis, this volume critically reflects on the changes brought to the Italian system of government by the reform of Title V of the Italian constitution, the reasons why further decentralisation has been resisted and offers a comparative overview of the place and contributions that the Italian experience has brought to the global debate on regionalism and federalism. The book is divided into two parts: Part I distils the essence of the evolution of Italian regionalism and the respective debate before and after 2001. While focusing on Italy, the various chapters situate it within the global framework of discussion. Part II reflects on how the Italian regional constitutional architecture contributes to the global debate, particularly focusing on the main innovations brought about by constitutional reform.

The book will be essential reading for researchers, academics and policy-makers working in the areas of constitutional law and politics, and federalism.

Erika Arban is Postdoctoral Fellow at Melbourne Law School, Laureate Program in Comparative Constitutional Law, and Lecturer in Comparative Federalism at the University of Antwerp.

Giuseppe Martinico is Professor of Comparative Public Law at the Sant'Anna School of Advanced Studies, Pisa.

Francesco Palermo is Professor of Comparative Constitutional Law at the University of Verona and Director of the Institute for Comparative Federalism at Eurac Research in Bolzano/Bozen.

Federalism and Constitutional Law

The Italian Contribution to Comparative Regionalism

Edited by
Erika Arban, Giuseppe Martinico, and Francesco Palermo

Routledge
Taylor & Francis Group
LONDON AND NEW YORK

First published 2021
by Routledge
2 Park Square, Milton Park, Abingdon, Oxon OX14 4RN

and by Routledge
605 Third Avenue, New York, NY 10158

Routledge is an imprint of the Taylor & Francis Group, an informa business

British Library Cataloguing-in-Publication Data
A catalogue record for this book is available from the British Library

Library of Congress Cataloging-in-Publication Data
Names: Arban, Erika, editor, author. | Martinico, Giuseppe, editor, author. | Palermo, Francesco, editor, author.
Title: Federalism and constitutional law : the Italian contribution to comparative regionalism / edited by Erika Arban, Giuseppe Martinico, Francesco Palermo.
Description: Milton Park, Abingdon, Oxon ; New York, NY : Routledge, 2021. | Includes bibliographical references and index.
Identifiers: LCCN 2020052756 (print) | LCCN 2020052757 (ebook) | ISBN 9780367611705 (hardback) | ISBN 9781003104469 (ebook)
Subjects: LCSH: Federal government–Italy. | Constitutional law–Italy. | Regionalism–Italy.
Classification: LCC KKH2373 .F433 2021 (print) | LCC KKH2373 (ebook) | DDC 342.45/042–dc23
LC record available at https://lccn.loc.gov/2020052756
LC ebook record available at https://lccn.loc.gov/2020052757

ISBN: 978-0-367-61170-5 (hbk)
ISBN: 978-0-367-61173-6 (pbk)
ISBN: 978-1-003-10446-9 (ebk)

DOI: 10.4324/9781003104469

Typeset in Galliard
by Taylor & Francis Books

Contents

Contributors

Editors

Erika Arban is Postdoctoral Fellow at Melbourne Law School, Laureate Program in Comparative Constitutional Law, and Lecturer in Comparative Federalism at the University of Antwerp. She is co-editor of the blog of the International Association of Constitutional Law (IACL) and the co-convenor of the IACL research group New Frontiers of Federalism. Before joining the Melbourne Law School, Erika lectured in public law at the University of Ottawa.

Giuseppe Martinico is Professor of Comparative Public Law at the Sant'Anna School of Advanced Studies, Pisa. Prior to joining the Sant'Anna School of Advanced Studies he was García Pelayo Fellow at the Centro de Estudios Políticos y Constitucionales (CEPC), Madrid, and Max Weber Fellow at the European University Institute, Florence.

Francesco Palermo is Professor for Comparative Constitutional Law in the University of Verona, and Director of the Institute for Comparative Federalism at Eurac Research in Bolzano/Bozen. He worked for the OSCE High Commissioner on National Minorities and was member and president of the Council of Europe's Advisory Committee on the Framework Convention for the Protection of National Minorities. From 2013 to 2018 he has served as a non-party member of the Italian Senate. Member of the Scientific Committee of the Fundamental Rights Agency of the EU for the term 2018–2023 and Constitutional Adviser to the Council of Europe's Congress of Local and regional Autonomies since 2019, author of over 300 publications, including 11 monographs and 31 edited volumes.

Authors

Antonia Baraggia is Assistant Professor of Comparative Public Law at the University of Milan in the Department of Italian and Supranational Public Law. She serves as Chair of the Executive Board of the Younger Comparativists Committee (YCC) in the American Society of Comparative Law. She has been a Visiting Fellow at Fordham University, McGill University, and at the Max Planck Institute for the Study of Religious and Ethnic Diversity in Göttingen. Her research focuses on global constitutional law, constitutionalism in times of crisis, socio-economic rights, and federalism in comparative perspective. She has authored three books and several publications in Italian and English.

Eva Maria Belser is Professor of Constitutional Law and Co-Director of the Institute of Federalism at the University of Fribourg, Switzerland. She conducts teaching and research in the field of Swiss and comparative constitutional law as well as international law. In addition to federalism, she is particularly interested in fundamental and human rights, democracy, the rule of law, and the welfare state.

Eleonora Ceccherini is Associate Professor of Constitutional Law at the University of Genoa, where she also teaches Comparative Public Law. She has carried out study and research activities in Spain, Canada, and the United States on fundamental rights and the judiciary.

Giacomo Delledonne is Postdoctoral Researcher in Comparative Public Law at Scuola Superiore Sant'Anna, Pisa (Italy). He has written extensively in five languages (Italian, English, French, Spanish, and German). His first monograph, *L'omogeneità costituzionale negli ordinamenti composti* (2017), was awarded the 10th *Opera Prima—Sergio P. Panunzio Prize*, organized by the Italian Association of Constitutional Law Scholars. Since 2014 he has been one of the convenors of the IACL Research Group on Subnational Constitutions in Federal and Quasi-Federal Constitutional States.

Cristina Fasone is Assistant Professor of Comparative Public Law, Department of Political Science, LUISS University, where she was the holder of a Jean Monnet Module (2016–2019) on "Parliamentary accountability and technical expertise: budgetary powers, information, and communication technologies and elections". She has been a Max Weber Fellow in Law 2013–2015, EUI, and a Visiting Scholar at Georgetown University Law Center, Victoria University of Wellington (NZ), Uppsala University, Complutense University of Madrid, University of Copenhagen, Durham University, and the University of Toruń.

Erik Longo (PhD) is currently Associate Professor of Constitutional Law at University of Florence (Italy). He has been visiting at the Center for Civil and Human Rights of the Notre Dame University, Program for Law, at the University of Sussex, School of Global Studies, and at the Queen's University, Belfast. From 2007 to 2019 he was professor of Constitutional Law at the University of Macerata (Italy).

Giovanni Piccirilli is Assistant Professor of Constitutional Law at the LUISS University of Rome, Law Department. In the same university, he is Deputy Director of the Centre for Parliamentary Studies. He was Emile Noel Fellow at the Jean Monnet Center, NYU School of Law. His main research interests are domestic and EU constitutional law, parliamentary practice, electoral studies.

Alice Valdesalici is Senior Researcher at the Institute for Comparative Federalism of Eurac Research. She got her PhD in Italian and European Constitutional

Law at the Graduate School of Law (University of Verona). She has been a visiting scholar at the Institut d'Estudis de l'Autogovern in Barcelona and at the Deutsche Forschungsinstitut für öffentliche Verwaltung Speyer. She has been Ronald Watts Young Researcher Award 2016, by the International Association of Centers for Federal Studies (IACFS). She is the author of various works on comparative fiscal federalism and co-editor of *Comparing Fiscal Federalism* (Brill 2018).

Alex Wilson is Senior Policy Analyst in the Members Research Service of the European Parliament. A recognised specialist on Italian politics, regionalism, and federalism, Alex has published in leading international journals across several academic fields. He co-edited the 2017 volume of *Italian Politics* (*Politica in Italia*), a prestigious series by the Istituto Cattaneo. Alex holds a PhD in Political and Social Sciences from the European University Institute

Jens Woelk is Full Professor of Comparative Constitutional Law at the University of Trento (Italy), at the Faculty of Law and the interdisciplinary School of International Studies. After obtaining his PhD in legal sciences at the University of Regensburg (Germany), Woelk worked at Eurac Research in Bolzano/Bozen (1994–2000). His research interests include federalism/regionalism, comparative constitutional law and European Union law, minority rights, and the constitutional transformation processes in Southeastern Europe. Woelk has participated in various projects and missions as an expert for the European Union and the Council of Europe.

Introduction

Why is the trajectory of Italian regionalism comparatively important and what does it have to offer?

Erika Arban, Giuseppe Martinico, and Francesco Palermo

In 2001, Title V of the Italian constitution – pertaining to the relationship between the central government and regional/local institutions – was significantly amended with a view to strengthening (at least on paper) peripheral powers. The reform further aimed at entrenching innovative features, including differential autonomy, the principle of subsidiarity, or metropolitan cities as layers of government. In the same wave of reforms, also a presidential system of government was introduced at regional level, making Italy the only European country where subnational governments are directly elected.

At the time it was discussed, this constitutional reform seemed to represent the first step towards a fully-fledged federalisation of the country. However, 20 years down the road, no further attempts to pursue such federalisation have been successfully carried out. Even the broader regional model envisaged by the 2001 reform has remained partially unaccomplished. Among the reasons that help explain this situation, there is a quite rooted *centralist* mentality and the absence of a widespread *federal* culture, coupled with a lack of political will – mainly but not exclusively at national level – to breathe new life into the regional edifice.

The year 2021 marks the 20th anniversary of this constitutional reform, and the recurrence offers an ideal opportunity for constitutional law scholars to critically reflect on the changes brought by it to the Italian constitutional system, the reasons why further decentralisation has been resisted and, more importantly, the contribution that Italian regionalism can bring to the global debate on comparative regionalism and federalism.

Italy is the country that has the longest-lasting regional system in place, since 1948. Yet, little is known about Italian regionalism outside Italian borders, and Italy rarely appears in comparative conversations. Likewise, many Italian constitutional scholars are mostly unaware of the contributions that Italy could offer to the broader debate on comparative federalism. This is where this volume comes into play, as it will look at the Italian case study in a comparative perspective, exploring what from the vibrant Italian experience has directly or indirectly influenced or even shaped the global developments of federal and regional states, and what could be learned from the Italian case, making contributions elaborated in Italy available to the international audience.

Within this broader comparative context, the book raises two sets of issues. First, it situates the regional form of government within the broader family of

DOI: 10.4324/9781003104469-1

federalism.[1] Regional states, of which Italy is the archetypal example, have emerged in the aftermath of World War II as an alternative to the "federal-unitary" dyad, although disagreement still exists among scholars on how to distinguish the regional model from the "purely" federal or "purely" unitary one. Sometimes referred to as "quasi-federal" or "hybrid" federal systems, regional states are imperfect or incomplete federal systems, as they lack some of the common features of federations and present a stronger centralist thrust. However, the expression "regional state" can be seen as a fictitious or imaginary one, as there are no constitutions that are labelled as such, differently than what happens with many federal constitutions. Regionalism is thus more of a normative construct. While scholars generally acknowledge that regional and federal systems similarly display a constitutionally entrenched division of legislative powers and the presence of an umpire (usually a constitutional court) settling conflicts of attribution between the various levels of government, they will look at the extent to which other typical "federal" indicators are absent in a regional model. For example, some scholars may argue that regional states usually lack a "federal" chamber representing the interests of the periphery at central level, or that the judicial powers of peripheral units in a regional system are more limited than in federations, or that regional subunits do not have constitution-making powers. However, this type of analysis is not very conclusive, since there are fully-fledged federal systems that do not have a typical federal upper chamber (e.g. Canada), or whose constituent units lack constitution-making powers (e.g. Canada and Belgium). More than individual indicators, what perhaps distinguishes a regional from a federal system is the presence (or lack thereof) of the so-called "federal culture". Being a very broad concept, there is of course much discussion about what federal culture really means, yet scholars tend to acknowledge the fundamental importance of this idea of sharing of powers in order to have a truly *pure* federation (Elazar, 1987, 192). When, for a variety of reasons, there is widespread resistance towards the federal idea, it is very unlikely that a *fully-fledged* federation be implemented. As a result, the eventual decentralisation that is being put in place might resemble something less than federal, i.e. a regional state. In fact, regional states often emerge in countries where the very concept of federalism is contested, so alternative denominations are needed to avoid the use of "federal" (sometimes the real "f-word") in constitutional or political debates.[2] But in which ways are regional systems capable of addressing problems that neither federal nor unitary states can solve? Rather than being rigidly anchored to the

1 In this volume, the expressions "regionalism", "regional state", and "regional form of government" are used indistinctively, as coterminous, to indicate a milder form of federal structure. However, it is important to note that, in the social sciences, the term "regionalism" is used with different meanings and also to refer to different phenomena, including forms of supranational integration like the EU. A more detailed analysis of the various concepts of regions and regionalism can be found in Palermo & Kössler, 2017, 20.

2 For example, the Spanish model is commonly referred to as *Estado Autonómico* (State of Autonomies); the South African system is called "System of Cooperative Government", while in Sri Lanka or Kenya the preferred denomination is "devolution". This testifies of the need to refer to something else than "federalism" for the heavily charged meaning of the term in several countries, due to their respective history or to the establishment of certain prejudices in the political discourse and in the very terminology.

plainly vertical or horizontal dynamics typical of unitary and federal paradigms, regional states seem to espouse a more cross-sectional relationship between the centre and the periphery, one that takes into account additional levels of government (i.e. local autonomies such as municipalities and/or provinces). In this way, they are more prone to experimentation and adaptability. Italy provides numerous examples of that, as this book shows.

Over the past two decades, the global trajectory of federalism and regionalism has deeply changed, marking significant improvements in some (mostly non-European) contexts and slowing down in others, especially in Europe, where instead secessionist movements have taken root, due to dissatisfaction with too timid decentralisation of powers.

This brings us to the second set of issues raised in this book. Regional states share tensions that are very similar to those of many *classic* federal states, therefore mechanisms and strategies applied in one model can be easily "exported" to the other. In this sense, the Italian regional system may represent a useful showcase as to how certain tensions (linguistic, cultural, socio-economic) have been addressed. In fact, many of the constitutional novelties introduced with the 2001 constitutional reform and extensively discussed in this volume deserve a more thorough analysis considering that more and more countries, especially but not exclusively in the *Global South*, are discussing decentralisation reforms (Breen, 2018). In describing Italian regionalism before and after the reform of Title V of the constitution, this volume situates the Italian case into comparative/global perspective by looking at how Italy has contributed to the global debate on regionalism and federalism, and how it has been shaped by it. Among the several themes commonly discussed in comparative regionalism/federalism there are: the role of courts in shaping division of powers and other doctrines; the implementation of principles such as subsidiarity and loyalty; the practice of fiscal federalism; the relationship between subnational levels of government and supranational structures such as the EU; intergovernmental relations and executive federalism; political parties and the role they play in the federal system; asymmetrical arrangements; the protection of ethno-linguistic groups; local governments and cities. The Italian experience has a lot to share about all this, but also about some more broadly constitutional issues such as the compromise character of the 1948 constitution; the devolutionary (rather than aggregative) formation of regions; the historic unitary legacy and the difficulties in accepting and understanding power-sharing.

From a methodological standpoint, the book adopts a theoretical/analytical approach, coupled with a comparative outlook, and mainly focuses on the legal/constitutional components of Italian regionalism: the work is compiled largely by public law scholars, thus looking at regionalism primarily from the perspective of comparative constitutional law. This is also rarely done, as most works on comparative federalism are drafted by political/social scientists. Therefore, attention is devoted especially to institutional aspects and to case law, without neglecting some aspects that are, conversely, not frequently looked at in the constitutional debate, such as the party system.

Conceptually, the volume is divided in two parts. Part I ("Federalism and Regionalism – The Italian Context") accurately distils the essence of the evolution of Italian regionalism and the respective debate before and after 2001. Part II of the book ("Italy's Major Contribution to the Discussion – Italian Regionalism in the Global Debate"), on the other hand, presents the elements of the Italian regional architecture that might have a broader comparative relevance and contribute to the global debate, particularly focusing on the main innovations brought about by the 2001 constitutional reform.

In Chapter 1, Erika Arban retraces the intellectual history of Italian regionalism starting from the Italian unification in the 1860s, but with particular emphasis on the debates on the regional form of government within the Constituent Assembly and the evolution of regionalism over the last seven decades. The chapter also sketches the general background against which the other chapters will be situated. As Arban points out, regionalism as construed in Italy shall be considered the result of a compromise, a model that is neither completely unitary nor federal, one that protects local autonomy and self-government within a largely asymmetric but fundamentally unitary state. The 2001 constitutional reform of Title V (on the relationship between the central state, regions, and local self-governments), which is amply discussed throughout the book, was not enough to transform Italy into a fully-fledged federation, although it significantly strengthened regional powers and introduced interesting constitutional innovations.

In Chapter 2, Cristina Fasone and Giovanni Piccirilli look at how the form of government has changed in Italian regions over the last 20 years, and the consequences for democratic accountability. As the authors indicate, in studying the transformations of the inter-institutional balance at regional level after the 1999 and 2001 reforms, scholars have extensively emphasised the role played by constitutional case law in devising a common model of "form of government" at least for ordinary regions. Against this background, the chapter retraces this scholarly debate for a non-Italian audience (considering that most of the literature is available only in Italian), highlighting similarities and differences of the Italian approach in relation to the comparative legal scholarship on subnational constitutionalism. Furthermore, it places the constitutional reform of 1999 (on the direct elections of regional presidents) in the broader context of the season of institutional reforms. Fasone and Piccirilli also assess the relationship between the developments in the regional forms of government and democratic accountability from several perspectives. In their conclusion, the authors argue that 20 years after the reforms, the attempt to streamline the accountability chain in the regions in favour of their presidents has been successful, even though this has led to the overstrength of the executive. The reform, however, has failed to deliver the expected autonomy to the regions: a combination of factors has contributed to limit the impact of potential institutional innovation and, as such, the change of the regional form of government cannot be considered as a test-bench for the much-awaited national institutional reforms.

In Chapter 3, Giacomo Delledonne delves into issues of federalism and regionalism in constitutional adjudication. The chapter assesses the role of constitutional adjudication in the evolution of the Italian regional state. Since the entry into force of the constitutional reform of 2001, the Constitutional Court has often been described as the umpire in a flawed multi-level order, in which the unfinished legislative and administrative implementation of constitutional amendments, the lack of political consensus, and the problematic wording of the relevant constitutional provisions all led to the Court being overwhelmed by workload. The chapter probes the question of whether and how the Court has contributed to the actual working of the system. Indeed, the case law of the Constitutional Court has contributed to making the system more functional. This was the case both before and after the constitutional reform of 2001. However, the implementation of some of the most important components of the Italian regional model, including the so-called fiscal federalism, being an unfinished business, the interpretive activity of the Court has mostly been conservative and has somehow slowed down the unleashing of the innovative potential of territorial pluralism. The chapter also considers the contribution of the case law of the Constitutional Court to the theoretical understanding of regionalism.

In Chapter 4, Eleonora Ceccherini discusses an essential feature of all multilevel systems: intergovernmental relations. From a comparative standpoint, cooperation among the levels of government can be achieved in many ways: by introducing a territorial Chamber, by participating in joint bodies, by intervening in the legislative and administrative proceedings with proposals, opinions, industry standard agreements, etc. In Italy, the 2001 reform did not operate a systematic review of the instruments promoting greater correlation and participation between the different institutional levels of the Republic, particularly with regard to the possibility of establishing a Senate specifically representing all autonomies: this solution has been left to potential future constitutional reforms. However, in many countries, this question represents the heart of all debate concerning the involvement of decentralised institutional levels. In Italy, the issue has been approached through the instrument of Conferences, i.e. bodies that are composed of representatives of the central, as well as of the regional, and local executive power. The chapter also reflects on the absence of any normative indication of the procedural rules regulating a debate session or defining voting formalities (i.e. definition or not of structural or operative quorum needed for the validity of the sessions; effectiveness or not of the resolutions adopted by the conferences). Finally, part of the essay is devoted to the analysis of horizontal cooperation among regions.

In Chapter 5, Alice Valdesalici concentrates on the impact of the 2001 constitutional reform on the "financial constitution" and its subsequent implementation through national legislation, with special focus on its impact on the regional level of government. Although the 2001 reform was intended to comprehensively address the institutional design of a (quasi-)federal state, the author suggests that, in reality, the financial dimension of Italian asymmetric regionalism has almost entirely monopolised the political attention and every aspect of the federalisation process. The financial aspects have become particularly important during and after the 2008–2012 economic crisis, because of the stringent EU constraints to national finances, the rocketed spread in the Eurozone (that made interests on state's debts more expensive than in the past), and the financial markets' pressures: all these factors have indirectly impacted both sub-national budgets and autonomy, resulting in a counter-wave of re-centralisation.

In Chapter 6, Alex Wilson discusses party system in Italy. The creation of regional governments in the ordinary regions in the 1970s meant that Italian parties had to adapt their organisations to serve this new political level. However, because of the centralised tradition of the Italian state and of its political parties, the limited competences and resources of regional governments, and an electoral system that encouraged party fragmentation, regional party systems largely mirrored the shifting coalitions at national level. The 1990s and 2000s saw the rise of regional leadership as part of a process of "personalisation" of electoral politics at sub-national levels. A stratarchical form of multi-level organisation emerged in most Italian parties, facilitated by the withering away of the party bureaucracies that had once sustained a centralised party model with strong local branches. Regional leaders proved less than crucial in influencing the different constitutional reforms pursued by their governing parties at national level, which were rejected in national referendums held in 2006 and 2016. The 2010s saw the tide turn against regional leadership for a number of reasons. Corruption scandals engulfed many regions and brought down prominent politicians, who also faced growing unpopularity as they enacted austerity measures imposed by the central government. The rise of the populist Northern League and Five Star Movement also impacted regional party systems, displacing the parties and leaders that had come to prominence in the 1990s. 2020 has seen regional presidents come to the fore again in dealing with the Coronavirus outbreak, which has an impact on regional healthcare systems but has also placed regional politics under the spotlight. It is not clear whether this experience will enhance or undermine the credibility of regional governments, or how it will influence the future debate about the organisational structure of the state and its parties.

In Chapter 7, Antonia Baraggia paints the role of sub-national entities within the European Union as one of the more fascinating conundrums of the EU integration process. The aspiration of the EU to build a quasi-federal constitutional space beyond the states seems to clash with the deepest expression of national identity: the presence of local and regional entities. For many years after the beginning of the EU integration process such a tension was dormant. Looking at the Italian case, however, at the beginning of the new century, after a slow and long process, the EU and the regions crossed their paths: on one side the Italian reform of Title V clearly emphasised the role of regions in the EU affairs; on the other, the Lisbon Treaty finally recognised the key role of sub-national entities in the EU decision making process, providing innovative procedures of participation and information duties and considering them one of the two pillars for the guarantee of democracy in the EU. The chapter critically examines the evolution of the role of Italian regions within the EU, in order to assess the factual realisation of the "promise" of the regional participation within the EU decisional processes.

In Chapter 8, Francesco Palermo illustrates the multidimensional and devolutionary asymmetry characterising Italian regionalism, both in terms of constitutional law and of powers transferred to and used by the regions. The chapter also argues that, over the past 70 years, the constitutional picture of Italian regionalism has become increasingly complex, considering that each special region has developed its own degree of autonomy, and the constitutional reform in 2001 has made it institutionally possible to differentiate the distribution of competences among the ordinary regions as well. The author sketches the trajectory and the current state of the art of the different forms of regional asymmetry, and contends that asymmetry in the books looks way different than it is in action, due to a highly different implementation of the constitutional instruments by the various regions. The chapter also explores the contribution of Italian asymmetric design to the development of federalism/regionalism worldwide. As a matter of fact, all recent federal/regional experiments place asymmetry at their core.

In Chapter 9, Erik Longo addresses the Italian experience and its comparative relevance with regard to local governance and metropolitan cities. The institutional framework of local governments and metropolitan cities is surely one of the most controversial parts of the 2001 constitutional reform, since the implementation of the 2001 reform for local governments has been inadequate and largely ineffective. Remarkable is the story of metropolitan cities: whereas the reform entrenched them into the constitution for the first time, they existed in legislation for 30 years before the reform, and it took further time to give them birth amid the enactment of a controversial law with many legal and institutional flaws. Some metropolitan cities have innovatively interpreted the reform leveraging its powers to create a new institutional environment, to foster a strong collaboration with municipalities in the metropolitan area, and to create an "experimental laboratory" for good administrative practices. Against this background, the chapter aspires to rethink the role of local government and metropolitan cities in the unique Italian regional system by inquiring how it concretely works today after 20 years from the constitutional reform. More broadly, the question is also about the place that local government can and should have in a federal/regional system, which is one of the most intriguing and controversial debates in contemporary comparative federalism.

In Chapter 10, Jens Woelk explores the principle of loyal cooperation in Italy and beyond. Instead of centralist orders and strictly hierarchical organisation guaranteeing the cohesion of the political and constitutional system of centralised states, in federal states a specific culture of solidarity and integration is needed in order to resolve the permanent and basic conflicts between different levels of government. In Italy's regional system, the principle of "loyal cooperation" has first been developed by the Constitutional Court, mainly for guaranteeing regional consultation and participation through procedural safeguards, thus balancing central government's interferences in the regional competence sphere. Based upon this case law, the principle has been constitutionalised in the reform of 2001, which gave Italian regions more powers and abolished supervision powers by the central government. The principle shall have the function of a counterweight in the powers of substitution by the central government (Article 120(2) Const.) and has been further developed by the Constitutional Court. Comparative analysis shows that loyalty principles are explained by the typical relationship of mutual dependence and interdependence of federal/central and federated/sub-national entities as well as their decision- and policy-making bodies. The respective allocation of competences and forms of supervision explain differences and the peculiar form of the principle in each federal or regional system.

In Chapter 11, Giuseppe Martinico delves into the principle of subsidiarity and its mutation within the Italian constitutional system over the last 20 years. Subsidiarity could be regarded as an example of a principle that was originally alien to the Italian constitution and was introduced under the pressure of EU law. In judgment no. 303/2003, the Italian Constitutional Court used the subsidiarity principle as a Trojan Horse to reshape the distribution of competences codified in the constitution. On that occasion, the Court has expanded the original scope of application of the subsidiarity principle by inventing a mechanism analogous to the idea of "national interest", which was present in the wording of the old Title V of the constitution but was discarded in the 2001 reform. It seems useful to recall the solutions suggested by the Italian Constitutional Court for the relationship between subsidiarity and loyal cooperation ("*leale collaborazione*"): the former requires a loyal cooperation between the territorial actors, concerted practices and bodies and, finally, a system of agreements between the institutional actors. The Italian subsidiarity episode described here tells us at least two things. Firstly, it confirms the centrality of the Constitutional Court in the destiny of Italian regionalism. Secondly, it makes it more difficult to trace the Italian constitutional principle of subsidiarity back to the EU (or even German) legal system. Whereas the Court of Justice of the EU traditionally avoids engaging in debates concerning subsidiarity, the Italian Constitutional Court has actively made use of subsidiarity to reshape Italian regionalism.

Finally, in Chapter 12, Eva Maria Belser touches upon those aspects of Italian regionalism which are most fascinating and inspiring in a comparative perspective. As Belser suggests, regionalism is a unique model of state organisation that is both captivating to study and challenging to understand. At the same time, it could be a good alternative for countries interested in reconciling unity and diversity while rejecting fully-fledged federalism. Belser further contends that regionalism as implemented in Italy adds most crucial elements to the toolbox of power-sharing, which in fact can be inspirational both to unitarians refusing federalism (because it goes too far in empowering subnational units), and to separatists (discarding federalism for not offering sufficient protection to individual units). By looking at the Italian experience with regionalism, Belser also tries to address the question of how to define regionalism, and what distinguishes it from unitary and federal systems. While providing such an answer can be difficult, any such attempt must consider asymmetry as a characterising element: in this sense, the Italian experimentation with special and ordinary regions is a case-in-point. In conclusion, Belser argues that regionalism should not be treated as the "little brother of federalism", but as a model that stands on a par and has a lot to offer to both unitary and federal states.

These various chapters can be grouped into four main themes. The first theme is *temporal*, as its objective is to retrace the history of the debate on regionalism as it has occurred in Italy (Chapter 1) as well as the potential future trajectories not only of the Italian regional system, but of regionalism more in general (Chapter 12). The second theme is *relational*, as it looks at the several vertical and horizontal relations of the various institutional actors. In this regard, it is worth mentioning intergovernmental relations (Chapter 4), financial relations (Chapter 5), and the relations between regions and the European Union (Chapter 7). The third theme focuses on *principles,* as it discusses some important features introduced in the Italian regional model in 2001, namely loyal cooperation (Chapter 10) and subsidiarity (Chapter 12). Finally, the fourth theme is *institutional,* as it looks at a number of significant institutional features of Italian regionalism, such as reforms (Chapter 2), constitutional adjudication (Chapter 3), party system (Chapter 6), asymmetries (Chapter 8), and local governments (Chapter 9).

The debate on how to reform Italian regionalism is not over, and the recent COVID-19 crisis has stressed some ambiguities of the system and reinforced criticism on the 2001 reform. Scholars have blamed the regional system for creating confusion and uncertainty, supporting the introduction of an explicit "supremacy clause". It has also been argued that the current constitutional text would already give the central government the necessary powers to manage (health and other) emergencies in a centralised manner, especially by means of Article 120 Const. However, this option has not been used so far. For sure, the debate on the division of powers between state and regions following the pandemic is very telling of the unexplored potential of Title V of the Italian constitution as amended in 2001.

These reflections are now offered to the wider community of scholars for further consideration and with a view to contributing to the global debate on comparative federalism and its trajectories. So far, the Italian contribution to this debate has been less prominent than it could and should have been. We hope that the following chapters may at least in part redress this flaw and open new avenues for comparative research.

This book has been a joint idea and endeavour by the editors. Our thanks goes to the authors who have kindly accepted to share their knowledge and to make this publication possible, to the publisher (and their anonymous reviewers) who has believed in the idea behind the volume, and not least to Antilia Wyss for her excellent and invaluable support in checking and formatting all chapters.

Literature

Michael Breen, *The Road to Federalism in Nepal, Myanmar and Sri Lanka: Finding the Middle Ground* (Routledge, 2018)

Daniel Elazar, *Exploring Federalism* (The University of Alabama Press, 1987)

Francesco Palermo and Karl Kössler, *Comparative Federalism. Constitutional Arrangements and Case Law* (Hart Publishing, 2017)

Part I

Federalism and regionalism

The Italian context

1 An intellectual history of Italian regionalism

Erika Arban[1]

I. Introduction: the pre-1948 period

In this chapter, I will retrace the intellectual history of Italian regionalism, with particular emphasis on the regional model emerged with the 1948 constitution and on the 2001 reform of Title V and subsequent amendments. In so doing, the chapter will paint the general background against which the other contributions in this volume will be situated.

As the term suggests, *regionalism* as a feature of the Italian constitutional edifice is premised on the idea of *regions* as political and administrative centres of power and as a compromise between federalism and centralism. Although Italian regionalism is ingrained in the 1948 constitution, the regional state did not emerge in a vacuum, as debates on regionalism started well before then, and were particularly lively at the time of the Italian unification in 1861.

After the Congress of Vienna of 1815, the Italian peninsula was divided in eight states: the Kingdom of Piedmont and Sardinia, Lombardy-Venetia (a province of the Austrian Empire), the Dukedom of Modena and Reggio Emilia, the Dukedom of Parma and Piacenza, the Grand-Duchy of Tuscany, the Princedom of Lucca, the Papal state (including part of Emilia, Romagna, Marche, Umbria, and Lazio), and the Kingdom of the Two Sicilies. Italy was thus a non-homogeneous entity (as famously stated by Metternich and cited in Putnam 1993, 121, "Italy was hardly more than a geographical expression"), a compound of diverse political structures with their own laws and institutional apparatus.[2] As a result, Italy was heterogeneous from a socio-economic standpoint but also linguistically: the Italian language, derived from Latin, was spoken only

1 Postdoctoral Research Fellow, Melbourne Law School, and Lecturer in Comparative Federalism, University of Antwerp, Faculty of Law. This research was fully funded by the Australian Government through the Australian Research Council (ARC) Laureate Program "Balancing Diversity and Social Cohesion in Democratic Constitutions."

2 This is similar to Germany at the time of the Holy Roman Empire and until after the French Revolution: in the words of Martin Loughlin, Germany was "an eccentric patchwork of over 300 political units (kingdoms, prince-bishoprics, duchies, free cities, and such like) structured largely according to feudal privilege and servitude" (Loughlin, 2010, 120).

DOI: 10.4324/9781003104469-2

by intellectuals, with the majority of the population communicating almost exclusively in dialects.

Throughout the nineteenth century, federalism was still a quite novel idea in Europe since, across the continent, the ideals of the French Revolution contributed to reinforce the image of a state characterised by a strong central government and administration that allowed the regime to dominate politics, thus defying all ideas of dispersion of powers espoused by federalism. However, in spite of the powerful influence of the French model, some European intellectuals had started to acquaint themselves with federalism, especially as experimented in the United States (1787 constitution) and Switzerland (which became federal in 1848, but whose "confederal" tradition dated back to the late thirteenth century).

During the *Risorgimento*,[3] intellectuals and patriots from the Italian peninsula were also discussing which form of state to give to Italy in pursuing unification. Federalism was particularly praised by some as a viable solution, considering the Italian socio-economic and cultural-linguistic divide, and therefore as a tool to reconcile unity and diversity. A convinced advocate of federalism for unified Italy within a larger European federation was the Milanese thinker Carlo Cattaneo (Arban 2017; Sabetti 2010).[4] Conversely, Giuseppe Mazzini, one of the heroes of *Risorgimento* and of Italian unification, was in principle opposed to federalism *per se*, although he did not support the idea of a strongly centralised model for Italy either (Ambrosini, 1946–47, 137). Mazzini believed that the unification of Italy should be premised on the recognition of *regions* as intermediate entities between the central government and municipalities, and characterised by "secondary territorial features, by dialects, and by a predominance of agricultural, industrial, or maritime attitudes" (Ambrosini, 1946–47, 137).

Also Camillo Benso di Cavour (one of the architects of Italian unification and the first Prime Minister of the new Kingdom of Italy) and Marco Minghetti (his minister of the interior) supported the idea of creating a regional model for Italy. In particular, Minghetti proposed the creation of regions not simply as entities enjoying administrative powers, but as autarchic entities endowed with normative powers (Ambrosini, 1946–47, 139). Like Mazzini, Minghetti also thought that the political unity of Italy did not necessarily have to coincide with its administrative unity (Ambrosini, 1946–47, 139), and believed that regions would "reconcile (…) the positions of those who wanted to preserve the great variety of trends, traditions, interests of those natural entities and of those who dreamt of an administrative unification" without threatening the "unity and forces of the nation" (Bin & Falcon, 2012, 69). In other words, his idea was to create a new system for Italy, different both from the unitary and centralised model, and from

3 The expression *Risorgimento* refers to the XIX century ideological and literary movement for Italian unification that culminated with the creation of the Kingdom of Italy in 1861: Encyclopaedia Britannica, *sub verbo* Risorgimento, at https://www.britannica.com/event/Risorgimento

4 Cattaneo famously contended that "We will have true peace only when we will have the United States of Europe" (Bobbio & Cattaneo, 2010, 27).

the federal model incarnated by the Swiss and the US systems (Ambrosini, 1946–47, 139).

However, when Italy was eventually unified, a unitary and centralised form of state was preferred, and all proposals on decentralisation withdrawn, as there was a palpable fear that regionalism would threaten the unity of the state which was still too fragile (Bin & Falcon, 2012, 69).

With the creation of the Kingdom of Italy in 1861, the *Statuto Albertino* became the Basic Law that unified the country. The *Statuto* pre-dated Italian unification since it was the "constitution" of the Kingdom of Piedmont-Sardinia that King Carlo Alberto granted to his people in 1848 in the aftermath of the European insurrections (Cassese, 2012, 3). The *Statuto* was not a real constitution, since it was not enacted by a "popular elected assembly" and "it had not been put forth to the representatives of the people for their approval" (Cassese, 2012, 3). It was simply *octroyé* – or conceded – by the King to the people (Cassese, 2012, 3). Similar to many constitutions of the time, the *Statuto* was a "flexible" document that could be modified by ordinary laws (Cassese, 2012, 3). Consequently, the Kingdom of Italy did not give itself a new constitution but simply inherited the document in force in the Kingdom of Piedmont-Sardinia (which led the unification process) (Cassese, 2012, 3). The *Statuto* remained in force until 1948, although its provisions had been largely disregarded (although not formally amended) at least since fascism.

The years following unification were complex for Italy. In fact, the political class in power lacked the required administrative skills, and a massive number of inexperienced people occupied the administrative roles of the newly formed state (Lepre, 1994, 31). Also, the various peoples that composed the Italian society remained linked to local traditions (Lepre, 1994, 75). Most importantly, the unification had not emerged as a result of a popular revolution, but it was imposed by the Kingdom of Piedmont-Sardinia from the top (Amoretti, 2002, 129), and this did not help forge a sense of belonging and of *Italian* identity.

For several decades after unification, regionalism remained largely off the agenda. It was only in the aftermath of World War I that regional aspirations were voiced again, when the newly constituted Peoples' Party (*Partito Popolare Italiano*) – under the leadership of the Sicilian priest Don Luigi Sturzo – sought to reform the entire state structure by strengthening local autonomies (Ambrosini, 1946–47, 140). The first proposal to actually implement a form of regionalism was discussed in Parliament in the early 1920s in reference to the so-called *Terre Redente,* those territories recently annexed to Italy after the war but that had already enjoyed some form of autonomy under the Austrian Empire (in particular, the territories of Trento and Trieste) (Ambrosini, 1946–47, 140; Ciuffoletti, 1994, 113). However, the advent of Mussolini and the fascist dictatorship in the early 1920s suffocated all aims for autonomy, and reiterated the authority of a strong, centralised state (Fabbrini & Brunazzo, 2003, 104). It was only at the time of the Constituent Assembly that regionalism was put back on the agenda, as the next section will illustrate.

II. The path to the 1948 constitution

A. The Constituent Assembly and the idea of regional state

In the confused aftermath of World War II, on 2 June 1946 the Italian people were called to vote on a referendum to choose between a republican and a monarchical form of state. The republican front won, so monarchy was rejected, and a republican form of state was implemented. In the same occasion, voters were also called to select the members of a Constituent Assembly, whose purpose was to draft a new constitution that would replace the already defunct *Statuto Albertino*. Within the Constituent Assembly, discussions arose on the form of state to give to Italy and on the creation of regions, among other things (Caretti & Tarli Barbieri, 2012, 15).

The Constituent Assembly was rife with towering constitutional scholars and statesmen who would leave an indelible imprint on Italian and comparative constitutionalism. The expression "regional state" was coined by Gaspare Ambrosini, a jurist, statesman, professor of constitutional law, and member of the Constituent Assembly (Bin & Falcon, 2012, 48; D'Atena, 2014, 68). However, as noted above, the idea of a regional state in Italy can be traced back to Mazzini, Minghetti, Cavour, and Sturzo, who conceived of regions as an intermediate level of government between the central and the municipal/provincial spheres: regionalism was thus seen as a compromise between the unitary scheme and the federal model, both rejected in their purest form as less than ideal solutions for Italy. A regional form of government had already been entrenched in the Spanish republican constitution of 1931, which created autonomous communities endowed with legislative powers (Bin & Falcon, 2012, 26). However, because of the civil war that broke up in Spain, this constitution had a short life and was never actually applied (Bin & Falcon, 2012, 48). It was, however, used by Italian constituents as the model for the regional state created in 1948 (Bin & Falcon, 2012, 26). Ambrosini had studied the 1931 Spanish constitution, as well as other models in Europe, such as the Soviet Union, the Austro-Hungarian scheme (Bin & Falcon, 2012, 48; D'Atena, 2014, 68), Swiss federalism, or the Weimar constitution (Mangiameli, 2014, 3; D'Atena, 2014, 68). Inspired by these experiences, Ambrosini formulated the expression "regional autonomy" and envisioned the region as a new entity enjoying legislative powers (Bin & Falcon, 2012, 48). Incidentally, it is worth noting that some scholars have criticised the use of the Spanish model for Italy and in general the overall understanding of foreign federal models by Ambrosini and other members of the Constituent Assembly (see in particular Basile, 1980, 94–95).

Ambrosini supported regionalism as it allowed to combine two elements: it would avoid excessive centralisation (thus contributing to make the whole bureaucratic system more agile and efficient) while at the same time it would strengthen local autonomies (Ambrosini 1946–47, 141). In fact, although the administrative model implemented in 1848 was one of the most advanced in Europe, it was never updated after unification and, by the mid-1940s, it had become obsolete: thus, the regional model envisaged by the Constituent Assembly also served the purpose of improving bureaucracy and the administrative system. To this end, Ambrosini believed that empowering municipalities (or even provinces) was not enough, as they were too small for certain tasks: it was thus necessary to create an intermediate entity – the *region* – as originally suggested by Mazzini and Minghetti. In this way, the regional system would perfectly balance the enhancement of local powers and autonomy with the pursuit of the overarching interests of the state as a whole (Ambrosini 1946–47, 142).

Ambrosini was opposed to a *federal* solution for Italy mainly because it would entail the elevation of regions to "member states" of the federation (Ambrosini 1946–47, 142). In his view, the creation of a pure federal system would require the "complete transformation or the disintegration (…) of the state structure" something that did not seem to reflect the main priority of Italy at the time (Ambrosini 1946–47, 143). His main concern with a federal solution was thus not so much the threat to the political unity of the state (as was the case at the time of unification): after all, he believed that the risk of breaking up the unity of the state after so many decades of unification was negligible (Ambrosini 1946–47, 143). Rather, what troubled Ambrosini was that the elevation of regions to the status of federated entities would split sovereignty: sovereign regions would then compete with the central government, interfering with the swift implementation of those programs of economic rebuilding and social reform that Italy so badly needed at the time (Ambrosini 1946–47, 143).

The regional state envisaged by Ambrosini entailed the creation of *regions* as entities endowed not only with administrative powers but also with legislative powers embedded in the constitution, although limited to subject matters of local nature (Ambrosini 1946–47, 144). These legislative powers could not be amended by ordinary law, but required a constitutional law, with a Constitutional Court playing the role of arbiter in case of conflict between state and regional laws (Ambrosini 1946–47, 145). Ambrosini also believed that the regional model could be applied asymmetrically, based on different local needs and priorities: consequently, some regions would have additional – or different – powers than others (Ambrosini 1946–47, 145). The region, as conceived by Ambrosini, would thus be (i) *autarchic*, meaning that it would have its own regional interests and the capacity to perform activities to pursue those interests; (ii) *autonomous,* since it would have its own legislative powers embedded in the constitution; (iii) representing local interests; and (iv) endowed with *financial* autonomy (Ambrosini 1946–47, 147).

Ambrosini also contended that such regional model would differ from a federal system on two main grounds: genesis and sovereignty (Ambrosini 1946–47, 146). Insofar as its genesis, he maintained that federal systems usually emerge from a covenant (*foedus*) among formerly independent states which, through this union, become member states of the federation. As such, they attribute to the federation powers and tasks in specifically enumerated subject matters, while retaining for themselves original sovereign powers on all residual subject matters (Ambrosini 1946–47, 146). Consequently, member states in a federation continue to enjoy original sovereign powers on these subject matters since they have not relinquished them when they formed the federation (Ambrosini 1946–47, 146). Conversely, a regional system is not based on a pact or covenant, because the state is not created by regions: rather, it is the state that creates regions as entities endowed with political autonomy, and decides which powers and functions the regions should enjoy (Ambrosini 1946–47, 146). Consequently, while regions can exercise their political influence and voice their requests, it is the state that ultimately decides (Ambrosini 1946–47, 146). And even if the rights attributed to the regions are constitutional rights (and therefore better protected and guaranteed compared to the rights of autarchic entities), it is the central government that gives these rights to the regions (Ambrosini 1946–47, 146). Therefore, the state could always change these rights and powers following the amendment procedure established for constitutional laws (Ambrosini 1946–47, 146). With regard to sovereignty, in a regional state there is only one sovereign entity – the state – and regions can never be sovereign, because they are radically different in nature from member states of a federation (Ambrosini 1946–47, 146): accordingly, regional autonomy can never evolve into a federal state (Ambrosini 1946–47, 146).

B. The 1948 constitution

The new Italian constitution entered into force in 1948, creating a regional state predicated on Ambrosini's ideas as a compromise between a fully-fledged federal and a completely unitary paradigm, although the expression "regional state" did not appear anywhere in the constitution. The new democratic and republican state was premised on local self-government and individual values. A cardinal principle of this constitutional scheme was crystallised in article 5, mandating that

> The Republic is one and indivisible. It recognises and promotes local autonomies, and implements the fullest measure of administrative decentralisation in those services which depend on the State. The Republic adapts the principles and methods of its legislation to the requirements of autonomy and decentralisation.

Italy was divided into 20 regions, 15 "ordinary" ones and 5 "special" regions enjoying "particular forms and conditions of autonomy pursuant to the special statutes" as provided by article 116. Following Ambrosini's proposal of asymmetry, the rationale behind the special status rested on the fact that these regions were either islands (like Sicily and Sardinia) with separatist or autonomist movements, or bordering areas with linguistic minorities and separatist tendencies (like Valle d'Aosta, Trentino-Alto Adige, and Friuli Venezia Giulia). Ordinary regions, on the other hand, were either "originally independent states before Italian unification" or "laid out according to different criteria" (e.g. the "geographical definition of railway areas") (Grottanelli de' Santi, 2006, 5; Palermo in this volume).

However, special forms of decentralisation had already been implemented in certain areas even before the Constituent Assembly. In fact, in 1944 Sicily and

Sardinia were provided with temporary institutions, such as a high commissioner (nominated by the Prime Minister) and a regional chamber representative of the various political, economic, union, and cultural organisations (Bin & Falcon, 2012, 71). In 1946, the statute (*statuto*) of Sicily was also approved, recognising ample legislative powers for this region (Caretti & Tarli Barbieri, 2012, 17). In 1945, Valle d'Aosta was transformed into an "autonomous district" enjoying particular forms of administrative autonomy in specific subject matters (Bin & Falcon, 2012, 72). Finally, in 1946, pursuant to the "De Gasperi-Gruber" understanding, special conditions of autonomy were granted to the German speaking communities living in the province of Bolzano (Palermo in this volume; Bin & Falcon, 2012, 72). The statute of Friuli Venezia Giulia, however, was approved only in 1963, after the definition of the status of the city of Trieste after the war.

One important difference between special and ordinary regions pertained to their statutes of autonomy. Statutes of special regions were approved by constitutional law and granted additional and distinct powers compared to ordinary regions to reflect the peculiar needs of these territories (Caretti & Tarli Barbieri, 2012, 44). These statutes governed the various organs and functions of these regions (Caretti & Tarli Barbieri, 2012, 18–19). Conversely, statutes of ordinary regions were deliberated by regional councils and approved by national (not constitutional) law. Special regions also enjoyed broader legislative powers than those listed in article 117 Const. for ordinary regions (who only had concurrent legislative powers). In the ambit of fiscal autonomy, the 1948 constitution acknowledged all regions full autonomy with regards to expenditures, and a much more limited autonomy with regards to revenues, although statutes of special regions allowed for a more favourable financial treatment (see Valdesalici in this volume). Finally, along with the 20 regions, the territory was also divided into provinces and municipalities.

C. The creation of the regional model

Despite these provisions on regionalism, the Italian territorial organisation continued to be characterised by a "strong centralist thrust" (Fabbrini & Brunazzo, 2003, 104). In fact, article 127 Const. contained a "national interest" clause that was often used by the national government to justify legislation on subject matters supposedly assigned to regions (Groppi & Scattone, 2006, 132). More importantly, the provisions on regionalism contained in the 1948 constitution required the legislative action of Parliament, but in the aftermath of 1948 the Italian Parliament was reticent in realising the regional state (Caretti & Tarli Barbieri, 2012, 22). In addition to an ideological clash between political parties, who had opposite views on regionalism (Del Duca & Del Duca, 2006, 802), there was the need to rebuild the country – dramatically devastated after the war – and put in place economic and social measures which required strong central action (Caretti & Tarli Barbieri, 2012, 23). Therefore, the creation of ordinary regions was not seen as a priority.

Consequently, with the exception of the five special regions, the regional state became a reality only in the early 1970s, when implementing legislation was finally enacted by Parliament, financial resources were transferred from the centre to the periphery for the functioning of these entities, and regional councils of ordinary regions were elected.

III. The 2001 constitutional reform

A. The resurgence of federal ideas in the 1990s

The regional model ingrained in the 1948 constitution was significantly amended in 2001 with the reform of Title V. Preceded by a series of other initiatives, this reform was the culmination of the resurgence of regional and federal ideas that took place in Italy during the late 1980s – early 1990s. Italian regionalism had started to reveal its limitations already after the creation of regional governments in the 1970s, mainly because of its strong centripetal trends (Caretti & Tarli Barbieri, 2012, 28). However, it was between the late 1980s and the early 1990s that a combination of political, economic, and international factors created a fertile ground for the resurgence of regional and federal ideas in the country.

A thorough analysis of the interplay of these events is beyond the scope of this chapter. Here, I will just briefly note that, from a political standpoint, during the 1980s some of the historical Italian political parties (notably, the Christian Democrats and the Socialists) started to lose consent, with a consequent increase in approval of newly formed parties, including regional coalitions, especially in the North (Amoretti, 2002, 133–134). This revival of regional sentiments caused a disturbance in the traditional assessment of more established national parties (Amoretti, 2002, 134). The weakening of traditional parties was favoured also by the emergence of the *Tangentopoli* scandals (a series of scandals in the early 1990s caused by political corruption that implicated several prominent political representatives), which produced a loss of credibility in national coalitions.

The surge of regional sentiments in the North of Italy was favoured also by a complex change of economic factors, both at domestic and international levels. Internally, the equilibrium created by national integration – which brought economic advantages both in the North and the South in the aftermath of World War II, leading to the economic prosperity of the 1960s (Mingione, 1993, 316) – started to fail in the late 1970s – early 1980s, when the political system at central level became more oriented towards the South (Mingione, 1993, 317). Voters in the North started to feel neglected by the system and began to turn to local parties to represent their interests. At international level, the European integration process also played a major role in mutating the overall socio-political and economic landscape: for instance, the increased importance acquired by regions across the European Union strengthened their lobbying and networking activities at the European level, favouring their overall visibility and power (Fabbrini & Brunazzo, 2003, 110).

In Italy, these changes found expression in the rise of *Lega Nord* (Northern League), a political party emerged from the combination of various local "leagues" with strong roots particularly in the wealthier and more industrialised North. It was this party who put regionalism back on the national political agenda, strongly promoting the transformation of Italy into a federal state. The idea was to acquire, through federalism, more financial or fiscal autonomy for Northern regions so that they could emancipate from the central government, especially insofar as decisions on economy, infrastructures and other services were concerned.[5]

B. Pre-2001 reforms

As noted, the 2001 reform was anticipated by a number of initiatives fuelled by demands for more autonomy coming mainly from *Lega Nord*. First, in January 1997 a bicameral commission was established with the task of preparing proposals for a broad constitutional reform which would affect, among other things, also local self-government (Caretti & Tarli Barbieri, 2012, 28). The propositions for constitutional amendment put forward by the commission were however deemed unsatisfactory and its work failed (Bull & Pasquino, 2007, 673).

In the same year, Law 59/1997 (the so-called First Bassanini Law, after the minister who proposed it) transferred to regions, provinces, and municipalities "all functions and administrative duties relative to care of the interests and promotion of the respective communities' development" (Del Duca & Del Duca, 2006, 809). The propelling force behind this was the European Union law principle of subsidiarity (Cartei & Ferraro, 2002, 446).

Very important was also the constitutional entrenchment (with constitutional law 1/1999) of the direct election of regional presidents, preceded by a reform in 1993 which introduced the direct election of mayors. Constitutional law 1/1999 also brought changes to regional statutes (Delledonne & Martinico, 2010–11, 891).

Finally, Law 56/2000 granted broader financial competences to regions (Cartei & Ferraro, 2002, 448).

C. The 2001 constitutional reform

The aforementioned reforms paved the way to the 2001 reform of Italian regionalism, which continued this regionalisation process. The reform was approved under the leadership of the centre-left majority then in power, and implemented

5 It is beyond the scope of this chapter to paint the trajectory of *Lega Nord* and its federalist agenda, as the literature on this topic, both in Italian and English, is gigantic. In addition to the literature used in this chapter, the following works can be consulted on the topic: Baldini & Baldi, 2014; Caravita, 2013; Cartei & Ferraro, 2002; Lecours & Arban, 2015; Mazzoleni, 2009.

with constitutional law 3/2001. This reform, however, was put together quickly and without much conviction, as the centre-left coalition that proposed it did so mainly to contrast the rising power of *Lega Nord*. In any event, the bill that contained the reform was approved by the House of Representatives in February 2001 and by the Senate in March 2001. It was then subject to "confirmative" referendum pursuant to article 138 Const.[6] The referendum was held on 7 October 2001 approving the constitutional amendment.[7] In the remainder of the volume, the most significant aspects of this reform will be analysed in great detail and also in comparative perspective. Here, I will briefly summarise the novelties of this reform.

The 2001 reform significantly amended Title V of Part II of the constitution (articles 114–133) entitled "Regions, Provinces, Municipalities" and pertaining to the relationship between central and peripheral governments.

First, the reform amended article 114 Const., providing that, in addition to the state, Italy is composed of municipalities, provinces, metropolitan cities, and regions, as "autonomous entities having their own statutes, powers and functions in accordance with the principles laid down in the Constitution". The amendment of this article was innovative in many ways. For example, it created a new level of local government, i.e. the metropolitan city, placed between municipalities and provinces. Compared to the "old" version of article 114, which provided that Italy was "divided" into regions, provinces, and municipalities, the "new" wording of article 114 also increased the number of the component units and changed the terminology (Italy is no longer "divided" but "constituted" of the listed component units), and reversed the order, starting from the entity closest to the citizens (municipality) (Ortino, 2003, 187–198).

Second, article 116(3) Const. was amended, allowing ordinary regions to "negotiate with the state particular forms and conditions of autonomy" in the ambit of organisation of the offices of justices of peace, education, environment, and cultural heritage. The forms and conditions of this enhanced autonomy have to be approved by state law, on the basis of an agreement between the state and the regions. For several years, this provision has remained dormant. It was only in 2015 that three regions (Emilia-Romagna, Lombardy, and Veneto), started the process to acquire increased autonomy by initiating negotiations with the central government, not without difficulties (see Palermo and Valdesalici in this volume).

Third, article 117 Const. on the division of legislative powers between the central government and regions was modified. It now mandates that legislative powers are exercised by the state and the regions, in compliance with the principles laid down in the constitution, with EU legislation and with international obligations. Article 117(2) lists in detail all subject matters falling within the

6 Pursuant to article 138 Const. if a constitutional law or a law amending the constitution has not passed with a majority of two-thirds in each of the two Chambers at the second voting, a referendum can be requested either by a fifth of the members of one house, or half a million voters, or five regional councils.

7 The turnout at the referendum was very low, as only 34.1 per cent of the voters participated in the consultation, with 65 per cent voting in favor of the reform.

exclusive legislative powers of the state.[8] Article 117(3) details subject matters of shared jurisdiction between the state and the regions.[9] In such areas, "legislative powers are vested in the Regions, except for the determination of the fundamental principles, which are laid down in State legislation". Regional laws are bound by the provisions laid down in the constitution, by international and EU obligations (Caretti & Tarli Barbieri, 2012, 75–76), and by the fundamental principles enshrined in the national legislation already in force (Caretti & Tarli Barbieri, 2012, 80). Article 117(4) mandates that regions enjoy residuary powers, thus reversing the previous arrangement which reserved to the state all "non-enumerated" powers. Finally, article 117(6) recognises to regions full regulatory powers in all subject matters that are not exclusive competence of the state (Caretti & Tarli Barbieri, 2012, 35). Article 117 represented a true innovation, especially in comparison to the previous arrangement, which listed those areas or subject matters where regions were authorised to legislate, assuming that all other competences belonged to the state. Scholars have pointed out how the new wording of article 117 made it more complicated to fully grasp the scope of the provision. For this reason, especially in the years immediately following 2001, the Italian Constitutional Court ("ItCC") was called to settle conflicts of attribution between

8 Exclusive "national" competences include: foreign policy and international relations of the state; relations between Italy and the European Union; asylum rights and legal status of non-EU citizens; immigration; relations between the Italian state and religious denominations; defense and armed forces; national security; armaments, ammunitions and explosives; currency; savings protection and financial markets; competition protection; foreign exchange system; state taxation and accounting systems; equalisation of financial resources; state bodies and relevant electoral laws; state *referenda*; election of members to the European Parliament; legal and administrative organisation of the state and of national public agencies; public order and security, with the exception of local administrative police; citizenship, civil status and register offices; jurisdiction and procedural law; criminal and civil law; administrative judicial system; determination of the basic levels of benefits relating to civil and social entitlements to be guaranteed across the national territory; general provisions on education; social security; electoral legislation, governing bodies, and fundamental functions of municipalities, provinces, and metropolitan cities; customs, protection of national borders, and international prophylaxis; weights, measures, and standard time; intellectual property law; statistical and computerised coordination of data of state, regional, and local administrations; protection of the environment, the eco-system, and cultural heritage. This listing was amended with constitutional law 1/2012 (see Valdesalici in this volume).

9 Subject matters of shared or concurrent jurisdiction include: international relations of the regions with other states and with the European Union; foreign trade; work safety and protection; education, except for vocational education and training and subject to the autonomy of educational institutions; professions; scientific and technological research and innovation support for productive sectors; health care; nutrition; sports; disaster relief; land-use planning; civil ports and airports; large transport and navigation networks; communications; national production, transportation, and distribution of energy; complementary and supplementary social security; harmonisation of public accounts and coordination of public finance and taxation system; enhancement of cultural and environmental properties, including the promotion and organisation of cultural activities; savings banks, rural banks, regional credit institutions, regional land, and agricultural credit institutions

regions and the state, and contributed with its judgments to clarify the division of powers (see Delledonne in this volume).

Fourth, article 118 Const. introduced the principle of subsidiarity in administrative functions. Article 118(1) now provides that "administrative functions are attributed to municipalities, unless they are conferred to provinces, metropolitan cities, regions, or to the state, pursuant to the principles of subsidiarity, differentiation, and proportionality, to ensure their uniform implementation" (see Martinico in this volume).

Fifth, article 119 Const. on fiscal federalism was also amended. Based on the "old" version of this article, regional finance comprised income deriving from regional taxes as well as from state grants. However, the capacity of regional governments to levy taxes was limited; furthermore, the central government could determine both the type of taxes levied and the amount of the tax. The new article 119 Const. has expanded, at least on paper, the fiscal capacity of regions (Valdesalici in this volume will thoroughly detail financial relations under the new framework).

Sixth, article 120(2) introduced state/regions "substitution powers" and loyal cooperation. This power is backed up by a similar power enshrined in article 117 (5), whereby the state can step in when regions and autonomous provinces fail to implement international agreements and EU measures (see Woelk in this volume).

Finally, article 127 Const. eliminated the control of the state on regional laws. Under the amended article, only an *ex post facto* review by the ItCC can be performed on regional laws allegedly infringing upon areas belonging to the state's legislative jurisdiction, and on state laws allegedly infringing upon the legislative jurisdiction of the regions. All references to the "national interest" have disappeared (Groppi & Scattone, 2006, 133) – except from the statutes of special regions – but practically re-introduced with the case-law of the ItCC (see Delledonne in this volume). Under the "old" provision, regional laws had to pass muster before their implementation and, if the national government deemed that the law infringed upon state's legislative powers or was in contrast with a national interest, it could send the act back to the regional government.

The 2001 reform also abolished article 124 Const., providing that "[a] commissioner of the government (…) supervises the administrative functions exercised by the state and coordinates them with those exercised by the Region". Constitutional Law 3/2001 also eliminated all forms of control over the legality of administrative acts of the Region by an organ of the state as enshrined in the "old" article 125 Const.

IV. Constitutional reforms after 2001

At least on paper, the reform of 2001 significantly strengthened the powers of local sub-units (particularly of regions) to the point that many observers believed that this constitutional change represented the first step towards a more radical federalisation of Italy (*ex multis:* Cartei & Ferraro, 2002; Del Duca & Del Duca, 2006, 799 and 839). However, in the aftermath of 2001, the Italian Parliament failed to implement, through national laws, most of the innovations introduced in the 2001 reform. This inertia led to two major consequences: first, a substantive dissonance between the constitutional text and the actual type of system in operation (Palermo, 2012) and, second, a progressive fading of the political and popular interest for further federal reforms. As a result, in the aftermath of 2001 a number of constitutional reforms have been – more or less successfully – discussed to reduce (rather than increase) the powers of the regions.

Although it was behind the federalist thrust in the 1990s, *Lega Nord* never fully endorsed the 2001 constitutional reform, as it considered it not "federal" enough (Mazzoleni, 2009, 143). Furthermore, there were also political reasons since, as recalled above, the 2001 reform was approved by a centre-left majority, and the centre-right majority which came then in power (of which *Lega Nord* was part) wanted to have their "own" reform. Consequently, they pushed for another reform of regionalism, and in 2005 the Italian parliament (led by a centre-right majority) passed a reform intending to modify certain critical aspects of the 2001 amendments (Bin & Falcon, 2012, 95). Among other things, the reform aimed at transforming the Senate into a "federal Senate" or "Chamber of Regions" (Caretti & Tarli Barbieri, 2012, 38; Bin & Falcon, 2012, 95–96) so that it would be elected by direct universal suffrage on a regional basis and thus guarantee territorial representation at the centre. The Senate would also be vested with legislative powers on a series of issues directly related to regions, thus leaving the Chamber of Deputies with legislative competences on matters of national concern (Bin & Falcon, 2012, 95–96). With regards to division of powers, the reform would assign exclusive legislative competences to regions in health services, organisation of schools and management of educational and training institutions, the definition of educational and training programs of specific interest to the regions and local police; similarly, regional powers over "residual" matters were also considered "exclusive" (Caretti & Tarli Barbieri, 2012, 38). This proposal was submitted to popular referendum in 2006 but it was eventually rejected by 61.3 per cent of the voters.

In 2012, some parts of the constitution, including aspects of regionalism, were amended with constitutional law 1/2012. Originated by the need to "improve the credibility of the Italian institutions in the global context" (Groppi, 2012), this law eroded the financial autonomy of regions, with a consequent impact on the whole architecture of local autonomies (Cecchetti, 2012, 3). The modifications amended articles 81, 97, 117 and 119 Const. First, article 81 introduced the principles of "balanced budget" and "sustainable debt" for the national budget and for the budgets of all public administration (regions, provinces, municipalities, and metropolitan cities). The applicability to all public administration of the principles of "balanced budget" and "sustainable debt" are reiterated by the amended article 97(1) Const. (Cecchetti, 2012, 5).[10] Second, article 81 reserves to a procedurally "reinforced" national law the power to set the fundamental norms and

10 Article 97(1) as amended mandates that "consistently with the EU legal system, public administrations shall guarantee a balanced budget and a sustainable public debt".

criteria to implement the principles of "balanced budget" and "sustainable debt": consequently, the national legislature is granted an exclusive power in this specific subject matter, including the budget of local governments (Cecchetti, 2012, 8), and is free to impose limitations and obligations to the expenses of local autonomies (Cecchetti, 2012, 1). Constitutional law 1/2012 brought some changes also to article 117 Const. on division of legislative powers. The subject matter labelled "harmonisation of public accounts" was severed from "coordination of public finance and taxation system". Therefore, while under the "old" version of article 117(3) (as amended in 2001), the two subjects were listed together under the shared competences of national and regional legislatures, now the item "harmonisation of public accounts" has been added to the list of subject matters of exclusive competence of the national legislator (article 117(2), Const.) (Cecchetti, 2012, 5). Substantial modifications were also brought to article 119 Const. on fiscal federalism, further limiting the autonomy of local governments (see Valdesalici in this volume).

Finally, in April 2016, the Italian Parliament approved another extensive constitutional reform – dubbed "Renzi-Boschi" from the names of its promoters – whose objective was to "overcome perfect bicameralism, reduce the number of MPs, reduce institutional expenses, eliminate CNEL (*Consiglio Nazionale dell'Economia e del Lavoro)*, and amend Title V of the Constitution" (Camera dei Deputati, 2016, 3). A substantive analysis of the merits and flaws of this reform is beyond the scope of this contribution (*ex multis*, see Caravita, 2016; Pace, 2016,) so I will just briefly comment on the proposed changes to the Senate and the amendment of Title V.

Similarly to the proposal of 2005, the 2016 reform intended to transform the role of the Senate into a chamber of regional representation. While the Chamber of Deputies would continue to be composed by members directly elected by – and representing – Italian citizens, the Senate would be transformed into a Chamber representing regional and territorial interests (Riforma Costituzionale, 2016, 6). The number of senators would be reduced from 315 to 100, with 95 senators appointed by Regional Councils among regional councillors and mayors, and 5 senators appointed by the President of the Republic for 7 years (Riforma Costituzionale, 2016, 6). Also the legislative role of the two Chambers would change, since only certain bills would require the approval of both Chambers, and the Senate would vote only on specific subject matters affecting local interests. The new Senate would also appoint two judges of the Italian Constitutional Court (Riforma Costituzionale, 2016, 6).

As for Title V of the constitution, the reform would remove provinces from the constitution as part of a broader restructuring of local self-government (Riforma Costituzionale, 2016, 7), and it would also radically change the distribution of legislative powers between regional and state governments as enshrined in article 117 Const.[11] Finally, the reform would reintroduce a "supremacy clause" allowing

11 Concurrent powers would be eliminated – thus leaving only exclusive regional or state powers – but the number of exclusive state powers would significantly expand (Riforma Costituzionale, 2016, 7).

a national law to legislate in the field of regional powers in case of overarching national interest (Riforma Costituzionale, 2016, 7). Article 116(3) on differential regionalism and article 120(2) on substitution powers would also be amended (Riforma Costituzionale, 2016, 7).

On 4 December 2016, the reform was rejected by popular referendum: the turnout was 65.48 per cent, with the "No" votes amounting to 59.1 per cent and the "Yes" votes amounting to 40.88 per cent.

V. Conclusion

The purpose of the regional design ingrained in the 1948 constitution – and revised in 2001 – was to depart from the strong centralised model existing since unification, without creating a fully-fledged federation. In fact, a *pure* or *classic* federal solution for Italy has often been resisted, mainly for fear that it would lead to the disintegration of the country. At the same time, a strongly centralised model was also deemed unsuitable, especially in light of the deep socio-economic, linguistic, and cultural fragmentation existing in Italy. As noted, the gist of Italian asymmetric regionalism is crystallised in article 5 Const., which reconciles the unity and indivisibility of Italy with the recognition and promotion of local self-government. The regional model was a product of the genius of Ambrosini, whose idea of regionalism was highly innovative and revolutionary for the time, both from a theoretical and normative standpoint.

When Ambrosini proposed regionalism during the Constituent Assembly, he was clearly describing a "third genus" which blended both unitary and federal elements. However, situating the regional model as a variant of the unitary or of the federal state is controversial, as the features of the regional paradigm are still unclear. For example, we can ask to what extent the classification between regional and federal model that Ambrosini offered still stands today. Ambrosini wrote at a time when federalism was not as elaborated and sophisticated as it is now. The US federal model entrenched in the 1787 constitution was considered quintessential, and was highly influential: in fact, the Swiss and Australian federal systems (created in 1848 and 1901, respectively) heavily borrowed from the US paradigm, as did the South American federations. These systems had all emerged from the "coming together" of formerly independent states, and the federal constitution had the nature of covenant (or *foedus*) among them and the federal government, as Ambrosini contended. However, recent experiences have proved that federal systems no longer emerge only from the "coming together" of formerly independent states; rather "holding together" federations (federal states emerging from the progressive "federalisation" of a formerly unitary state such as, for example, Belgium, Spain, or South Africa) are becoming very popular. Also, the way legislative powers are divided between the centre and the periphery significantly varies among federations, and specifically enumerated powers for the federal government are no longer the rule, as is no longer the rule that in a federal model residual powers always belong to the constituent units. Finally, even if sovereignty is virtually split in a federal system, the powers enjoyed by the federated entities, however labelled, are not absolute (as sovereignty suggests), as they should always abide by the constitution and often in case of conflict between a federal and a state law, the former prevails.

Ambrosini's intuition of regionalism – premised on Mazzini and Minghetti – has remained particularly rooted in Italy, so when federal ideas had a resurgence in the 1990s and discussions were made to transform Italy into a more federal model, Ambrosini's scheme still loomed large. In fact, the 2001 reform strengthened at least on paper the powers of regions, but did not go all the way to the creation of a pure federal model. At the time we are writing, the expression *federalism* (in all its possible declinations) has practically disappeared from the political agenda of all major political parties, including the *Lega Nord* (now informally called simply "Lega") which was once its main supporter.

In any event, the regional model conceived by Ambrosini for Italy has influenced also other European models, most notably Spain, Poland (Groppi & Scattone, 2006, 132) and, to a certain extent, the UK with its devolution scheme (Grottanelli de' Santi, 2006).

Literature

Gaspare Ambrosini, 'Relazione sulle Autonomie Regionali' [report prepared for the Constituent Assembly of 1946–47]. http://legislature.camera.it/_dati/costituente/lavori/relaz_proposte/II_Sottocommissione/30nc.pdf

Ugo Amoretti, 'A New Look at Federalism. Italy Decentralizes' (2002) 13 (2) *Journal of Democracy* 126

Erika Arban, 'Carlo Cattaneo and Gaetano Salvemini: The Modernity of their Federalism' (2017) 3 (2) *The Italian Law Journal* 277

Gianfranco Baldini and Brunetta Baldi, 'Decentralization in Italy and the Troubles of Federalization' (2014) 24 *Regional and Federal Studies* 87

Silvio Basile, 'La cultura politico-istituzionale e le esperienze "tedesche"', in Ugo De Siervo (ed.), *Scelte della Costituente e cultura giuridica, I, Costituzione italiana e modelli stranieri* (Il Mulino, 1980)

Roberto Bin and Giandomenico Falcon (eds.), *Diritto Regionale* (Il Mulino, 2012)

Norberto Bobbio and Carlo Cattaneo, *Stati Uniti d'Italia* (Donzelli, 2010)

Martin Bull and Gianfranco Pasquino, 'A Long Quest in Vain: Institutional Reforms in Italy' (2007) 30 *West European Politics* 670

Camera dei Deputati, Servizio Studi, 'La Riforma Costituzionale'. Schede di Lettura, n. 216/12, May2016 [report prepared by the Research Office of the Chamber of Deputies], online at http://documenti.camera.it/leg17/dossier/pdf/ac0500p.pdf

Beniamino Caravita, 'Italy: Between the hybrid state and Europe's federalizing process', in John Loughlin, John Kinkaid, and Wilfried Swenden (eds.), *Routledge Handbook of Regionalism and Federalism* (Routledge, 2013)

Beniamino Caravita, 'La Riforma Renzi - Boschi: Le Ragioni Del Sì' (2016) *Rivista AIC* 2 published on 17 June: https://www.rivistaaic.it/images/rivista/pdf/2_2016_Caravita.pdf

Paolo Caretti and Giovanni Tarli Barbieri (eds.), *Diritto Regionale*, 3rd ed. (Giappichelli, 2012)

Gian Franco Cartei and Vincenzo Ferraro, 'Reform of the Fifth Title of the Italian Constitution: A First Step Towards a Federal System' (2002) 8 *European Public Law* 445

Sabino Cassese, 'The Italian constitutional architecture: from unification to the present day' (2012) 17 *Journal of Modern Italian Studies* 2

Marcello Cecchetti, 'Legge costituzionale n. 1 del 2012 e Titolo V della parte II della Costituzione: profili di contro-riforma dell'autonomia regionale e locale' (2012) *Federalismi.it*, http://www.federalismi.it/ApplOpenFilePDF.cfm?dpath=document\editoriale&dfile=EDITORIALE_21122012092949.pdf&content=Legge+costituzionale+n.+1+del+2012+e+Titolo+V+della+Parte+II+della+Costituzione:+profili+di+contro-riforma+dell%E2%80%99autonomia+regionale+e+locale&content_auth=Marcello+Cecchetti

Zeffiro Ciuffoletti, *Federalismo e regionalismo: da Cattaneo alla Lega* (Laterza, 1994)

Antonio D'Atena, 'Between Spain and Germany: The Historical Models of Italian Regionalism', in Stelio Mangiameli (ed.), *Italian Regionalism: Between Unitary Traditions and Federal Processes* (Springer, 2014)

Louis Del Duca and Patrick Del Duca, 'An Italian Federalism? – The State, its Institutions and National Culture as Rule of Law Guarantor' (2006) 54 *American Journal of Comparative Law* 807

Giacomo Delledonne and Giuseppe Martinico, 'Legal Conflicts and Subnational Constitutionalism' (2010–2011) *42 Rutgers Law Journal* 881

Sergio Fabbrini and Marco Brunazzo, 'Federalizing Italy: The Convergent Effects of Europeanization and Domestic Mobilization' (2003) 13 *Regional and Federal Studies* 104

Tania Groppi, 'The Impact of the Financial Crisis on the Italian Written Constitution' (2012) 4 *Italian Journal of Public Law* 1

Tania Groppi and Nicoletta Scattone, 'Italy: The Subsidiarity Principle' (2006) 4 *International Journal of Constitutional Law* 132

Giovanni Grottanelli de' Santi, 'The Italian Variant of Federalism', in Jörg Fedtke and Basil Markesinis (eds.), *Patterns of Regionalism and Federalism. Lessons for the UK* (Hart Publishing, 2006)

André Lecours and Erika Arban, 'Why Federalism Does Not Always Take Shape: the Cases of Italy and Nepal' (2015) 25 *Regional and Federal Studies* 183

Aurelio Lepre, *Italia, Addio? Unità e disunità dal 1860 a oggi* (Mondadori, 1994)

Martin Loughlin, *Foundations of Public Law* (Oxford Scholarship Online, 2010)

Stelio Mangiameli, 'The Regions and the Reforms: Issues Resolved and Problems Pending', in Stelio Mangiameli (ed.), *Italian Regionalism: Between Unitary Traditions and Federal Processes* (Springer, 2014)

Martino Mazzoleni, 'The Italian regionalization: a story of partisan logics' (2009) 14 *Modern Italy* 135

Enzo Mingione, 'Italy: the resurgence of regionalism' (1993) 69 *International Affairs* 316

Sergio Ortino, 'Ripensare lo Stato nel ripensare le nuove forme politiche', in Silvano Labriola (ed.) *Ripensare lo Stato* (Giuffrè, 2003)

Alessandro Pace, 'La Riforma Renzi - Boschi: Le Ragioni Del No'(2016) *Rivista AIC* 2, published on 17 June, https://www.rivistaaic.it/images/rivista/pdf/2_2016_Pace%204.pdf

Francesco Palermo, 'Italy: A Federal Country without Federalism?', in Michael Burgess, G. Alan Tarr (eds.), *Constitutional Dynamics in Federal Systems. Sub-national perspectives* (Forum of Federations and McGill-Queen's University Press, 2012)

Robert Putnam, *Making Democracy Work. Civic Traditions in Modern Italy* (Princeton University Press, 1993)

Filippo Sabetti, *Civilization and Self-Government. The Political Thought of Carlo Cattaneo* (Lexington Books, 2010)

2 The new "form of government" in the reforms of the Italian regional system

Cristina Fasone[1] *and Giovanni Piccirilli*[2]

I. Introduction

The mutual relationship between the legislative and the executive branch and their interaction in the formation of the general political direction constitute the core of the "form of government", a classical topic in the Italian scholarly debate (Elia, 1970). It was elaborated with reference to States, in order to describe the fundamental dynamics of a given national polity, but then has been extended also to local and regional levels, in order to describe the fundamental functioning of their institutional system.

How have regional "forms of government" changed in Italy over the last twenty years and at what consequence in terms of democratic accountability? Studies on the transformations of the inter-institutional balance at regional level triggered by the constitutional reforms of 1999 and of 2001 abound. Scholars have emphasised the role played by constitutional case-law in devising a common model of "form of government" at least for regions with ordinary statutes (of autonomy) (*statuti regionali*) compared to the new open-texture constitutional provisions which, for the very first time, include the wording "form of government" (Article 123 Const.). Comparative analyses on the implementation of this model across regions have been carried out in the first decade, in particular, since the entry into force of the reforms. Subsequently, the last decade has witnessed the blossoming of regional constitutional law textbooks in almost every region, also dealing with the specific equilibrium reached in the form of government.[3] This rich debate, also on the desirability to apply the very notion of "form of government" to regions in a country that cannot be considered as federal, is available mostly in Italian.

The contribution aims, first, to reconstruct this scholarly debate, highlighting similarities and differences of the Italian approach on the regional form of

1 Assistant Professor of Comparative Public Law, Department of Political Science, LUISS Guido Carli, Rome.

2 Assistant Professor of Constitutional Law, Law Department, LUISS Guido Carli, Rome.

3 See the book series on 'Diritto costituzionale regionale' (Regional constitutional law) published by Giappichelli: https://www.giappichelli.it/giappichelli/serie/view/code/gcr/ visited on 12 August 2020.

DOI: 10.4324/9781003104469-3

government in relation to the comparative legal scholarship on subnational constitutionalism. Second, it places the constitutional reform of 1999 in the broader context of the (never-ending) season of institutional reforms or attempts thereof at national and subnational level. In particular, the chapter looks at the accomplished reform of the form of government in the regions, in continuity with the local electoral law passed in 1993 and with the repeatedly failed attempts to replicate a similar modification of the form of government at State level. Third, the contribution articulates its assessment of the relationship between the developments in the regional forms of government and democratic accountability from three perspectives: 1) the design of the new regional form of government as envisaged in Const. law no. 1/1999; 2) the evolution of the regional inter-institutional relationships – in particular between the president and the legislative assembly – in the practice and in the case-law; 3) and the regional sources of the law and their autonomy. Finally, it concludes that twenty years after the reforms the aim to streamline the accountability chain in the regions in favour of their presidents has been achieved, even though this has led to the overstrength of the executive. The "presidentialisation" of regional politics is partly derived from transnational trends and developments and is partly context-dependent. The constitutional reform, however, has failed to deliver the expected autonomy to the regions: a combination of factors has contributed to diminish the rate of actual institutional innovation and, as such, the change of the regional form of government cannot be considered as a test-bench for the much-awaited national institutional reforms.

More theoretically, this contribution aims to speak to the strand of scholarship on subnational constitutionalism seeking to advance the knowledge of the international academic community about the evolution and reform of the regional form of government in Italy, also in relation to the national one.

II. The study of the regional form of government in Italy in the framework of the debate on subnational constitutionalism

The notion of form of government, by which we refer to the relationship amongst the constitutional bodies entitled to give the political direction to a certain polity (Mortati, 1973), in particular between the legislative and the executive branch,[4] has been analysed by generations of Italian constitutional scholars and represents one of the classic topics of investigation in national constitutional law.

The notion, as such, is much less used in comparative constitutional law, with a few exceptions in the Spanish-speaking world (Pérez Calvo, 2014) and in continental Europe (Steffani, 1983; Troper, 1994). Almost non-existent in the Anglo-Saxon context and occasionally used in a much broader sense (MacCormick, 2006, 8), it is replaced by functional substitutes, i.e. the study of the constitutional features of parliamentarism and presidentialism, and by the emphasis on some landmark constitutional principles, like separation of powers and checks and

4 According to Elia (1970), the relationship also includes other players, like the electoral body, political parties, and, potentially, social formations.

balances (see, notably, Ackerman, 2000), without resorting to the more encompassing and comprehensive "relational" notion of form of government. The reasons for this "geographical" difference are not clear. Partly it may be because of the different path towards the autonomisation of constitutional law in continental Europe and in the Anglo-Saxon context with an earlier and deeper distinction from political philosophy. The difference in the approach may also depend on the higher institutional instability of the continental European countries and the normative ambition of the notion "form of government". The latter aims not only to describe a certain institutional system, but also to provide a direction for its evolution and interpretation.[5] The more chaotic institutional history of continental Europe, with frequent changes of the constitutional regime, led political élites and scholars to resort very often to constitutional engineering – compared to the UK or the US – and, hence, to make reference to the flexible and normative notion of "form of government".

In Italy, the debate in the constitutional assembly (1946–1947), the choice for a "pure" parliamentarism, based on a weak level of rationalisation (Mirkine-Guetzévitch, 1928), and the well-known governmental instability it triggered at the national level, have probably contributed to feeding the line of scholarship devoted to the investigation of the form of government in the country. Not surprisingly, at least since when ordinary regions were established, in 1970 – but, to some extent, also before with regard to the five regions with special statutes[6] – this rich elaboration on the form of government has also applied at subnational level. Indeed, municipalities and regions were affected by a comparable level of governmental instability as the State institutions and governments. Moreover, in a regional State "in the making", gradually taking up the features of a quasi-federal system (Palermo, 2012), regional and local forms of government could only develop in line with the broader national context, as they are inevitably affected by the political and institutional dynamics of the latter. Also for this "inevitable" strong interdependence doubts were raised regarding the possibility to apply the notion of form of government at Italian subnational levels, given the alleged lack of autonomy – from the centre – regional and, even more so, local authorities had in shaping the political directions for their own communities (Andò, 1971; Pitruzzella, 1989).

Although there is still some resistance (Luciani, 2010), the Italian constitutional reform of 1999 has to a large extent led to overcome any hesitation about the use of the notion of form of government in relation to regions. Article 123 Const., as amended, openly refers to the "form of government" as one of the basic and indispensable elements to be regulated under the revised regional statutes of autonomy (see further, section 4). As a consequence of such an explicit constitutional acknowledgement, monographs and textbooks dealing precisely with the

5 See the difference between *forma formata* (how it works) and *forma formans* (how it should be) (Luciani, 2010).

6 Friuli-Venezia Giulia, Sardinia, Sicily, Trentino Alto-Adige (with the two autonomous Provinces of Trento and Bolzano), Aosta Valley.

topic abound. These publications, which would potentially make an interesting contribution to the study of subnational constitutionalism, in that they highlight (mostly) similarities and (a few) differences amongst Italian regions in this respect, are published mostly, if not only, in Italian.

However, to date few contributions available to the English-speaking community have directly or indirectly dealt with the regional form of government in Italy. They have predominantly focused on the issue of the institutional autonomy left to Italian regions (Palermo and Kössler, 2018, chapter 1), on the role of the constitutional case-law in preserving such an autonomy (Delledonne and Martinico, 2009), and on the position of regional legislatures vis-à-vis the executives (Fasone, 2012).

In the last decade, it appears that, beyond Italy, scholars of subnational constitutionalism elsewhere have also become increasingly interested in the study of the subnational governmental dynamics and the notion of "form of government" has been expressly cited. Michael Burgess and G. Alan Tarr (2012, 9), for example, referred to the "form of government" as a case study to detect the degree of "constitutional space" left to subnational units by federal constitutions in contrast to a situation where the form of government is mandated by the centre.

Moreover, similarly to the perspective that is followed here, several scholars in the field of federalism and subnational constitutionalism have highlighted the (expected) mutual influence in the shape and functioning of the forms of government across the federal and the regional subunits of the same State and between these subunits and the national form of government (see, e.g. Dinan, 2008). For example, Robert F. Williams (1988) has noticed that the framers of the US Constitution drew inspiration from state constitutions when designing the federal form of government, by modelling the US president on the governor of New York and rejecting the idea to equip citizens with the power to directly instruct their representatives, given the inability of such mechanisms to work properly at State level.

III. Common premises and continuity with the renovation of the Italian institutional system in the 1990s

The modification of the regional form of government is an important milestone in the long-standing debate about institutional reforms in Italy. It can be said that it is the only part actually attained in the general rethinking of the equilibrium between legislative and executive branches, in a general picture of repeatedly failed reforms.

The instability of the Italian government at State level is renown: between 1948 and 1992, Italy had almost 50 different presidents of the council of ministers. The situation in the regions was probably even worse. The Constitution replicated at every level of government (municipalities, provinces, regions, and the State) the same idea of "pure" parliamentarism, possibly accentuating its fragilities with regard to the regions: Article 122 Const., in its original version, foresaw the parliamentary election of the president of the region and its "government" (*Giunta*), to be selected within its members. Hence, the lack of an autonomously structured party system at regional level (Bifulco, 2009) made regional elections a sort of second order ones, so that the stability of regional majorities was strictly dependent on the evolution at national level: as soon as a political crisis in Rome led to a change of government, similar changes followed at regional level, amplifying the lack of stability and autonomy of the regional politics.

In this complex scenario, the constitutional amendment passed in 1999 represents only the last part of a process started at the beginning of the decade which had the most dramatic moment in 1993 and related to a comprehensive renovation of the Italian political and institutional system.

Soon after the fall of the Berlin Wall, the Italian political system started to change, abandoning the consociational logic which had featured the first decades of the Republic and that had been conditioned by the presence of one of the biggest communist parties of the Western World. Notwithstanding its progressive autonomisation from the USSR, the Italian Communist Party was considered as unfit to participate in the government (Elia, 1970) but was anyway involved in the legislative bargain. As the international scenario evolved, the Communist Party changed its name and platform, aiming to become a potential legitimate candidate to enter the government in a more open and competitive democracy.

At the same time, the draft and then the entry into force of the Treaty of Maastricht and its budgetary constraints led to the abandonment of the deficit-spending policies that devastated Italian public finances in the 1970s and 1980s. The vast majority of the political parties were hit by the corruption scandals, which reached their climax in 1993 and basically cancelled some of the former protagonists of Italian political life (the socialist party in the first place, whereas the Christian Democrats suffered various transformations and eventually dissolved in a variety of marginal parties). Moreover, the people via two referendums (in 1991 and, decisively, in 1993) pushed for a dramatic change of the electoral law, paving the way to a shift from a proportional system to a mixed one, mostly based on single member constituencies (Manzella, 2003, 7).

Elements of renovation also emerged from specific choices taken by the same political system: in the first months of the same year a fundamental novelty was brought with the new electoral law for municipalities and provinces (no. 81/1993). For the first time, mayors and presidents of provincial districts could be elected directly by citizens, without the intermediation of city or provincial councils. This innovation, combined with the drop-in legitimacy of the political parties, boosted the verticalisation and presidentialisation of politics that had some premises in the 1980s and in particular with the leadership of Bettino Craxi, but now had institutional mechanisms for its consolidation (Calise, 2005).

In sum, 1993 brought an electoral reform for the national parliament, introducing a mostly first-past-the-post system; a massive reshuffle in the political parties led to the creation of new political subjects and identities, abandoning the rooted ideologies of the past; a broad acceptance of the popular request of more direct and immediate democracy, expressed through referendum and civic movements; the first experiences of direct election of executive offices, with the significant municipal election in many big cities (including Milan, Turin, Rome, Naples, and Palermo). The renovation was later sealed by the victory of Berlusconi in the 1994 general elections, with a party set up in less than six months and a coalition including the Northern League (*Lega Nord)* as a strategic partner, which was crucial for the overwhelming victory in that part of the country.

Regions were not directly involved in the wave of novelties introduced in 1993 but they immediately took centre stage in the subsequent phase. In the big discussion for a new institutional design, regions and the federalisation of the form of State suddenly became one of the major issues of the political debate, also due to the pivotal role it had in the transition of the Italian Republic by the Northern League. The latter had already achieved some results in the late 1980s, but it is in 1992 (and in the subsequent new phase) that it had its real *exploit*. As said, it was part of the winning coalition in 1994, and was able to stay in government after having withdrawn the support to Berlusconi. Progressively it became one of the major political parties in the big regions of the North (the most productive and richest part of the country). Its claims for autonomy and even secession of the northern Italy put the discussion on the role of the regions and the devolution of competences at subnational level at the top of the political agenda. This discussion was held in the turmoil of the transition from the old party system to the new equilibrium polarised by Berlusconi.

As frequently occurred in the turning points of Italian history – in which institutional engineering is often considered a sort of miracle cure – electoral reforms have been used to anticipate elements and ideas of broader constitutional innovations. Thus, shortly before the 1995 regional elections, a narrow modification of the electoral law for the regions (set forth by law no. 43/1995) was passed in order to get the functioning of regional bodies closer to the model designed for municipalities and provinces, which was acquiring consensus in the population. As said, due to constitutional provisions requiring the election of the president of the region and of the regional government (*Giunta*) among the members of the assembly (*Consiglio regionale*) it was impossible to transpose directly the model of law no. 81/1993 with the direct election of the president of the region. Consequently, the approach was more indirect and caused many criticisms about its possible unconstitutionality (Di Giovine and Pizzetti, 1996). The electoral law for the regions was amended in order to award a bonus of one-fifth of the available seats to the most voted "regional list" which had a designated leader (*capolista*) indicated on the ballot. The combination of these factors was in the sense of indirectly designating the candidate to the presidency of the region and to support his/her majority with the bonus of seats. As the constitutional framework lacked further mechanisms of rationalisation, the same law proposed an innovative attempt to stabilise majorities: in case of whatever clash between the executive and the regional legislature within two years after the elections, the legislative term would have been shortened to 24 months. This sophisticated mechanism (also claimed to be unconstitutional: Volpi, 2000) aimed to improve the stability of the regional government and pushed for a progressive homogenisation of the electoral discipline and what has been later labelled as "the Italian model of government"

(D'Alimonte, 2007), which would be based on majority assuring electoral laws and the direct or indirect election of the leader of the political coalition.[7]

This strategy of enhancing political stability of regions through the sole modification of the electoral law was evidently partial and, as said, quite problematic from the constitutional point of view. It had to be completed with a constitutional amendment that was in a first moment absorbed in the general discussion about the comprehensive constitutional reform being debated at that time.

After the general elections in 1996, the moment for a bipartisan discussion on the topic seemed to be promising. The centre-left majority approached the topic of regional autonomy with a twofold strategy: on the one hand, by innovating ordinary legislation regulating the distribution of administrative functions,[8] with the aim of promoting the regional and local self-government; on the other, by setting up in the national Parliament a bicameral committee for constitutional reforms, with the very ambitious aim of a complete redraft of the second part of the Constitution, related to the institutional relationships.

Notwithstanding the constructive debate of the first months and even the drafting of a constitutional reform bill in the fall of 1997, the committee failed because of the lack of political agreement in 1998. However, the parts related to regions were those on which it seemed that both majority and opposition could converge. In the view of the regional elections to be held in spring 2000, a first part of the constitutional reform, limited to the procedure of the approval of regional statutes and to their contents, was passed with the Const. law no. 1/1999. A further and broader constitutional amendment was later approved (with a narrower majority and the first-ever request of a constitutional referendum) in 2001, with a complete rethinking of the division of legislative competences between the State and the regions, as well as a deep valorisation of territorial and local autonomy, so to give full implementation to the constitutional principles already enshrined in Article 5 Const. (Berti, 1975).

IV. A primer on the design of the Italian regional form of government after 1999

The current form of government of the Italian regions derives from the implementation of Const. law no. 1/1999, what appeared at first as a major constitutional breakthrough given the period of constitutional stalemate just described. The 15 ordinary regions were given the power to adopt their own statutes and to define their form of government and institutional arrangements in compliance with the Constitution. Subsequent constitutional amendments granted the same possibility to the special regions.[9] The reform created high expectations at first,

7 See the chapter by Alex Wilson in this volume.

8 See, in particular, law no. 59/1997 and the legislative decrees adopted on its basis.

9 See Const. law no. 2/2001, which allowed the special regions to regulate the form of government outside of their statutes of autonomy, by approving *ad hoc* laws by the absolute majority of the regional council's members.

with regard to the enhanced autonomy of the regions. As the practice has revealed, however, regions were not guaranteed a great margin for manoeuvre nor have they been able to use the margin granted properly (Gianfrancesco, 2009). This has led to a trend towards the homogenisation of the regional forms of government, potentially divergent, towards a common model, then followed also with some adaptations by most of the regions with special statutes.

Const. law no. 1/1999 foresaw the direct election of the president of the region by the people – at subnational level, a unique case amongst European countries in comparative perspective – as a "transitional" requirement for the ordinary regions, pending the adoption of the new ordinary statutes under Article 123 Const. as revised. However, this "transitional" element could well endure over time, as in fact it did, should the region in question decide to codify it in the new statute. As a consequence, this transitional feature turned out to be a permanent and typified element of the regional form of government, up to the point that only Aosta Valley and the autonomous province of Bolzano, within Trentino-Alto Adige, have decided to keep the parliamentary form of government (Palermo, 2020, 1068–1073).

With a view to counter the very negative evaluation of the performance of regional governments from the 1970s to the 1990s (D'Atena, 1988) – too unstable executives and too much conditioned by the changes of political majority in the legislative assemblies – the main elements of the new form of government at regional level, as envisaged (only temporarily) by Const. law no. 1/1999, were: the direct election of the president of the region together with that of the council; the power of the president of the region to appoint and remove the other members of the regional executive, without any participation of the council;[10] the power of the council to force the president to resign; the "joint destiny" of the regional council and the president, who stand together or fall together (see *infra* in this section), which makes definitely unlikely the removal of the president in charge by the assembly through the withdrawal of confidence.

This "new" form of government entails aspects which are typical to national presidential systems (the direct election of the president of the region, in the first place, as well as his/her possibility to appoint and dismiss the other members of the executive) and others taken from more traditional parliamentarism (the confidence relationship, in particular). It has also been labelled as "neo-parliamentarism" (Ceccanti, 1998) with the aim of underlining the step further made from the previous system, whereas other commentators emphasised the lack of continuity between the elected president and the majority in the council, concluding for a classification of the form of government closer to presidentialism (Tarli Barbieri, 2004).

Indeed, the power of regional council to self-dissolve, as per Article 126 Const., should not be overstated and can be used in several different hypotheses. The first two hypotheses have been described as an "institutional suicide" (Gianfrancesco, 2009, 218), when the majority of the members of the council decides to resign (as

10 As also confirmed by the ItCC judgement no. 12/2006.

happened in Lombardy in 2013,[11] see Coduti, 2013) or when a motion of no confidence against the president of the region is approved (some statutes also add the refusal to approve the question of confidence tabled by the president: Coduti, 2010). However, the practice of these remedies has been extremely limited: only one case for the former, not a single occurrence of the latter. This is because regional councils are very reluctant to use their prerogatives to sanction the president because of the impact on their term of office, too. The same effect of a new election of both the regional council and the president can be caused by the permanent inability, death, or voluntary resignation of the president (so mixing political disagreement and "external" causes of impossibility to stay in office).[12]

Particularly with this regard, one can wonder whether the attempt to rationalise the regional form of government has not gone beyond its scope by questioning the democratic legitimation of the so-called "*simul stabunt, simul cadent*" clause. If, for any reason, the president is deemed to be permanently unable to stay in office or has to be removed (see Piccirilli and Perniciaro, 2011), the council is forcefully dissolved. Either the two institutions act side by side or they cannot stay in office. However, the system of sanctions that penalises the council does not operate vis-à-vis the president, who, for example, can change the political majority supporting him/her in the council without any consequences in terms of institutional balance (Viceconte, 2010).

As it will be further confirmed in section V, as a sort of "retaliation" compared to the pre-1999 regime, regional assemblies are definitely in a weaker position within the regional form of government, while the *finalité* of the reform, to improve executive stability, has been achieved overall.

V. The functioning of the inter-institutional relationships at regional level

As soon as the new statutes were to have been approved, regions could have chosen either to maintain the standard form of government provided in Const. law no. 1/1999 or to adopt a different one (for instance moving back to the election of the president of the region by the council), if consistent with the Constitution. As anticipated, the former was the default option set by the Constitution and the one confirmed by the new statutes approved.

This outcome was the consequence of two main factors. On the one hand, the regions had become accustomed to the new form of government introduced in 1999 – also because it assured a double channel of direct legitimation, of the council and of the president – and were not willing to go back to the past or to

11 Oddly, upon request of the same president of the region, as a more convenient political move than his resignation.

12 Interestingly all these elements have been put in continuity with the original content of Article 126 Const. according to which the regional council could be dissolved by the president of the republic in case of acts in contrast with the Constitution or severe violations of the law. This provision has been however supplemented with the possibility to also remove the president of the region.

test alternatives (the failure could have meant the sanction of the Constitutional Court – hereinafter, ItCC – and/or subsequent amendments to the statutes); on the other hand, the attempt by some regions, essentially the councils, who approved the statutes, to insert variations on the "pre-packaged" form of government was obstructed by the ItCC by adopting an extremely narrow reading of the regional autonomy on this point.

In general, the latter played the role of limiting the development of a more innovative autonomy by regions. This line of case-law will develop more clearly with regard to the 2001 constitutional reform, in relation to which the ItCC progressively reaffirmed the centrality of State legislation with a narrow interpretation of regional legislative competences (Calzolaio, 2012), but the premises of this centralistic nuances can already be found with regard to the institutional innovations attempted by statutes of autonomy.

For example, the ItCC limited the use of iconic denominations for regional bodies, with the aim of stressing the uniqueness of the State representation and of its branches of government. It was evident in judgement no. 106/2002, in which it denied the possibility of using the word "Parliament" with reference to the regional councils, because only "the" (State) Parliament is the place of national representation (Article 67 Const.).

Later on the ItCC developed a quite disappointing case-law about the potential innovation of the regional form of government. Even basic attempts to deviate from the binary choice between the transitional model provided for by the Const. law no. 1/1999 and the original pure parliamentarism have been rejected. For example, the statute of autonomy approved by Calabria proposed the indication on the ballot of a vice-president, so to let the voters know beforehand the person who would have replaced the directly elected president in case of death or permanent inability. With judgement no. 2/2004 the ItCC declared this innovation as unconstitutional, embracing an extremely narrow reading of Article 126 Const.

Thus, in the end, the position of regional councils in the regional form of government has certainly not been enhanced by the constitutional reform (Olivetti, 2003; Cavaleri, 2010).[13] The aim of the reform was acknowledged by the ItCC itself: to simplify the regional political systems – with the aspiration to move from an extreme fragmentation of political groups to a bipolarisation – and to make the functioning of the political institutions more stable (see, again, ItCC judgement no. 2/2004). Therefore, regional councils became far less free to determine the destiny of the executives compared to the past. The real winners of the constitutional reform were the presidents of the regions.

According to Article 126 Const. and to the new statutes, the council can challenge the existence of the confidence relationship, basically in two ways: first, by approving a motion of no confidence by the absolute majority of its members or, second, where foreseen, by rejecting a question of confidence tabled by the president. As a matter of fact, in judgement no. 12/2006 the ItCC disputably denied

13 Neither was the position of the governing bodies of the regions (*Giunte regionali*), in search for a new role between the powerful presidents and the councils.

the existence of the confidence relationship between the council and the president and affirmed that the relation is rather based on "political consonance" (Buratti, 2010; Catalano, 2010), as the result of two contextual elections confirming the same majority. However, while it is certainly true that a vote of confidence is not required when the new executive is set up and would probably be inconsistent with the Constitution, nonetheless it is the Constitution itself that calls that relationship, once established, as based on confidence. Otherwise Article 126, which entitles regional councils to adopt "a reasoned motion of no confidence against the president of the executive" would be misleading.

In the same judgement, no. 12/2006, the ItCC also declared unconstitutional the provision of the statute of Abruzzo on the individual motion of no confidence to the members of the regional executive different from the President. The conclusion is that such a motion can be voted but, if approved, cannot trigger the removal of the person contested from his office. It seems conceived as a kind of symbolic sanction, limiting the opportunity for the council to effectively control the action of the executive.

As anticipated, some regions have also introduced the question of confidence to be put by the president in the council (e.g. in Campania, Friuli-Venezia Giulia, Liguria, and Calabria, where a previous decision of the executive as a whole is required). As with the analogous tool provided at national level (by parliamentary rules of procedure, not by the Constitution), the question of confidence enables the head of the executive to call his majority to order on crucial measures for the governmental political program. For how they are regulated, questions of confidence are very unlikely to be rejected (Coduti, 2010). It will be almost impossible for a president to fail and to be forced to resign (and in fact it never happened). The technique used to regulate the question of confidence at regional level led to the opposite effect compared to the discipline contained in the rules of procedure of the national parliament. While these rules allow putting a question of confidence on virtually every matter, regional statutes and legislation list the bills or the measures on which such a motion can be presented. Finally, regional norms on the vote of the question of confidence require the absolute majority for its rejection and the simple majority for its approval, which then becomes the rule.

The design and implementation of the new regional form of government was also complemented by the electoral legislation. Due to the shift of the competence in regional electoral matters from those reserved to the State to those shared between State and regions following Const. law no. 1/1999 (which amended Art. 122 Const.), State law no. 165/2004 was approved as framework law fixing fundamental principles to be respected by the regions when regulating the details of their electoral systems (Caravita, 2005; Perniciaro, 2013). With this regard, the strict relation between Articles 122 and 123 Const. can be immediately seen. Indeed, by setting the general framework of the regional electoral systems, and especially prescribing the direct election of the president of the regions, where not otherwise provided for in the statutes, Article 122 directly conditions the regional forms of government, to be defined in each statute, according to Article 123 Const. (Catalano, 2010). Amongst the principles fixed by law no. 165/2004, there are two which are particularly important: the first requires the contextual election of the regional councils and of the presidents of the region; the second demands that the regional electoral systems assure the formation of stable majority in the council as well as guaranteeing the adequate representation of minorities (Article 4, para. 1, let. *a)* law no. 165/2004). Therefore, on the one hand, the risk of a divided government (i.e. opposite majorities in the council and for the president) is minimised; on the other hand, the president can count on a certain and reliable majority to govern, even though the duty to protect minorities impedes the adoption of pure majority electoral systems. The adoption of the new statutes has not affected the outlook significantly. The rate of innovation in this regard has been low and all ordinary regions have opted for two solutions: either accepting the national legislation and completing the content of the national framework law no. 165/2004 for certain limited aspects (such as incompatibility) or, as happens only in Liguria and Piedmont at present, applying the "original" law no. 108/1968, as modified by law no. 43/1995 (Trucco and Bailo, 2020, 1052–1053).

It is relatively easy to see that the balance of powers between regional councils and presidents (executives) of the regions does not really run in favour of the legislative assemblies (Buratti, 2010, 139–175). It has been argued that the only effective tool these assemblies have to "sanction" their own executive would be to vote a motion of no confidence (Bin, 2001; Catalano, 2020). While this is the natural landing place of the constitutional reform's original design to bring stability into the regional form of government, regional councils can still exert their influence on the executive through the legislative process, in particular by enhancing the role of the committee stage (Griglio, 2010), and by using more traditional tools of parliamentary oversight, like hearings, inquiries, and investigations, or addressing specific concerns to the executive by mean of motions or resolutions. It has also been supported that regions can become democratic laboratories to better link the democratic scrutiny at institutional level, through the councils, with bottom-up processes of public deliberation (Maccabiani, 2010, 161–188). Whether this would be sufficient to re-calibrate the asymmetric powers between the regional legislative assembly and the president and its executive and to ensure adequate mechanisms of democratic accountability is however questionable.

VI. The autonomy of regional sources of law

The transition to the new form of government that has been described above was possible thanks to a major innovation in conceiving the autonomy of regional sources of law and, in particular, the regional statutes of autonomy.

The original understanding of the 1948 Constitution was in the sense of attributing legislative capacity to the regions, but it was subject to the *ex ante* control of the State. Even the statutes – that were openly described by the Constitution as disciplining the "internal organisation of the region" (Article 123(1)) – were subject to State approval anyway[14] not only in the case of the 5 special regions (whose statutes are materially constitutional sources as they derogate to the constitutional text and so they have to be passed with the same procedure as constitutional

14 See the same Article 123(2) Const. in its original version.

amendments), but also for the 15 ordinary regions. Until 1999, the latter could pass a draft charter, but the final approval had to be made by the national parliament, so to stress the limits – both on the law and on the merit – to which regional autonomy was subject.

The new version of Article 123 Const., as amended in 1999, set forth a procedure for the adoption of statutes inspired by Article 138 Const., on the constitutional amendment process: the statute has to be approved twice by the regional parliament, with a certain temporal distance between the first and the second vote,[15] with a specific majority required in the latter.[16] Hence, after the final approval, the text can be both brought before the ItCC by the Government, with due motivation related to its "harmony" with the Constitution; and also be submitted to popular referendum, upon request of one-fifth of the regional parliament or one-fiftieth of the population of the region.

In sum, the effects of the 1999 reform on the procedure for the adoption of the regional charters was in the sense of moving the intervention of the State out from the decision-making stage, in order to transform it in a sort of external control on the product of the will of the regional bodies which was autonomously exerted.

The subsequent reform in 2001, related to the law-making capacity of the regions, went in a similar direction. Apart from increasing the number and the significance of the matters of regional competences, it completely changed the idea of regional legislative autonomy. Internal and *ex ante* checks were removed, equalising State and regional laws both with reference to the general limits to which they are subject[17] and with regard to the mechanisms to sanction the violation of the constitutional framework. The 2001 constitutional amendment removed the preliminary check of the government on regional laws, allowing the State to claim the unconstitutionality of regional laws only after their entry into force, with the same (close: 60 days) deadline in which regions can claim the unconstitutionality of State laws. Hence, the general limit of the "national interest" (a sort of supremacy clause) was abrogated, although it was subsequently reinstated through constitutional case-law.[18] In sum, many asymmetries that were present in the original text of the Constitution were removed, although some others remained in the proceedings before the ItCC: for example, notwithstanding the equalisation of the introduction of questions of constitutionality between State and regions, the latter could only claim violation of their domain of competences, whereas the State could also claim for substantive and procedural violation beyond

15 60 days for the regional statutes of autonomy, 3 months for the constitutional amendments.

16 Absolute majority in both cases, with the peculiarity that, with regard to constitutional amendments, supermajorities beyond two-thirds of the members avoid the possibility to ask for a final popular referendum.

17 See Article 117(1) Const. which states that both State and regional laws have to comply with the Constitution, the international obligations, and the constraints deriving from the EU membership (Pinelli, 2001).

18 For further details on this point see the chapter by Giacomo Delledonne in this volume.

the specific respect of the separation of competences enshrined in Article 117 Const. (Padula, 2005).

However, the overall experience of regional legislation after the reforms in 1999 and 2001 has been quite disappointing. Perhaps due to the persistent asymmetries with the State legislature, Italian regional councils have not used their new legislative powers at length and, on the whole, the quality of regional legislation has often been considered poor, some hyper-sectoral, and others not at all homogeneous in the content, not differently from national legislation (Carli, 2010, 1–7). The legislative process is usually dominated by the executive and concerns almost exclusively the executive's bills. In addition, regional councils have lost their monopoly as a rule-making authority at regional level. Regulations (namely acts lower than legislation used to enact, implement, or supplement it) were originally reserved to the councils. After 1999 their adoption has been left open by the Constitution with regard to the definition of the competent authority that is usually transferred by the new statutes from the councils to the executive bodies, with few exceptions (Abruzzo and partially Marche) (Gianfrancesco, 2009, 231; Tarli Barbieri, 2010). Nevertheless, regional executives, even after Const. law no. 1/1999, are forbidden from adopting acts having force of law. The case-law of the ItCC was already well settled in the previous phase,[19] but also in the revised constitutional context the general opinion in the literature was against this option. The rigidity of the new form of government did not allow more nuanced ways to trigger the responsibility of the executive apart from leading to the self-dissolvement of the same regional legislature. Therefore, considering the reference to the "responsibility of the government" made by Article 77 Const. under which (national) decree-laws have to be adopted, the 1999 constitutional amendment and the regional form of government prescribed there gave further arguments against the possibility of their approval at regional level (Belletti, 2002). The final word against the possibility for the regions to adopt decree-laws (as well as to delegate legislative power to the regional government) was said by the ItCC: although in a rather general context, judgement no. 361/2010 restated that all legislative powers at regional level have to be vested in the councils, without the possibility to transfer them to the executive (Ruggeri, 2010). Regional presidents have nevertheless made wide use of regional orders (*ordinanze*), administrative acts able to limit and restrict rights, for example in the context of the COVID-19 pandemic in the field of civil protection and public health (Luciani, 2020, 130).

VII. Conclusion

Twenty years after the constitutional reform of 1999, the empowerment of regional governments and their presidents is evident. This result can be considered a success, as it was one of the main aims of the 1999 constitutional reform. It is also coherent with the general, transnational trend of presidentialisation of politics,

19 See judgements nos. 59/1959 and 32/1961.

with the deep transformations of the political communication and culture. However, regional councils, the democratic institutions where pluralism and protection of minorities are deemed to be best guaranteed at regional level, are clearly on the losing side.

Yet, it would be unfair to attribute the weakening of regional councils only to the 1999 constitutional reform: parliaments in general – not only in Italy and not just at regional level – are struggling in a world in which their fundamental task of intermediation is perceived as less and less important. The most recent demands for direct and e-democracy made the challenge even bigger and harder for parliaments. In addition to this, there are also context-dependent reasons that played a role in such developments in Italy, notably the lack of autonomous political party systems at regional level and the case-law of the ItCC, which run in favour of the homogeneity among regions.

Nevertheless, it has to be acknowledged that Italian regions (and their representative bodies in particular) mostly missed the opportunity to develop a wider autonomy both in political and institutional terms, thereby confirming the lack of such a culture of autonomy, at least at the regional level (Toniatti, 2018). It is true that they have been limited in this process by the centralistic attitude of the ItCC, which has restricted the institutional innovation to the binary choice between the "old" parliamentary asset and the pre-packaged option set by the "transitional" form of government directly provided for by the Constitution. Anyway, they showed a very limited rate of innovation in the methods and the contents of legislation. The direct election of the president of the region created local "potentates", but did not offer new models of leadership to national politics: it is significant that not a single former directly elected president of a region later led the national government as president of the council of ministers.

The lesson that can probably be drawn from this evolution is that constitutional engineering alone cannot be sufficient to attain deep transformations, in particular if referred to subnational entities which anyway are bound to a wider and more complex national cultural and political context, from which it can be hard to gain sudden autonomy. And whose politics and policies are mostly shaped by second-order political personnel that very rarely take centre stage at national level.

Even a radical change in the form of government (i.e. the mutual relationship between the executive and the legislature) or a complete redraft of the electoral laws cannot produce, alone, the innovation in the society that is expected to be achieved if it is not accompanied by a coeval shift at political and institutional level, when it comes to their implementation.

The fact that, as said, the institutional reforms of the regional systems were conceived as a premise to a more comprehensive reform at State level (so that they were designed in continuity with that debate) leaves the observer quite disoriented. It seems that the famous metaphor of the "laboratory" hinted by US Supreme Court's Justice Louis Brandeis to describe the potential of the member states (regional) choice for the democratic development of national constitutional law cannot apply to Italian regions.[20] In contrast to the practice registered in the field of comparative subnational constitutionalism about the spillover effects of subnational choices at federal-State level and the vertical and horizontal mutual influence (see section 2), in Italy the development of the regional form of government is a case of horizontal homogenisation nudged, if not forced, by the national level.

Literature

Bruce Ackerman, 'The New Separation of Powers' (2000) 113 *Harvard Law Review* 633

Salvatore Andò, 'Autonomia statutaria e forma di governo regionale', (1971) 25 *Rivista trimestrale di diritto procedurale e civile* 926

Michele Belletti, 'Un altro argomento contro i decreti legge regionali' (2002) 22 *Quaderni costituzionali* 812

Giorgio Berti, 'Art. 5', in Giuseppe Branca (ed.), *Commentario della costituzione*, I (Zanichelli, 1975) 277

Raffaele Bifulco, 'Partiti politici e autonomie territoriali', in Associazione dei costituzionalisti (ed.), *Partiti politici e società civile a sessant'anni dall'entrata in vigore della Costituzione* (Jovene, 2009) 239

Roberto Bin, 'Il Consiglio regionale. Funzioni di indirizzo e controllo' (2001) 1 *Le istituzioni del federalismo* 85

Andrea Buratti, *Rappresentanza e responsabilità politica nella forma di governo regionale* (Jovene, 2010)

Michael Burgess and G. Alan Tarr, 'Introduction: Sub-national Constitutionalism and Constitutional Development', in Michael Burgess and G. Alan Tarr (eds.) *Constitutional Dynamics in Federal Systems. Sub-national Perspectives* (Forum of Federations and McGill-Queen's University Press, 2012) 3

Mauro Calise, 'Presidentialization, Italian Style', in Thomas Poguntke and Paul Webb (eds.), *The Presidentialization of Politics: A Comparative Study of Modern Democracies* (OUP, 2005) 88

Simone Calzolaio, *Il cammino delle materie nello Stato regionale. La definizione delle competenze legislative nell'ordinamento costituzionale* (Giappichelli, 2012)

Beniamino Caravita (ed.), La legge quadro n. 165 del 2004 sulle elezioni regionali (Giuffrè, 2005)

Massimo Carli, 'Procedimento legislativo regionale e qualità della legislazione', in Paolo Caretti and Emanuele Rossi (eds.), *Osservatorio sulle fonti 2009. L'attuazione degli statuti regionali* (Giappichelli, 2010) 1

Stefano Catalano, *La "presunzione di consonanza". Esecutivo e Consiglio nelle regioni a Statuto ordinario* (Giuffrè, 2010)

Stefano Catalano, 'Giurisprudenza costituzionale in materia di forma di governo regionale a vent'anni dalla legge costituzionale n. 1 del 1999' (2020) 2 *Osservatoriosullefonti.it* 991

Paolo Cavaleri, 'Ambiguità del ruolo attribuito ai Consigli regionali dai nuovi statuti ordinari', in Eduardo Gianfrancescoet al. (eds.), *Il Filangieri, Quaderno 2009. Nuove regole per nuovi Consigli regionali* (Jovene, 2010) 337

20 See the dissenting opinion of Justice Louis Brandeis in *New State Ice Co. v. Liebmann*, 285 US 262, 311: 'It is one of the happy incidents of the federal system that a single courageous state may, if its citizens choose, serve as a laboratory, without risk to the rest of the country.'

Stefano Ceccanti, 'Il modello neo-parlamentare: genesi e sviluppi', in *Scritti in onore di Serio Galeotti*, I (Giuffrè, 1998) 183

Daniele Coduti, 'La questione di fiducia tra statuti regionali e regolamenti consiliari', (2010) 2 *Osservatoriosullefonti.it* 1

Daniele Coduti, 'Crisi, scioglimento anticipato e nuove elezioni nelle Regioni Lazio e Lombardia: una lettura in parallelo' (2013) 2 *Istituzioni del federalismo* 509

Roberto D'Alimonte, 'Il nuovo sistema elettorale. Dal collegio uninominale al premio di maggioranza', in Roberto D'Alimonte and Alessandro Chiaramonte (eds.), *Propozionale ma non solo. Le elezioni politiche del 2006* (Il Mulino, 2007) 51

Antonio D'Atena, 'Regione (in generale)', in *Enciclopedia del diritto*, XXXIX (Giuffrè, 1988) 344

Giacomo Delledonne and Giuseppe Martinico, 'Handle with Care!: The Regional Charters and Italian Constitutionalism's "Grey Zone"' (2009) 5 *European Constitutional Law Review* 218

John Dinan, 'Patterns of Subnational Constitution-making in Federal Countries' (2008) 39 *Rutgers Law Journal* 837

Alfonso Di Giovine and Francesco M. Pizzetti, 'Osservazioni sulla nuova legge elettorale per i Consigli regionali' (1996) 24 *Le Regioni* 11

Leopoldo Elia, 'Governo (forme di)', in *Enciclopedia del diritto*, IX (Giuffrè, 1970) 634

Cristina Fasone, 'What Role for Regional Assemblies in Regional States? Italy, Spain and the United Kingdom in Comparative Perspective' (2012) 4 *Perspectives on Federalism* 171

Eduardo Gianfrancesco, 'La forma di governo regionale nella recente esperienza italiana', in Josep Maria Castellà Andreu and Marco Olivetti (eds.), *Nuevos Estatutos y Reforma del Estado. Las experiencias de España e Italia a debate* (Atelier, 2009) 193

Elena Griglio, 'Il ruolo delle commissioni permanenti nei "nuovi" Consigli regionali: Piemonte, Lombardia, Emilia-Romagna e Toscana' (2010) 1–2 Studi parlamentari e di politica costituzionale, special issue, Eduardo Gianfrancesco and Nicola Lupo (eds.), *Le riforme dei regolamenti dei Consigli regionali* 119

Massimo Luciani, 'Governo (forme di)' in *Enciclopedia del diritto. Annali*, III (Giuffrè, 2010) 538

Massimo Luciani, 'Il sistema delle fonti del diritto alla prova dell'emergenza' (2020) 2 *Rivista AIC* 109

Nadia Maccabiani, *Codeterminare senza controllare. La via futura delle Assemblee elettive regionali* (Giuffrè, 2010)

Neil MacCormick, 'The European Union and the Idea of a Perfect Commonwealth' (2006) 68 *Hume occasional paper*

Andrea Manzella, *Il parlamento* (3rd ed., Il Mulino, 2003)

Boris Mirkine-Guetzévitch, *Les Constitutions de l'Europe nouvelle* (Delagrave, 1928)

Costantino Mortati, *Lezioni sulle forme di governo* (Cedam, 1973)

Marco Olivetti, *Nuovi statuti e forma di governo delle regioni. Verso le Costituzioni regionali?* (Il Mulino, 2003)

Carlo Padula, *L'asimmetria nel giudizio in via principale. La posizione dello Stato e delle Regioni davanti alla Corte costituzionale* (Cedam, 2005)

Francesco Palermo, 'Italy: A Federal Country without Federalism?', in Michael Burgess and G. Alan Tarr (eds.) *Constitutional Dynamics in Federal Systems. Sub-national Perspectives* (Forum of Federations and McGill-Queen's University Press, 2012) 237

Francesco Palermo, 'La forma di governo regionale a vent'anni dalla riforma: cosa resta della specialità?' (2020) 2 *Osservatoriosullefonti.it* 1063

Francesco Palermo and Karl Kössler, *Comparative Federalism. Constitutional Arrangements and Case Law* (Hart, 2018)

Giovanna Perniciaro, *Autonomia politica e legislazione elettorale regionale* (Cedam, 2013)

Alberto Pérez Calvo, *Las formas de gobierno del Estado constitucional*, 2nd ed. (Editorial Reus, 2014)

Giovanni Piccirilli and Giovanna Perniciaro, 'Il "fallimento politico" del Presidente della Giunta regionale. Note critiche sul decreto legislativo in materia di "premi e sanzioni"' (2011) 4 *Rivista AIC* 1

Cesare Pinelli, 'I limiti generali alla potestà legislativa statale e regionale e i rapporti con l'ordinamento internazionale e con l'ordinamento comunitario' (2001) 126 *Foro italiano* 194

Giovanni Pitruzzella, 'Forme di stato e forme di governo. II) Forma di governo regionale', *Enciclopedia giuridica* XIV (Treccani, 1989)

Antonio Ruggeri, 'Dalla giurisprudenza di fine anno una opportuna precisazione in tema di disciplina (con legge costituzionale) del sistema delle fonti. (nota a Corte cost. n. 361 del 2010)' (2010) *Forum di Quaderni costituzionali* 1

Winfried Steffani, 'Zur Unterscheidung parlamentarischer und präsidentieller Regierungssysteme' (1983) 14 *Zeitschrift für Parlamentsfragen* 390

Giovanni Tarli Barbieri, 'La forma di governo nel nuovo statuto della Regione Toscana: prime osservazioni' (2004) 10 *Diritto pubblico* 707

Giovanni Tarli Barbieri, 'La potestà regolamentare: un bilancio delle scelte statutarie e della loro successiva attuazione', in Paolo Caretti and Emanuele Rossi (eds.), *Osservatorio sulle fonti 2009. L'attuazione degli statuti regionali* (Giappichelli, 2010) 9

Roberto Toniatti, *La cultura dell'autonomia: le condizioni pre-giuridiche per un'efficace autonomia regionale* (University of Trento, 2018)

Michel Troper, *Pour une théorie juridique de l'État* (Presse Universitaire de France, 1994)

Lara Trucco and Francesca Bailo, 'Forma di governo regionale e legislazione elettorale' (2020) 2 *Osservatoriosullefonti.it* 1047

Nicola Viceconte, *La forma di governo nelle Regioni ad autonomia ordinaria. Il parlamentarismo iperrazionalizzato e l'autonomia statutaria.* (Jovene, 2010)

Mauro Volpi, 'Considerazioni di metodo e di merito sulla legge costituzionale n. 1 del 1999' (2000) 31 *Politica del diritto* 203

Robert F. Williams, 'Experience Must Be Our Only Guide: The State Constitutional Experience of the Framers of the Federal Constitution' (1988) 15 *Hastings Constitutional Law Quarterly* 403

3 Federalism and regionalism in constitutional adjudication

Giacomo Delledonne[1]

I. Introductory remarks: the link between regionalism and constitutional adjudication

According to a widely supported opinion (e.g. D'Atena, 1988; D'Orazio, 1981), regionalism and a centralised system of constitutional adjudication are the two most important innovations introduced in the Second Part of the Constitution of the Italian Republic in 1947. Both the transformation of Italy into a regional state (as defined by Ambrosini, 1944; see Arban in this volume) and the establishment of a specialised Constitutional Court can be understood in light of the anti-authoritarian flavour of the Italian Constitution. The regions were conceived according to a classically liberal, and perhaps slightly outdated, conception (see section III) and would serve as territorial counterpowers. The Italian Constitutional Court (ItCC), in turn, would put a check on the legislature and, consequently, on the parliamentary majority.

Moreover, there is also a direct link between these two innovations. The establishment of regions with primary law-making powers went hand in hand with raising the question of how regional laws would be reviewed and the distribution of legislative competences in Article 117 of the Italian Constitution (Const.) would be enforced (Malfatti, 2006). In its early wording, the Constitution provided for a double system of review of regional laws, either on substantive grounds or on the basis of compatibility with the Constitution; the former would be performed by the Parliament, the latter by the Constitutional Court. In the Italian system of constitutional adjudication, the review mechanism under which the state may challenge regional laws and the regions, in turn, may challenge laws enacted by the state or by other regions takes the name of principaliter review (*controllo di costituzionalità in via principale*). The principaliter review of state and regional laws, which can be defined as a form of abstract review (see Ferreres Comella, 2004) and is regulated in Article 127 Const. and Article 2 of constitutional law no. 1/1948,[2] has been an integral part of the Italian model of constitutional review since the entry into force of the Constitution.

1 Postdoctoral Researcher in Comparative Public Law, Scuola Superiore Sant'Anna, Pisa. Email address: giacomo.delledonne@santannapisa.it.

2 Regulation of the Constitutional Court in the text of the Constitution is far from exhaustive. According to Article 137(1) and (2) Const., a constitutional law is supposed to regulate, among other things, access to constitutional adjudication. Ordinary

DOI: 10.4324/9781003104469-4

The link between the re-organisation of Italy as a regional state and the establishment of centralised constitutional review should come as no surprise. Most of the times, those who have investigated the 'genealogy' of Italian regionalism as regulated in Title V of the Second Part of the Constitution have pointed to Austria and the Second Spanish Republic (D'Atena, 2012; Basile, 1980, 92–96). In some respects, the wording and the spirit of Article 127 Const. and Article 2 of constitutional law no. 1/1948 remind of the founding moment of the European model of constitutional adjudication, the hard-fought compromise on the tasks of the *Verfassungsgerichtshof* (Constitutional Court) during the elaboration of the Federal Constitutional Law of Austria in 1920 (Caruso, 2020, 65–68; Buratti, 2008, 248; see also Caravita, 1983, 56). This model, in turn, played a role in Hans Kelsen's subsequent reflection about the role of constitutional courts as impartial umpires between the federal government and state government (Vinx, 2015, 174–221).

Since the entry into force of the constitutional reform of 2001, the Constitutional Court has often been described as the umpire in a flawed multi-level order, in which the unfinished legislative and administrative implementation of constitutional amendments, the lack of political consensus, and the problematic wording of the relevant constitutional provisions all contributed to overwhelming the workload of the ItCC in the first years after the entry into force of the reform (section II). This chapter will assess the role of constitutional adjudication in the evolution of the Italian regional state and its contribution to the (self-) understanding of Italian regionalism. The chapter will be structured as follows. After focusing on the distinctive features of principaliter review and its impact on the overall activity of the Constitutional Court (section II), the analysis will focus on the first research questions (section III). Has the case law of the ItCC contributed to the actual working of the Italian model of regional state? How has this happened? After that, attention will switch to another set of problems (section IV): how has the case law of the ItCC contributed to the theoretical understanding of regionalism? What role did its judgements play after the entry into force of the 2001 amendment, which some commentators at first described as paving the way to the advent of federalism?

II. Principaliter review of state and regional laws: defining features and trends

This section focuses on the basic aspects of principaliter review. To begin with, it should be remarked that regionalism-related issues may also surface when the Constitutional Court scrutinises laws in the framework of the incidental review.

---

laws, in turn, lay down the other provisions necessary for the functioning of the Court. Constitutional law no. 1/1948, enacted shortly after the entry into force of the Constitution and ahead of the termination of activities of the Constituent Assembly, brought about the incidental, 'concrete' review of constitutionality, which is not mentioned in the Constitution, and regulated the principaliter review in greater detail than had been the case in Article 127 Const.

Moreover, the ItCC also adjudicates (prevalently) non-legislative conflicts between the state and regions and between regions. However, principaliter review provides the state and the regions with an opportunity to raise a constitutional challenge before the Constitutional Court immediately after a law has entered into force.

Although some aspects of the constitutional regulation of principaliter review have remained unchanged since 1948, the constitutional amendment that came into force in 2001 revised Article 127 Const. in order to strengthen the institutional position of the regions before the Constitutional Court. Most notably, the constitutional amendment suppressed the power of the Italian Parliament to review regional laws on substantive grounds, which, in fact, had never been exercised. Today, the Italian Government may challenge a regional law before the Constitutional Court within 60 days from its publication, 'when it deems that the regional law *exceeds regional competence*'. A region, in turn, may question the constitutional legitimacy of a state or regional law before the Constitutional Court 'when it deems that said law … *infringes upon its competence*'. Again, the challenge may be raised within 60 days of the publication of the relevant piece of legislation. As the wording of Article 127 suggests, there is no complete equality between the state and the regions. Such assumption has been further confirmed by the Constitutional Court. When the Italian Government raises a constitutional challenge against a regional law, it can allege the violation of all constitutional provisions, even if unrelated to the constitutional allocation of powers.[3] By contrast, when one region challenges a law enacted by the state or by another region, it has to prove that the relevant provisions infringe upon its competence. Whenever the region argues that other constitutional provisions have been violated, it has to prove that such violation 'redounds on its competence'[4] (*criterio della ridondanza*). Having in mind both the wording of Article 127 Const. and the subsequent case law of the Constitutional Court, the regions have not been put on an equal footing with the state.

In quantitative terms, principaliter review was long seen as a minor component of the ItCC's workload. Before 2001, 'the incidental method of judicial review not only was the most important and frequent way of raising questions of constitutionality of legislation before the ItCC but also occupied a great part of its docket' (Barsotti et al., 2016, 54). In turn, by the end of the 1980s no more than 10 percent of the judgements rendered each year by the ItCC resulted from principaliter review (Dal Canto and Rossi, 2014, 140). The constitutional reform of 2001 marked a crucial turning point. Since then, the relative weight of the principaliter review has gradually increased. In the last decade, each year the ItCC has rendered 30 to 50 percent of its judgements in response to principaliter constitutional challenges, with a peak in 2012 and 2013, when the economic crisis clearly impacted on the relationship between the state and the regions (see Martinico and Pierdominici 2014, 125–30). In 2012, 47.5 per cent of the judgements rendered by the ItCC derived from constitutional challenges raised by the state or

3 Constitutional Court, judgement no. 274/2003. See also Randazzo, 2012, 183–86.
4 See e.g. judgement no. 233/2009 of the Constitutional Court.

by the regions in the framework of the principaliter review; in the subsequent year, these fell, albeit slightly, to 45.7 per cent. Since 2014, the quantitative relevance of the judgements resulting from principaliter challenges has varied from 31.7 per cent to 40.9 per cent of the number of judgements issued by the ItCC each year.[5]

The growing importance of the *controllo di costituzionalità in via principale* has not been without influencing the public perception of the Constitutional Court. Thanks to the incidental review, the ItCC had gradually emerged, although with some controversy, as an institution whose chief mission is to protect fundamental rights (Pizzorusso, 1990, 381–82). Since 2001, the annual reports on the activity of the ItCC have signalled that a 'conflict-resolving Court' (*Corte dei conflitti*), focusing on the distribution of competences between the state and the regions, was rivalling the long-established perception of a 'rights-protecting Court' (*Corte dei diritti*).[6]

In comparative perspective, the quantitative relevance of the principaliter review within the docket of the Italian Constitutional Court is striking (Rossi, 2018, 647; Claes and de Visser, 2012, 96–97). The reasons for this apparently structural trend do not seem to be exclusively related to the poor drafting of the constitutional provisions that allocate powers and resources between the state and the regions, most notably Article 117 Const. (see D'Atena, 2003, 16–17). At least three additional factors should be mentioned. First, the legislative implementation of the 2001 reform has been an unfinished business. This is particularly true for Article 119 Const., which lays down the foundations of an Italian model of 'fiscal federalism' (see Valdesalici in this volume). Second, the incomplete implementation of the reform has been particularly problematic with regard to the cooperation between the institutional layers and to regional participation in the law-making processes at state level. Pending a comprehensive reform of the Senate, Article 11 of constitutional law no. 3/2001 tried to strengthen the role of the Bicameral Committee for Regional Affairs and to have representatives of the regions, the autonomous provinces and the local government authorities taking part in its meetings. In many respects, the frequent resort to the instrument of principaliter review shows that the system suffers from the limited room for institutional cooperation between the state and the regions (see Woelk in this volume). Third, the launch of two far-reaching projects for constitutional reform, both of which significantly affected Title V of the Second Part of the Constitution and were ultimately unsuccessful, has also contributed to undermining the political consensus around the 2001 amendment and to creating opportunities for conflict. In sum, the growing relevance of the principaliter review after 2001 is not only a product of interpretive uncertainty in the immediate aftermath of the reform.

5 See the statistical data attached to the 2019 annual report, presented by Marta Cartabia on 28 April 2020 (available at <www.cortecostituzionale.it/documenti/relazione_cartabia/4_servizio_studi_stat.pdf>).

6 See e.g. Valerio Onida's remarks at the presentation of the 2004 annual report, on 20 January 2005 (available at <www.issirfa.cnr.it/la-giustizia-costituzionale-nel-2004-conferenza-stampa-del-presidente-valerio-onida-20-1-2005.html>).

On the whole, the growing relevance of principaliter review has also triggered a partial departure from its defining purpose. According to critics, the last decade has witnessed a trend towards the politicisation and instrumentalisation of principaliter review. More and more often, regional governments controlled by parties that are in the opposition at state level raise constitutional challenges against major pieces of legislation promoted by the Italian government. A prime example is provided by the two so-called 'Security Decrees' promoted by Matteo Salvini in his capacity as Interior Minister in the first Conte government (2018–19).[7] In these cases, the regions do what parliamentary minorities are not enabled to do in Italy and try to take advantage of the doctrine of redundancy in order to challenge state legislation shortly after it has entered into force (Tega, 2019). Of course, this use of the principaliter review is partially foreign to its original purpose (see Caruso, 2020, 170–74).

III. Making the regional system work: the stabilising function of the case law of the Constitutional Court

In a powerful piece, Paolo Carrozza (2003) pointed at an inherent paradox of the constitutional regulation of federalism (and regionalism). Since the end of the eighteenth century, when the Constitution of the United States was drafted, the allocation of powers and competences between the federal government and the subnational units has generally been based on a recurring technique, that is, enumerated powers. More recently, bottom-up federalising processes and holding-together federations have also resorted to this well-ingrained constitutional technique. However, the allocation of competences, most notably, legislative competences, is tightly connected with at least two historically located assumptions: first, that the distribution of law-making power is the key to the balance within federations, and, second, that the respective spheres of competence of the two (main) institutional layers can be clearly separated or, to say the least, distinguished. Over the course of the twentieth century, the transition from dual federalism to cooperative federalism challenged both assumptions.

Having in mind the interpretive and political difficulties mentioned in section II, the ItCC has developed an interpretation of Title V of the Second Part of the Constitution that tries to take account of the multiple interferences between state

7 Decree-law no. 113 of 4 October 2018 and decree-law no. 53 of 14 June 2019 introduced measures related to migration and asylum policies. Shortly after the first Security Decree was converted into law and entered into force, regions run by centre-left administrations, including Emilia-Romagna and Tuscany, raised constitutional challenges before the ItCC. Although immigration and the right of asylum fall within the exclusive competence of the state, the regions argued that a number of provisions in decree-law no. 113/2018 redounded on their own competences in the fields of health protection, vocational training, and social assistance and, consequently, were unconstitutional. According to the ItCC, the regional arguments failed to pass the redundancy test (judgement no. 194/2019). Some of the measures introduced by the first Security Decree were later struck down in the framework of incidental review (judgement no. 186/2020).

and regional competences and the 'semantic flaws' (Carrozza, 2003) of the enumerated powers clauses in Article 117 Const. This is not entirely new: under the 'old' Title V, the ItCC contributed to attenuating the idea of a strong separation between state and regional competences in order to address the consequences of regional non-compliance with Community law obligations. Because of the well-known territorial blindness of the European Communities and later of the European Union (see Baraggia in this volume), each Member State is the only entity responsible to comply with Community law requirements. Shortly after the 15 ordinary regions were established in 1970, the Italian Parliament regulated a number of situations in which the state was empowered to act in substitution of the regions in order to ensure compliance with European directives and regulations related to 'agriculture'. According to critics, the substitution power, which allowed the state to take action in matters falling within the competence of the regions, had no solid constitutional basis. However, the Constitutional Court upheld the legislative provisions that regulated the substitution power: the state being the sole responsible for ensuring compliance with Community law, it also needs appropriate instruments for addressing regional non-compliance.[8] In so doing, the ItCC indirectly pointed at the flaws of a predominantly dual regional model and the need to mitigate the rigidity of the constitutional system of distribution of competences. State substitution powers were finally entrenched in Article 120(2) Const. in 2001.

The aim of this section is not to retrace exhaustively the case law of the Constitutional Court concerning the distribution of (mainly but not exclusively) legislative competences in the last two decades; rather, it aims to discuss some relevant points in order to highlight the contribution of the ItCC itself to the functionality of the regional system.

After 2001, the Constitutional Court had to make sense of the multiple situations in which state and regional competences coexist. Contrary to some historic federal constitutions, the Italian Constitution does not contain a supremacy clause. To date, attempts to entrench a supremacy clause of the likes of Article 31 of the German Basic Law have been unsuccessful.[9] However, the ItCC remarked that the coexistence of state and regional competences is a 'recurring' occurrence.[10] In the case law of the ItCC after 2001, *prevalence* is a criterion used to resolve this knot (see extensive discussion by Buoso, 2008). Having regard to the 'essential core'[11] of a piece of legislation that 'lies at the intersection of multiple competences',[12] the ItCC identifies the relevant matter and the corresponding competence. A recent example of how the ItCC resorts to the criterion of the prevalent competence can be found in a judgement issued in 2018. The regional

8 Constitutional Court, judgement no. 142/1972. See Martinico, 2012, 362.

9 A supremacy clause was part of the draft constitutional amendment promoted by the Renzi government. The discussion on the virtues of a supremacy clause was revived by the handling of the Covid-19 pandemic crisis in spring 2020.

10 Constitutional Court, judgement no. 80/2007.

11 Constitutional Court, judgement no. 50/2005.

12 Constitutional Court, judgement no. 51/2005.

government of Veneto had raised a challenge against a state law that had introduced a number of mandatory vaccinations. The Court recognised that the legislative provisions at stake could be ascribed to matters falling within state and regional competences, 'such as health protection and education'.[13] Still, the prevalent relevant matters all fell within state competence. Consequently, the state law on vaccinations did not infringe upon regional competences.

In some cases, the interlacement of state and regional competences is so complex that the criterion of the prevalent competence is of limited use. Quite often, this is the case with state laws that launch major reforms in order to regulate 'complex social phenomena'.[14] If the ItCC finds it impossible to identify a prevalent competence, the *principle of loyal cooperation* applies: the state legislature has to provide for appropriate tools that ensure regional participation and, consequently, the protection of regional competences. The ultimate goal of loyal cooperation is to reconcile the protection of regional autonomy with the need for unitary regulation of a specific issue. The non-observance of the principle of loyal cooperation may lead to the invalidation of the impugned law, as it happened in 2016 with the reform of public administration (see Woelk in this volume); judgement no. 251/2016 is of great relevance because the ItCC hinted at the need for 'strong' regional involvement in the state law-making processes, 'which, at the moment, is not reflected in our constitutional order' (Lugarà, 2017, 8).

On a different note, the ItCC had to make distinctions among the legislative matters enumerated in Article 117(2) Const. Some of the exclusive state powers listed in Article 117(2) Const. have to do with *objects*: this is the case, for instance, with 'defence and armed forces', 'jurisdiction and procedural law', and 'customs'. Some others, in turn, refer to *policy goals*; this means that the state is given competence in order to pursue a specific goal. The main examples of functional competences are 'competition protection', 'protection of the environment, the ecosystem and cultural heritage', and 'determination of the basic standards of benefits relating to civil and social rights to be assured throughout the national territory'. As the ItCC noted, some of the competences enumerated in Article 117 Const. are not '"matters" in a narrow sense'.[15] Moving from this starting point, scholarship and the Constitutional Court have further elaborated a specific category, that is, *transversal matters* (see Scaccia, 2004). The choice of the adjective means that several different interests are related to these legislative matters; in this vein, both the preservation and exploitation of the environment are relevant for the 'protection of the environment [and] the ecosystem'. At first sight, the existence of transversal matters means that in the pursuit of the corresponding goals the Italian Parliament may enact laws that apply to the whole of the national territory and overlap with regional competences. However, the ItCC has also

13 Constitutional Court, judgement no. 5/2018.
14 Constitutional Court, judgement no. 251/2016.
15 Constitutional Court, judgement no. 407/2002. In this respect, it should be noted that there is some continuity between the case law of the Court before 2001 and its decisions since the entry into force of the constitutional amendment.

clarified that transversal matters do not only legitimise state legislative interventions to the detriment of regional competences. Much to the contrary, due to their cross-cutting nature, they may also allow the regional legislatures to take action. When it comes to environmental protection, although the state can dictate unitary regulations, the regions keep the power to 'adopt ... norms that define higher standards'.[16] Similarly, the determination of basic standards related to civil and social rights does not prevent the regional legislatures from setting even higher standards.[17] Basically, the great relevance of transversal matters in the structure of Title V of the Second Part of the Constitution after 2001 should be interpreted in accordance with the tenets of cooperative regionalism (Benelli and Bin, 2009, 1203–07).

Finally, the Constitutional Court has tried to instil dynamism and flexibility in the enumerated competences of Article 117 Const. In spite of the apparent rigidity of the lists of exclusive powers and shared powers, in a landmark judgement in 2003 the ItCC held that the principle of subsidiarity, referred to in Article 118(1) and (4) Const., applies not only to administrative functions but also to legislative competences (see Arban, 2015, and Martinico in this volume).

The implementation of the constitutional reform of 2001 being a largely unfinished business, the case law of the Constitutional Court has not always been immune from criticism. More particularly, a generous reading of the 'transversal' clauses in Article 117(2) Const., justified by the need for unitary regulations throughout the national territory, has sometimes led to a certain insensitivity to legislative diversity, which should be one of the basic aspects of regionalism. Critics of the 'neo-centralising' attitude of the Constitutional Court have warned against judgements in which the ItCC based its arguments on pervasive state competences like the protection of competition and private law and, consequently, all but annihilated the room for regional legislation in the area of commerce (Tosi, 2016).

By force of circumstances, the attitude of the ItCC towards state legislation became more deferential in the years following the outbreak of the economic and financial crisis, which marked the beginning of an anti-regional backlash peaking in the draft constitutional amendment promoted by the Renzi government in 2016. In those years, the ItCC extensively resorted to a generous interpretation of the 'fundamental principles' laid down by the state in the area of 'coordination of public finance and tax system' (Article 117(3) Const.). In fact, these provisions, labelled fundamental principles, often included very detailed measures that applied to the regions (see Salerno, 2012, 570–71). The Court generally upheld these measures, even the more detailed ones, with a reference to the power of the Italian Parliament to define fundamental principles relating to the coordination of public finance and the tax system. Although the economic crisis cannot be used as an excuse for derogating from the ordinary allocation of competences, some judgements of the ItCC in those years can be described as being part of a trend towards

16 See, among others, judgements no. 105/2008, no. 61/2009, and no. 7/2019 of the Constitutional Court.

17 See, among others, judgement no. 322/2009 of the Constitutional Court.

a relative weakening of regional autonomy (see Groppi, 2014, 22–23).[18] The extraordinary circumstances produced by the crisis severely put to test the idea, based on comparative analysis, that 'courts are more inclined to take a non-centralist stance when representation of subnational governments at the federal level is weak' (Popelier, 2016, 44). In the subsequent years, the global attitude of the Court became more balanced, as the example of judgement no. 251/2016, mentioned above, suggests.

In some ways, the adjudicating activity of the ItCC has mostly been fruitful: in fact, the widespread image of a Court overburdened by pending cases does not correspond to constitutional reality. Constitutional challenges raised by the regions or, more frequently, by the state are a major component of its workload (see section II) but their number has more or less stabilised. Moreover, the quantitative relevance of the principaliter review depends not so much on the obscurity of the constitutional provisions, to whose systematic interpretation the ItCC has greatly contributed, as on the inherent political weakness of the Italian political system and the lack of appropriate mechanisms, including the preventive ones (Gianfrancesco, 2011), for averting competence disputes. However, the implementation of some of the most important components of the Italian regional model, including the so-called fiscal federalism, being an unfinished business, the interpretive activity of the ItCC has mostly been conservative and has somehow slowed down the unleashing of the innovative potential of territorial pluralism.

IV. Focusing on the theoretical foundations of the Italian regional model

Although federalism is never mentioned in the text of Title V that is currently in force, the constitutional reform of 2001 was preceded and followed by a lengthy discussion about the possible transition of Italy from regionalism to something closer to federalism. The rewriting of Article 117 Const., with all the competences not explicitly mentioned in paragraphs 2 and 3 reserved to the regions, and the strengthened financial autonomy of the regions and local government authorities fuelled the perception of a shift towards federalism in the constitutional order.

The 2001 reform was preceded by another constitutional amendment, two years before. As part of a wider reform process, constitutional law no. 1/1999

18 A convincing example is provided by a judgement rendered in 2012, in which the Constitutional Court upheld a number of anti-crisis provisions in decree-law no. 138/2011. In particular, in order to meet public finance targets the regions were called on to cut the number of members of their legislatures and executive organs. The cut would happen in proportion to the respective population of each region. Beforehand, the number of members of the regional organs was seen as one of the components of the regional 'form of government', which is regulated in the statute of autonomy (see also paragraph IV). However, the Court partly rejected the constitutionality challenges raised by the regions; in so doing, it relied not only on the 'one person, one vote' argument but also on the fact that the impugned measure was part of an effort to limit public expenditure (judgement no. 198/2012). See also Tarli Barbieri, 2013, 109–12.

amended Article 123 Const., which defines the contents of the charters of autonomy (*statuti*, hereinafter statutes) of the 15 ordinary regions and the limits on regional statute-making autonomy. Therefore, the ordinary regions were called on to enact new statutes of autonomy in substitution of the previous ones. In the wake of this reform, some analyses argued that the 'second-generation' statutes would become more similar to regional constitutions in the proper sense of the word than to mere instruments of government, as had been the case under the previous state of affairs (see Olivetti, 2002).

The 'second-generation' statutes were drafted at a time when requests for greater regional autonomy, especially in the north of Italy, were on the top of the national political agenda. These requests were sometimes intertwined with identity-based claims. In some cases, the use of identity-based arguments was instrumental in supporting the call for extended legislative or financial autonomy (see Pitruzzella, 2002). From a different angle, the Italian case was part of a wider trend, resulting from the weakening of nation states and the strengthening of local identities throughout Europe (see Carboni, 2019). The discussion about the contents and structure of the 'second-generation' statutes was influenced, and possibly misguided, by this political and intellectual climate.[19]

Article 123(1) Const., which was amended in 1999, enumerates the indefectible contents of the regional statutes; by now, they are supposed to contain norms concerning 'the form of government and basic principles for the organisation of the region and the conduct of its business', as well as 'the right to initiate legislation and promote referenda on the laws and administrative measures of the region as well as the publication of laws and regional regulations'. The limits on the regional statute-making power apparently became less stringent; under Article 123 (1) Const., it is now required that the contents of the statutes be 'in harmony with the Constitution'. The ensuing question is whether the contents mentioned in Article 123(1) Const. are *the only admissible contents* of a regional statute. In fact, the regional legislatures went another way and decided to entrench provisions relating to founding principles, regional identity, and fundamental rights (see Delledonne and Martinico, 2011, 891–93). These regional 'bills of rights' sometimes included rights that were not recognised, at least explicitly, by state laws. In particular, the statutes of Emilia-Romagna, Tuscany, and Umbria recognised certain domestic partnerships, including sex-same partnerships. From the establishment of the Italian Republic and until quite recently, these regions were generally seen as left-wing strongholds; consequently, the recognition of sex-same partnerships in their draft statutes was also instrumental in putting pressure on the (conservative) Italian government.

After the statutes of Emilia-Romagna, Tuscany, and Umbria were passed, the Italian government challenged many of their most significant provisions before the

19 Interestingly, due to the peculiar legal regime of their statutes of autonomy (see Palermo in this volume), the five special regions, including the ones in which the presence of distinct local identities is most evident, were marginally affected by this discussion.

Constitutional Court.[20] The national government argued, among other things, that the provisions in the statutes that recognised same-sex partnership clashed with the value, entrenched in Article 29 Const., of the family based on marriage. Furthermore, the regional legislatures were not supposed to rule on other issues than the 'form of government' and the basic organisational principles. The underlying legal controversy lends itself to multiple interpretations: the evolution of family law and the emergence of 'new rights', a political conflict between a conservative state government and three left-wing regional administrations, and, most importantly for the purpose of this chapter, the role of the new regional statutes within the constitutional order. More or less implicitly, the ItCC had to answer the question what the statutes would stand for, whether basic charters regulating the institutional systems of the regions or something resembling regional constitutions with significant substantive content. Depending on the viewpoint, the answer provided by the ItCC in the judgements on the three statutes may sound disappointing or extremely meaningful.[21]

The Constitutional Court avoided taking sides in the debate concerning the recognition of domestic partnerships. Meanwhile, it made some points on the legal regime of the statutes within the Italian constitutional order. The ItCC did not strike down the impugned provisions in the three statutes, but interpreted them in a way that diminished their legal and political meaning. It described these provisions as 'an expression of the several political convictions in the regional community'.[22] Their function, the Court said, is to express those convictions in the statute and, consequently, to legitimise the region as an authority that represents the regional community and its diverse interests and aspirations. However, these 'statements' (*enunciazioni*), as the Constitutional Court called the impugned provisions, have no legal force, their function being properly (and only) 'political' and 'cultural'.[23] Since these statements have 'no legal effect' (and, consequently, can remain in force), 'a regional law pretending to implement them would be illegitimate'.[24] The ItCC distinguished the cultural statements in the statutes from the 'programmatic norms' of the Constitution, a doctrinal category which enjoyed great popularity between the time when the Constitution came into force in 1948 and the beginning of the Court's activity in 1956 (see Barsotti et al., 2016, 30–34). However, a statute of autonomy is not a regional constitution but an act that regulates some specific objects by virtue of a provision of the

20 Under Article 123(2) and (3) Const., each statute of autonomy is adopted by the regional legislature with a law approved by a majority of its members. After that, the Italian government may challenge the statute before the Constitutional Court before its publication in the official bulletin of the region. After that, the statute may be submitted to referendum at the request of one-fiftieth of the registered voters of the region or one-fifth of the members of the regional legislature.

21 See judgements no. 372/2004, no. 378/2004, and no. 379/2004 of the Constitutional Court.

22 Constitutional Court, judgement no. 372/2004.

23 Ibid.

24 Constitutional Court, judgement no. 365/2007.

Constitution, that is, Article 123(1). The ItCC defined the contents of the statutes as reserved and specialised. Accordingly, the ItCC described the statutes of the Italian regions as something very different from the constitutions of the subnational units in long-established federations: their scope is limited and they are subject not to quite broad homogeneity requirements but to an obligation to be in compliance with all the provisions of the Italian Constitution (Tarchi and Bessi, 2006, 2465).[25]

The distinction between federalism and regionalism, with emphasis put on the distinctive traits of the latter, is a common thread of other judgements, in which the ItCC tackled some of the basic concepts of constitutionalism. In all these judgements, the Constitutional Court construed categories like 'Parliament', 'people' and 'sovereignty' in a way that set Italian regionalism apart from historic federations.

A case in which the north-western region of Liguria was involved illustrates this point. In 2000, even prior to the adoption of a new statute of autonomy, the Regional Council of Liguria changed its name to 'Parliament of Liguria'. The Italian Government raised a constitutional conflict against Liguria. In its judgement the ItCC sided with the state. The ItCC conceded that the 2001 reform had considerably modified the place of the regions within the constitutional order; therefore, the Italian Parliament could no longer be defined as the only institution in which popular sovereignty comes together by virtue of Article 1(2) Const. Nevertheless, 'the word "Parliament" cannot be used in regional systems. … Parliament is the only place where the national political representation (Article 67 Const.) is located …'.[26] Due to the uniqueness of the functions performed by the (state) Parliament, the Constitution prohibits the regional legislatures from 'taking possession' (*appropriarsi*)[27] of the word 'Parliament'.

In a subsequent judgement, the ItCC held that not all provisions relating to fundamental rights and local identities can be labelled as 'cultural statements' and, consequently, treated as basically harmless. In judgement no. 365/2007, the ItCC scrutinised a regional ordinary law of Sardinia that set up an ad hoc regional assembly (named 'Council for the new statute of autonomy and sovereignty of the Sardinian people'). The task of this Council was to prepare a draft for the new special statute of the island. According to the impugned law, the Council had to take into account 'the principles and characters of regional identity … autonomy and sovereignty; … to promote the rights of Sardinian citizens with regard to the specific traits of the island … to define autonomy and regional sovereignty'. The Italian government questioned the constitutionality of the law before the ItCC. In the government's view, these provisions would clash both with the principle of

25 The comparative landscape of subnational constitutions in federal and regional orders, which lies outside the scope of this chapter, is quite diverse (see Popelier, 2014). The idea of subnational constitutions implicitly reflected in the judgements of the ItCC seems to be based on comparative examples like the constitutions of the states of the United States, the German *Länder*, and the Swiss cantons.

26 Constitutional Court, judgement no. 106/2002.

27 Ibid.

equality and with the constitutional definition of the Republic as 'one and indivisible' (Article 5 of the Constitution). Faced with such strong arguments, the Sardinian defence claimed that the legislation in question could be interpreted as a collection of merely political statements, thus making it 'basically harmless' and not illegitimate. The Court firmly rejected the analogy, since the law on which it rendered its judgement was aimed at setting up a procedure to revise the regional statute – that was not the same as being inserted among the general principles in a regional charter.[28] Furthermore, the Court signalled that in federal orders the subnational units 'retain forms and institutions that are affected by their pre-existing condition as sovereign entities'.[29] The Italian Republic, in turn, was structured as a regional state, and this nature has not been affected in 2001 by the 'significant strengthening of many functions that the Constitution attributes to the regions and the local government authorities'.[30] The distinctive trait of regionalism, including when it comes to special regions like Sardinia, is autonomy, and it would be clearly improper 'to juxtapose two radically different conceptions'[31] like sovereignty and autonomy. Some scholars criticised this judgement because of the relative inaccuracy of the theoretical and comparative arguments (Passaglia, 2007); still, the attempt of the Court to make a clear distinction between regionalism and federalism deserves the greatest attention.

Finally, the ItCC focused on the relationship between regionalism, on the one side, and the notion(s) of people (and minorities), on the other side. In 2009, the regional legislature of Piedmont passed a law that entitled the 'Piedmontese language' to the same protection granted to other minority languages under state law no. 482/1999. By virtue of Article 6 Const., the protection of historic minority languages is one of the fundamental principles of the Italian constitutional order. When the ItCC struck down this regional law, it said that only the Italian Parliament has the power to identify a national community and the minority groups within it. In other terms, the state is better placed to protect diversity as well as the reasons for common belonging, and to reconcile pluralism with uniformity. This means that the regional legislature cannot identify '"its own" community' as a linguistic minority, since the population of each region cannot be treated as 'an unlikely "fraction"' of the Italian people.[32]

These judgements of the ItCC, as different as they are, share a common thread. They highlight the distinctiveness of Italian regionalism vis-à-vis federalism (or, better said, an abstract conception of federalism). In stressing the original traits of the Italian model against the background of general categories, they may have contributed to enhancing its visibility, both in the political debates and outside Italy.

28 Constitutional Court, judgement no. 365/2007.
29 Ibid.
30 Ibid.
31 Ibid.
32 Constitutional Court, judgement no. 170/2010. See also Delledonne, 2011.

V. Concluding assessment

The Constitutional Court, possibly against its will, has played a significant role in defining some of the foundations of the Italian regional model since 2001. On the one side, it has elaborated criteria for interpreting the new provisions in Title V; in so doing, it has emphasised the cooperative traits of Italian regionalism and clearly contributed to the functionality of the system. On the other side, it has repeatedly stressed that there is some continuity between the state of affairs before 2001 and the current constitutional framework. Although some scholars, mainly with a political science background, claim that decentralised, regional, federal, and confederal orders are part of a continuum (Baldi, 2003), the ItCC has stuck to the well-established dichotomy between federalism and regionalism and drawn consequences from it.

The strong role of the Court can be explained having in mind the weakness of the political actors and/or their inability to perform their tasks. This, however, has not been without collateral damage. Due to perceived pro-state bias of the ItCC,[33] its structure and, consequently, its legitimacy within the composite legal order have occasionally been questioned.

The most ambitious projects for constitutional reform in the last 25 years all aimed to modify the composition of the Constitutional Court. If any of these reforms had come into force, the Senate of the Republic would have been transformed into a supposedly 'regional' second chamber and the power to appoint some of the judges of the Constitutional Court would have been exercised by the Chamber and the Senate separately (see Cardone, 2016). For all their differences, these attempts were sharply criticised because they seemed to think of the judges of the Constitutional Court as representatives not so much of the general interest but of distinct constituencies. In this vein, the judges elected by a senate composed of representatives of the regional and local governments would have been seen as inherently more sensitive to the regional and local interests. A possible objection is that in a number of federal and regional systems throughout the world the subnational entities participate in the (s)election of the judges of supreme and constitutional courts through the second chamber, and this has not been to the detriment of the courts themselves and their institutional prestige (Palermo and Kössler, 2017, 194–98; see also Popelier, 2016).

Again, this discussion shows that the ItCC plays a major role in the day-by-day operation of Italian regionalism. At the same time, the typical institutional logic of 'mature' (so to speak) federalism is not generally accepted in the Italian constitutional discourse.

Literature

Gaspare Ambrosini, *Autonomia regionale e federalismo. Austria, Spagna, Germania, URSS* (Edizioni Italiane, 1944)

33 However, comparative analyses of the role of courts in federal systems show that the denunciation of the unitary bias of courts is a recurring trend (Aroney and Kincaid, 2017).

Erika Arban, 'Re-centralizing subsidiarity: Interpretations by the Italian Constitutional Court' (2015) 25 *Regional and Federal Studies* 129

Nicholas Aroney and John Kincaid, 'Comparative Observations and Conclusions', in Nicholas Aroney and John Kincaid (eds.), *Courts in Federal Countries: Federalists or Unitarists?* (University of Toronto Press, 2017)

Brunetta Baldi, *Stato e territorio. Federalismo e decentramento nelle democrazie contemporanee* (Laterza, 2003)

Vittoria Barsotti, Paolo G. Carozza, Marta Cartabia, and Andrea Simoncini, *Italian Constitutional Justice in Global Context* (Oxford University Press, 2016)

Silvio Basile, 'La cultura politico-istituzionale e le esperienze "tedesche"', in Ugo De Siervo (ed.), *Scelte della Costituente e cultura giuridica*, vol. 1, *Costituzione italiana e modelli stranieri* (Il Mulino, 1980)

Filippo Benelli and Roberto Bin, 'Prevalenza e "rimaterializzazione delle materie": scacco matto alle Regioni' (2009) 37 *Le Regioni* 1185

Elena Buoso, 'Concorso di competenze, clausole di prevalenza e competenze prevalenti' (2008) 36 *Le Regioni* 61

Andrea Buratti, 'Dottrina costituzional-comparatistica ed elaborazione dello Stato regionale in Assemblea costituente', in Marco Fioravanti (ed.), *Culture e modelli costituzionali dell'Italia repubblicana* (Pellegrini, 2008)

Beniamino Caravita, *Corte 'giudice a quo' e introduzione del giudizio sulle leggi*, vol. 1, La Corte Costituzionale Austriaca (Cedam, 1983)

Giuliana Giuseppina Carboni, *Il regionalismo identitario. Recenti tendenze dello Stato regionale in Spagna, Italia e Regno Unito* (Wolters Kluwer Cedam, 2019)

Andrea Cardone, 'La composizione della Corte costituzionale, tra riforme "dirette", "indirette" e mancate' (2016) 36 *Quaderni costituzionali* 21

Paolo Carrozza, 'Le "materie": uso delle tecniche di enumerazione materiale delle competenze e modelli di riferimento del "regionalismo di esecuzione" previsto dal nuovo Titolo V della Costituzione', in Giuseppe Franco Ferrari and Giampaolo Parodi (eds.), *La revisione costituzionale del Titolo V tra nuovo regionalismo e federalismo. Problemi applicativi e linee evolutive* (Cedam, 2003)

Corrado Caruso, *La garanzia dell'unità della Repubblica. Studio sul giudizio di legittimità in via principale* (Bononia University Press, 2020)

Monica Claes and Maartje de Visser, 'The Court of Justice as a Federal Constitutional Court: A Comparative Perspective', in Elke Cloots, Geert De Baere and Stefan Sottiaux (eds.), *Federalism in the European Union* (Hart Publishing, 2012)

Francesco Dal Canto and Emanuele Rossi, 'Il giudizio di costituzionalità delle leggi in via principale' in Roberto Romboli (ed.), *Aggiornamenti in tema di processo costituzionale (2011–2013)* (Giappichelli, 2014)

Antonio D'Atena, 'Tra Spagna e Germania. I modelli storici del regionalismo italiano', in Stelio Mangiameli (ed.), *Il regionalismo italiano tra tradizioni unitarie e processi di federalismo. Contributo allo studio della crisi della forma di Stato in Italia* (Giuffrè, 2012)

Antonio D'Atena, 'Materie legislative e tipologia delle competenze' (2003) 23 *Quaderni costituzionali* 15

Antonio D'Atena, 'Regione', in *Enciclopedia del diritto*, vol. 39 (Giuffrè, 1988)

Giacomo Delledonne, 'La Corte costituzionale si pronuncia sulla "lingua piemontese": fra tutela delle minoranze linguistiche e incerti limiti di un "costituzionalismo regionale"' (2011) 39 *le Regioni* 718

Giacomo Delledonne and Giuseppe Martinico, 'Legal Conflicts and Subnational Constitutionalism' (2011) 42 *Rutgers Law Journal* 881

Giustino D'Orazio, *La genesi della Corte costituzionale* (Edizioni di Comunità, 1981)

Victor Ferreres Comella, 'The European model of constitutional review of legislation: Toward decentralization?' (2004) 2 *International Journal of Constitutional Law* 461

Eduardo Gianfrancesco, 'Il giudizio in via principale oggi: prevenire è meglio che reprimere. Sì, ma come?', in Corte costituzionale (ed.), *I ricorsi in via principale. Atti del seminario svoltosi in Roma, Palazzo della Consulta, 19 novembre 2010* (Giuffrè, 2011)

Tania Groppi, 'Lo Stato regionale italiano nel XXI secolo, tra globalizzazione e crisi economica' (2014) 12 (21) *federalismi.it* 1, available at www.federalismi.it

Roberta Lugarà, 'Sentenze additive di procedura… legislativa? Il problematico seguito della sent. n. 251 del 2016' (2017) 8 (1) *Rivista AIC* 1, available at www.rivistaaic.it

Elena Malfatti, 'Art. 127' in Raffaele Bifulco, Alfonso Celotto and Marco Olivetti (eds.), *Commentario alla Costituzione* (Utet, 2006)

Giuseppe Martinico, 'The Impact of "Regional Blindness" on the Italian Regional State', in Elke Cloots, Geert De Baere and Stefan Sottiaux (eds.), *Federalism in the European Union* (Hart Publishing, 2012)

Giuseppe Martinico and Leonardo Pierdominici, 'Crisis, emergency and subnational constitutionalism in the Italian context' (2014) 6 (2) *Perspectives on Federalism* 116

Marco Olivetti, *Nuovi statuti e forma di governo delle regioni. Verso le Costituzioni regionali?* (Il Mulino, 2002)

Francesco Palermo and Karl Kössler, *Comparative Federalism: Constitutional Arrangements and Case Law* (Hart Publishing, 2017)

Paolo Passaglia, 'La Corte, la sovranità e le insidie del nominalismo' (2007) 52 *Giurisprudenza costituzionale* 4052

Giovanni Pitruzzella, 'Problemi e pericoli del "federalismo fiscale" in Italia' (2002) 30 *Le Regioni* 977

Alessandro Pizzorusso, 'Italian and American Models of the Judiciary and of Judicial Review of Legislation: A Comparison of Recent Tendencies' (1990) 38 *The American Journal of Comparative Law* 373

Patricia Popelier, 'Federalism Disputes and the Behavior of Courts: Explaining Variation in Federal Courts' Support for Centralization' (2016) 47 *Publius: The Journal of Federalism* 27

Patricia Popelier, 'Subnational multilevel constitutionalism' (2014) 6 (2) *Perspectives on Federalism* 1

Barbara Randazzo, 'La "manutenzione" del giudizio in via principale', in Carmela Decaro, Nicola Lupo, and Guido Rivosecchi (eds.), *La 'manutenzione' della giustizia costituzionale. Il giudizio sulle leggi in Italia, Spagna e Francia* (Giappichelli, 2012)

Emanuele Rossi, 'Il giudizio in via di principale tra motivi di crisi e prospettive di rilancio' (2018) 38 *Quaderni costituzionali* 647

Giulio Maria Salerno, 2012, 'Dopo la norma costituzionale sul pareggio di bilancio: vincoli e limiti all'autonomia finanziaria delle Regioni' (2012) 32 *Quaderni costituzionali* 563

Gino Scaccia, 'Le competenze legislative sussidiarie e trasversali' (2004) 10 *Diritto pubblico* 461

Rolando Tarchi and Demis Bessi, 'Art. 123', in Raffaele Bifulco, Alfonso Celotto, and Marco Olivetti (eds.), *Commentario alla Costituzione* (Utet, 2006)

Giovanni Tarli Barbieri, 'La potestà legislative regionale in materia elettorale alla luce delle più recenti novità legislative e giurisprudenziali' (2013) 41 *Le Regioni* 97

Diletta Tega, 'Giudizi su conflitti che riguardano diritti. I parametri sostanziali nel giudizio in via principale' (2019) 39 *Quaderni costituzionali* 131

Rosanna Tosi, 'Il neo-centralismo della Corte costituzionale: dei canili e di altre storie' (2016) 44 *Le Regioni* 619

Lars Vinx (ed.), *The Guardian of the Constitution: Hans Kelsen and Carl Schmitt on the Limits of Constitutional Law* (Cambridge University Press, 2015)

4 Intergovernmental relationships in Italy

A feeble but useful model

Eleonora Ceccherini[1]

I. Introduction

Every federal or regional state faces problems in the relationships between the different institutional levels, because any significant government activity requires the *combined* and *coordinated* effort of both the central state and the territorial communities, especially in the absence of a second chamber representing the interests of subnational entities.

Mature federal/regional states tend to discourage a clean-cut separation of competences between the central state and subnational entities, paying attention to the coordination needs. All decentralised systems[2] have had to develop tools to coordinate the exercise of powers distributed among the decision-making entities (Carrozza, 1989, 473).

From a comparative point of view, the path used to achieve such cooperation are various: a Second Chamber representing territorial autonomies, the regional participation in joint bodies, the inclusion of regions into the legislative and administrative proceedings through proposals, advisory opinions, agreements, and compacts (Poirier and Saunders, 2015, 540).

Despite several attempts to turn the Senate into a fully-fledged territorial Chamber, this has never happened; for this reason, Italian regionalism has developed other arrangements to enhance the cooperation between the state and the regions at legislative level. These are in particular the intergovernmental relations involving the executives of State and Regions acting in institutionalised bodies (institutionalised cooperation) or procedures (functional cooperation). This chapter explores the intergovernmental institutional and procedural relations in the Italian system, highlighting their functioning and their peculiarities.

In this regard, two points are worth being underlined. First, there is an increase of intergovernmental relationships in decentralised States overall. This trend can be considered as an attempt to give the subnational level a collective voice in the

1 Associate Professor of Constitutional Law, University of Genoa.
2 This chapter adopts the closest terminology to the Italian regional system. It therefore uses terms such as central State (the national level of government), decentralised systems (including federal and regional systems), Regions/regional (indicating the subnational level of government), and the like.

DOI: 10.4324/9781003104469-5

national policy process. Above all, where no regional second chambers exist, bodies and procedures can be the only means by which Regions and local entities can influence the national policy.

Second, the institutions of intergovernmental relations are important for the development of coherent policy, but they usually reduce the role of elected assemblies: in fact, the decisions reached in this context are compromises among executives, and neither the national parliament nor the regional legislature are responsible for the decisions taken while being bound by them.

II. Cooperative regionalism

The first stage of the relations between the central government and regional authorities in Italy was shaped by a "separatist" theory, according to which regional autonomy could only unfold within the limits of clearly defined competences and functions and should be "parallel" to national legislation and administration. In fact, certain constitutional provisions have been largely ignored, especially those stressing the need to coordinate the respective areas of competence.

However, a shift inverted the direction of the development of regionalism when it started to operate, from the 1970s onwards. The judgements delivered by the Italian Constitutional Court (ItCC), the spirit of the legislative evolution affecting relations between State and Regions, as well as the scholarship on the matter all contributed to the definition of a new model for central-regional relations, based on the principle of loyal cooperation (see the chapter in this volume by Woelk), which gave birth to the so-called 'cooperative regionalism'. Such a principle is based on the assumption that the activities constituting areas of exclusive competence of any one of the governmental levels are limited (Lopez Aranguren, 2002, 30).

It was the ItCC that inspired the codification of the principle of loyal cooperation, which has its foundation in article 5 Const.[3] As early as in judgement n. 49 of 1958, the ItCC invoked a tight collaboration among institutional levels both in the legislative and administrative activity. Hence, loyal cooperation became the cornerstone of State-Regions relations, informing all relations between the different institutional levels. Several rulings explain the concept adamantly. A case in point was judgement n. 341 of 1996, as it held that

> the duty of loyalty, which must shape all relations between State and Regions, intrinsically affects the areas of expertise in which the two institutional levels reciprocally influence each other's functions, that is when one level may not exercise its authority because the other has failed to perform its duties. Therefore, it becomes essential (…) to draw on the beneficial, composing

3 The Republic, one and indivisible, recognises and promotes local autonomies; implements in those services that depend on the state the fullest measure of administrative decentralization; and accords the principles and methods of its legislation to the requirements of autonomy and decentralization.

effect of an instrument based on the distinction and enunciation of differing competence, but more so, at times, on their interference and reciprocal connection.

This is precisely the purpose of the principle of loyal cooperation (see the chapter by Woelk): it is for this reason that such a principle must inform all interactions between the levels of government, far before formal decisions are made, as it actually delineates the context in which such relations must be carried out.

Also, when the content of a measure is to be defined by way of an agreement, the ItCC underlined the need to promote regional involvement whenever said measure appears to interfere with regional competence.[4] In keeping with the principle of loyal cooperation, all levels of government must in fact be involved in an effort to codetermine the content of the act subject to agreement. In order to do so, they must be made aware of alternative and substitutive mechanisms aimed at overcoming any obstructionist position.

But even in the absence of specific provisions imposing cooperation, the duty to reach an agreement must not degenerate into a mere non-binding advisory activity (ItCC judgement 351/1991). Also, should the State deviate from the content of the agreement, it would have to provide adequate reasons, which constitute the "minimum requirement validating the State's unilateral decision" (ItCC judgement 116/1994). Besides, the principle of loyal cooperation has expanded to incorporate the possibility to invalidate a state-adopted measure when it had been approved without taking into account the suggestions submitted by the Region in which the measure was to be implemented (ItCC judgement 232/2004).

Moreover, loyal cooperation can also be ensured when making use of national reference centres, working as informational and technical interface (ItCC judgement 270/1998) or when the State avails itself of subordinate offices within regions (or autonomous provinces, ItCC judgement 483/2001).

It is evident that the ItCC introduced this principle not only to strengthen a specific model of relations based on cooperative regionalism, but also to provide stronger safeguards, limiting the State's ability to unilaterally alter the competences of Regions. To this aim, the ItCC made a significant effort to introduce procedures aimed at harmonising state actions and regional competence. It tried to balance two different aims: on the one hand, to ensure the effectiveness of the State's involvement to avoid any instance of inactivity or legal vacuum; on the other hand, to exclude any unilateral decision that could substantially reduce regional competence.

This approach was further upheld by the ItCC's seminal judgement 303/2003: the Court maintained that a State law may transfer to the central government powers that belong to the Regions, based on the principle of subsidiarity, but this is only possible if an agreement with the interested Region has been previously reached. In other words, the constitutionally defined areas of competence can be

4 Judgements no. 747/1988, 186/1989, 444/1994, 389/1995, 207 and 289/1996, 393/1999, 31/2006.

overcome through a negotiation between the involved institutional parties. By bargaining, the State can revoke the legislative and administrative competence of any given Region in a specific subject matter, if it considers it necessary to ensure the unity of the entire system (see the critical remarks by Martinico in this volume).

Prior to this judgement from 2003, the principle of loyal cooperation was invoked only in areas of concurrent state and regional competence, and it was instrumental in enhancing the ability of both institutional levels to exercise their respective functions. After that judgement, however, the very same principle has become a tool to allow for permanent devolution (rather: re-centralisation) of competences, even disregarding constitutional wording (Bartole, 2004, 278).

In subsequent rulings, the ItCC further elaborated the doctrine of what it labelled "attraction in subsidiarity" (*chiamata in sussidiarietà*), i.e. a flexible criterion to determine which level of government is responsible for which activity, based on the prevalence of the interest at stake, irrespective of the formal constitutional division of powers: if the prevailing interest is national (as it is more frequently the case), then the power should belong to the State; if it is regional, then the Region is responsible for regulating the matter. With judgement 6/2004, the ItCC pointed out that such criterion is legal only if there is a strong agreement between the State and the concerned Region. This means that the State can attract regional powers only based on a previous agreement with the concerned Region(s).[5]

The principle of loyal cooperation between State and Regions has therefore been introduced and developed by the ItCC, which considers it immanent to the regional nature of State, even in the absence of explicit provisions in the Constitution. The 2001 constitutional reform codifies the principle of loyal cooperation, but it does so only in article 120 Const., which refers to the specific (and sensitive) aspect of the regulation of the national government's power to act instead of

> regions, metropolitan cities, provinces and municipalities if the latter fail to comply with international rules and treaties or EU legislation, or in the case of grave danger for public safety and security, or whenever such action is necessary to preserve legal or economic unity and in particular to guarantee the basic level of benefits relating to civil and social entitlements.

As far as the prime instrument for intergovernmental cooperation is concerned, the State-Regions-Autonomous Provinces Conference (see infra), the 2001 reform also failed to constitutionally entrench it, despite the fact that it proved a beneficial element in the implementation of the principle of loyal cooperation. The ItCC

5 We have to mention that later the ItCC in judgement n. 378 of 2005 overruled in part its previous case-law, arguing that Regions do not have a right to veto, and so the attraction in subsidiarity can take place also without reaching a formal agreement. The lack of accommodating would not breach the procedure.

confirmed the importance of such conference in several decisions, among others in judgement 116/1994, when the ItCC held that

> the Conference (…), far from representing an organ of the central state or of the local governments (…), is rather the privileged seat for any debate and political negotiation between State and Regions (and Autonomous Provinces) (…) to facilitate a collaborative *liaison* between said institutions. As such, the Conference can be regarded as an institution operating within the national community, as an instrument for the achievement of cooperation between State and Regions (and Autonomous Provinces).

Therefore, ItCC established a sort of a 'third level' in between State and Regions (Capotosti, 1991, 1).

The ItCC has repeatedly asserted that the relations between State and Regions must be based on loyal cooperation and other corollaries, such as the criterion of reciprocal equality and loyalty. The reiteration of such principles by the ItCC on the one hand aimed at enforcing a cooperative model of intergovernmental relations and on the other limited the State's attitude to unilaterally modify regional competences.

Cooperative regionalism triggers a tight network of relations between the different levels of government and is substantiated in a variety of involved actors and procedures. These relations can be classified based on the role played by the different actors. When the State has a dominant position, the relation is rather a coordination; when the levels are on equal footing, cooperation is in place (Bifulco, 1995, 20).

III. The "system of conferences"

Institutional cooperation among levels of government led to the establishment of a wide range of bodies that gather national, regional and local governments. Such a network of bodies is commonly known as the "system of conferences" (Carpani, 2006, 20), consisting of the permanent State-Regions-Autonomous Provinces Conference (hereinafter, State-Regions Conference), the State-Municipalities-Local Autonomies Conference (State-Local Authorities Conference) and, finally, the State-Regions-Autonomous Provinces-Municipalities-Local Autonomies Conference, also known as "unified Conference".

Such joint bodies are regulated by legislative decree n. 281 of 1997, and are composed of representatives of the central, regional and local executive powers: relations are in fact almost entirely executive in nature.

a) The State-Regions Conference

The permanent Conference for relations between State, Regions, and autonomous Provinces is chaired by the Prime Minister and is composed of the Presidents of Regions and of autonomous Provinces: depending on the subject under discussion, the competent national and regional Ministers may attend the Conference. The President is assisted by the Minister for Regional Affairs.

The Conference has been established by Prime Minister Decree in 1983, initially as a non-permanent body, which was summoned only upon discretion of the Prime Minister. Article 12 of Law n. 400/1988 has expanded the powers of and regulated the Conference, making it a permanent body that meets periodically. Finally, legislative decree n. 281/1997 introduced a systematic regulation of the Conference, making it a body with general (and not sectorial) competence. Such competence includes:

1. advisory opinions on government acts of regional interest, in particular legislative initiatives or proposals for regulations;
2. appointments to bodies carrying out activities or services relevant to the exercise of concurrent competence between State, Regions and autonomous Provinces;
3. codetermination of the content of national acts of coordination;
4. provision of information by assuring the exchange of data between the national Government and the Regions;
5. definition of criteria for the distribution of financial resources to Regions and autonomous Provinces;
6. opinion on draft budget laws;
7. cooperation determining the government's position in EU bodies in areas of regional interest and opinion on the annual community law (see chapter by Baraggia);
8. any other area determined by law and any time the Prime Minister considers it appropriate to ask for the opinion of the Conference.

The permanent State-Regions Conference has therefore evolved from a mere advisory body to the government into a forum for co-determining the national government's policies in an ever-wider range of areas.

b) The State-Municipalities-Local Autonomies Conference

To foster local autonomies (as mandated in the constitutional text), legislative decree n. 281/1997 included a provision for the creation of a State-Municipalities-Local Autonomies Conference. Article 9 of the decree states that such Conference

> has the duty to coordinate the relations between the State and Local Autonomies in order to study, inform and exchange opinions concerning problems connected to the general political direction; the latter may influence the functions of municipalities and provinces. The Conference is the seat for discussion and analysis of problems concerning the local body system and functioning of legislative initiative of government general acts.

Furthermore, the Conference has the duty to promote information and initiatives to improve the efficiency of public services and to promote agreements or planning contracts.

This Conference is chaired by the Prime Minister and is composed of the presidents of the associations representing municipalities (ANCI) and provinces (UPI); 14 majors (5 of which from mountain communities) and 6 provincial presidents appointed by UPI (Gaspari, 1998, 105). Some ministers (such as the Ministers of Interior Affairs, of Regional Affairs, of Economy and Finance, of Infrastructures and Transport, of Health) may also join the discussion.

c) The unified conference

As mentioned above, from a legislative standpoint, the process of strengthening Italian local entities led to a substantial equalisation between regional bodies and the system of local autonomies, especially in their relations with the State. Legislative decree n. 281/1997 also provides for the creation of a unified Conference (State-Regions-Autonomous Provinces-Municipalities-Local Autonomies Conference). In this way, regions and other local autonomies are placed at the same level, without giving regions a primary role in defining the various functions of local entities (Di Cosimo, 1998, 11).

Pursuant to article 9 of legislative decree 281/1997, the unified Conference "adopts deliberations, makes agreements, gives advice, appoints representatives for matters and tasks of joint interest of regions, provinces municipalities and mountain communities". In addition to the government's approval, resolutions within the unified Conference are adopted "with the consent of members of the two autonomies groups that compose the State-Regions Conference and the State-Municipalities-Local Autonomies Conference. The approval is expressed with unanimous vote of the members of the two aforementioned groups."

Some regions have argued that article 9 of Law n. 59/1997 and legislative decree n. 281/1997 refer to the unconstitutional equalising of regions and local entities. However, with judgement 408/1998, the ItCC has rejected such claim and argued that state legislation may set discretionary choices related to the relations between state, regions, and local autonomies; and that both the creation of a State-Regions Conference and of a State-Cities and Local Autonomies Conference are expressions of a bound constitutional choice. Moreover, the ItCC has pointed out that it is not unconstitutional to choose a unified conference with representatives of regions and local autonomies when there is a need to discuss issues of common interests; on the contrary, the ItCC evidenced that unifying the Conferences would be

> appropriate for a better integration of the different points of view and of the different needs coming out as referred to the autonomies. A smaller space is left for rigid division or oppositions that could bring obstacles or resistance to the decentralisation process.

d) The State-Cities and Local Autonomies Conference in the regional legislation about local functions

The effort to contrast the trend towards the equalisation between local governments and regions is partly realised with the attempt, coming from the regions, to define their own coordinating role towards municipalities and provinces located in their territory. This is favoured by article 4(1) of Law 59/1997, which acknowledges that regions may assign to municipalities and to other local entities all functions related to matters listed in article 117 Const., requiring a unified exercise at regional level, after hearing the organs representing local autonomies when set up by regional legislation (Cosulich, 1998, 67).

By looking at the regional legislation creating these organs, it is possible to identify some common elements. First, only members of the regional and municipal executive may be part of these bodies; next, the competence is general and not sectorial, as they usually give advice on plans concerning a reorganisation of the functions of local bodies and ensure that the law actually referred to local interests; finally, they have powers of coordination and connection between the region and local autonomies.

e) The Conference of Services

Unlike the previous ones, this organisation is temporary and specific. In fact, while the others are permanent organs with general competence, the Conference of Services is a mixed entity whose members are involved in planning and realising specific projects: once the project is completed, the body is dissolved (Sandulli, 2016, 40).

The Conference of Services usually comprises a conducting phase (which specifies the programs of the participants) and a procedural phase (which shortens the carrying out of certain projects). This Conference is a meeting place in which local administrations can participate and reach two different types of conclusions: first, they may get information from bodies and, second, they may reach a formal agreement through the unanimous vote of the different subjects, which will be transferred to the deciding administrations.

The Conference is a tool to collect "accords", "concerts", "permissions", or "named approvals" of other administrations. In fact, mechanisms to find agreements are those producing a complication in administrative procedures and the disposition allows the deciding administration to call the conference to obtain approval from other administrations and without waiting for the beginning of the different sub-process.

The Conference allows confrontation between involved subjects and coordination of the involved interests in a fair way.

f) The Production Room

The so-called Production Room (*Cabina di regia)* is an example of the efforts of the central and regional administration to rationalise the action of the government in matters where regional and local interests are involved. Compared to the other bodies described above, this is a technical body where the function of coordination is prevalent. In this case, the various parties are not on equal footing, as the position of the central government is prominent.

The "Production Room" was first set up with article 6 of Decree Law n. 23/1995 with the purpose of having a unified centre of reference for all issues connected to structural interventions. At the same time, Production Rooms were set up at a regional level, with councillors and managers of the administrations concerned involved in carrying out the different phases of European Union programs (e.g. planning, management, monitoring, and accounting reports).

The function of production has been directed to channel and to direct financial programs, in particular EU structural funds for depressed areas (Sorrente, 1998, 87; Carzaniga, 1998, 105). They are bodies aiming at strengthening and coordinating the central and regional administrative structures to mobilise and use the financial flow coming from Brussels that often were not used or not completely exploited by the administrations.

The structure of the national Production Room was amended by Law n. 190/2014; it can be defined as the national referral structure for the coordination and promotion of action utilising European structural funds.

The Production Room model has been exported to other policy areas, such as public contracts.

IV. Functional cooperation

Thus far, this chapter has explored the intergovernmental cooperation that has led to the creation of bodies both with general and sectorial competence. We will now focus on those forms of cooperation between levels of government generating acts and procedures. Such acts and procedures are the results of meetings between representatives of different administrations. In the Italian experience, this phenomenon is labelled 'concerted' or 'negotiated' administration, and it triggers procedures of coordination and connection between different bodies. This helps speed up the administrative process and, consequently, the improvement of public performance (Desideri and Torchia, 1986, 40).

Among these agreements, it is worth noting consents and conventions stipulated between privates and public administrations, in addition to those contracted between two or more public subjects.

While agreements between privates and public administrations arise from an identity crisis and a role characterising the administrative act that was meant to be unilateral, the agreements between public subjects come from the need to reassemble functions and competencies whereas a radical application of rules and principles of institutional pluralism generated break-ups and confusion of powers and competencies. In the first case, there is a need for the democratisation of the parties; in the second case, what dominates is the search for greater efficiency. In fact, the multiplication of constitutionally entrenched centres of power (pursuant to articles 5 and 114 Const.) and the diffusion of power to subjects operating at different levels of government caused – and is still causing – a certain confusion of competences.

The purpose of coordinated administrative tools is to guarantee a synergic organisation of the administrative action when a fragmented disarticulation of competencies exists between two or more public bodies in relation to the same goal and project. Consequently, the main goal of any planning agreement is to preventively involve all public subjects entrusted with the same function; this helps simplify and rationalise the administrative activity by forcing public subjects to sit at a negotiating table, take common decisions that are binding on the bodies that concluded the agreement, and then execute the pact that was freely reached.

In Italy, the acts of the concerted or negotiated administration are ruled by law. Among the several concertation tools that have been introduced by the legislature, the most relevant are:

1 'Planning Conference' (*conferenza di programmazione*) – this is a participatory body that was introduced by some regional acts. The regional or provincial Council may call it or by agreement with Municipalities whose public subject and associations cooperate a) to the sectorial analysis comparing their programs with the regional and provincial programs, b) to the definition of planning hypothesis, c) to control the carrying out of planned intervention. In fact, the specific task of the planning conference is to define due time and ways to check the real application of interventions and eventually their updating. The Planning Conference may be preliminary to the stipulation of a planning agreement. Here, the practical dimension – meaning the common goal or intention to adopt a coordinated approach to be realised with common procedures – is a central feature.
2 'Planning Agreements' (*intese di programma*) – such agreements were introduced by decree law n. 32/1995 (converted into Law n. 104/1995). They are interesting because the availability of financial resources is included among the necessary requirement to reach an agreement. According to the act, Planning Agreements are "agreements between institutional subjects with competences in a specific sector. Such subjects are engaged to cooperate by supplying the financial resources needed to realise a series of actions and specific interventions. The latter are functionally connected in a pluriannual frame, even if they are not completely clear in terms of feasibility".
3 'Planning Contracts' (*contratti di programma*) – they refer to the general model of agreement on procedures as provided by article 11 of Law n. 241/1990. Such contracts are stipulated between the public administration and private entities (usually corporations), to attract entrepreneurial actions towards the programmatic policy that shall answer to the goals of public interests in connection with the various types of public utility performance. Usually, the initiative is taken by a private party by bringing a project to the competent administration. Such procedure offers two advantages: on the one

hand, the investment programs and financing respond to specific public goals; on the other hand, the success of incentives given to those who are really capable of using them in a profitable way. The distinctive aspect of this procedure is that, even if the starting depends on the entrepreneur proposal, the public administration has a chance to influence the private initiative. At the same time, the private entity finds in this contractual scheme the advantage of the public financing of its own initiative.

4 'Territorial Agreements' (*patti territoriali*) – they are coordination tools between the public administration and social parties. The aim is to define strategic goals for local development by locating the means to realise the agreements and the actions to support. They indicate where to make interventions in specific sectors. Also, the Territorial Agreement defines an operating program to set in specific terms the actions to be realised, and a working program and its different chronological phases. Compared to the previous ones, the peculiarity of this negotiated administration tool is the meeting of public and private subject not so much for a specific project but for the definition of wide goals which are preparatory to the definition of operative activities.

5 'Program Agreements' (*accordi di programma*) – they are used to create a cooperative seat in the public activity where to define and carry out interventions requiring an integrated and coordinated action of several administration organs, both local and national, as provided for by law 267/2000. This tool is useful when there is a need to coordinate a plurality of shared activities among several bodies, or when there is a need to unify the administrative action and improve its efficiency and efficacy. These are provisions aiming at finding consensus among a plurality of subjects, in particular, of state, regional and local administrations for complex interventions. It is also possible to include in the agreement an arbitration process, a substitutive intervention, and sanctioning procedures if consent is infringed.

V. Final remarks

The involvement of decentralised organs in the general policy of the central state is evidenced by the acceptance of the principles of cooperative regionalism, according to which all significant governmental activities shall be conducted through joint and coordinated undertakings by central and local entities (Rolla, 2016, 143). The chapter described different types of relations between the centre and local governments, and discussed the main models, instruments and mechanism of collaboration. This network of relationships is still weak. The positive outcome depends on the capacities of political organs and of civil servants, who should show a will to collaborate (Del Prete, 2020, 69). Among the various bodies and procedures, special attention should be given to the system of conferences, as it represents the most relevant expression of intergovernmental relations. On balance, the system of conferences as developed in Italy reveals both elements of success and shortcomings (Castiello and Mazzola, 2014, 1).

A. Definite shortcomings...

As noted *supra*, among the reasons that led to the creation of a system of conferences (in particular, the permanent Conference for relations between State, Regions, and autonomous Provinces) there was the need to provide local autonomies with the opportunity and the means to take part in decision-making activities at central level. This need became even more pressing after the strengthening of Italian regionalism. This, however, was not sweeping enough to inspire a constitutional reform capable of introducing a new second Chamber representing Regions, and consequently, to allow territorial autonomies to play a substantial part in national legislative proceedings. As a result, given the absence of a regional Senate, the permanent State-Regions-Autonomous Provinces Conference seemed to be a viable option, although it cannot be regarded as an effective substitute for a representative assembly (Allegretti, 1996, 431; *contra* Ruggiu, 2006, 853).

The absence of a territorial chamber leaves the system without an important element of cohesion, although the comparative experience of several decentralised systems shows that the role of the Senate as a territorial chamber representing the sub-units has lost its appeal and has shown signs of weakness (Palermo, 2018). Nevertheless, abandoning the prospect of a representative body in favour of a system of intergovernmental relations may not lead to greater ease of relations between the central State and territorial communities, and more so, it would deny them all safeguards and protection.

It is indeed reasonable to question the possibility that the Government or the various levels of bureaucracy will adequately safeguard the rights of territorial autonomies.

This leads to the second weak element of the Conference: a proof of the substantially non-fungible nature of the Senate representing Regions and of the current State-Regions-Autonomous Provinces Conference is given by the fact that the latter is composed of representatives from both national and regional governments. The decision-making procedure within the Conference, which is limited to its governmental components, is indeed the object of notable criticism, especially in relation to its democratic *deficit*. Given that the centre of gravity has moved from the democratically elected legislative bodies to the governmental ones, this can only lead to a decrease in the democratic quality of the system, thus reducing the role of legislative councils. In any event, intergovernmental relations come about more as an effect of the pre-eminence of executive bodies within the legal order, rather than as a cause of the same circumstance. Therefore, it would be fruitful to reconsider the relations linking the legislative power to the executive authority from a general point of view, rather than to question the Conference, considering that this body merely represents a manifestation of the changes affecting such relations.

To overcome part of the criticism, it would probably be more reasonable to change certain rules and practices concerning the functioning of the State-Regions-Autonomous Provinces Conference, especially by stimulating a greater involvement of the representative bodies and inducing greater openness in the performances of such committees. With regard to this element, the issue specifically concerns the relations between regional governments and their respective Councils, which are substantially barred from any decision-making process within the Conference. Consequently, it would be desirable that each regional Council conducts a preliminary debate on the matters included in the Conference's agenda, so that the elective body could be informed of the issues discussed. In this way, the Council would be enabled to appropriately direct the activities of the regional government, even though the representatives in the Conference are not bound by their electoral mandate. This could be reasonably achieved by promoting a systematic and rational planning of the activities of the Conference, and by establishing a duty of the Prime Minister to communicate the agenda to the President of the Region and to the President of the Regional Council, so that they can inform the assembly. With regard to the second element, a measure that would contribute to reduce the criticism concerning the Conference's democratic quality refers to the inadequate publicity of the session's outcome. A solution to this problem that would entail that the minutes of all sessions and the meeting records give a clear and faithful account of the relevant debate (Marini, 2003, 339).

A third critical aspect of the system of Conferences concerns its nature of body of the Prime Minister's Office. As mentioned above, the Conference intends to solve the lack of regional involvement in decision-making at central level, and hence provides local autonomies with an adequate instrument of participation in activities at state level. In this sense, it is unquestionable that the Conference is a body of the central government: in fact, structured within the government, it is the President of Council of Ministers who acts as chair (and, as such, he is required to summon its meetings), and finally its secretariat depends on the government. In light of this structure, the Conference does not truly represent the "voice" of the regions at central State: rather, it is a body aimed at verifying whether the point of view of the regions is consistent with that of the central government (Marini, 2003, 339). For this reason, the Conference operates more as a mediation instrument with regard to the Government's resolutions affecting regional interests and competence, rather than as an organism allowing regional involvement in the definition of the Government's political policy.

Finally, the State-Regions-Autonomous Provinces Conference can exert great influence on regions, taken as a group or individually. In the first case, such persuasive impact comes about when the Conference operates in areas that have been constitutionally reserved to Regions, given that the central state's influence can throw the relation off balance, progressively eroding the area of regional competence. In the second case, the state can overshadow the autonomy of an individual region by substituting the latter's opinion with one expressed within the Conference. On this matter, the ItCC held unconstitutional a provision relating to "the involvement of the Conference – regarded as a privileged place for political debate and negotiation between state and regions on matters generally affecting regional interests – in a decision pertaining to a single concerned region" (judgement n. 124 of 1994). Likewise, with ruling 121/1997, the same Court argued that the opinions expressed by the Conference and by Trentino-South Tyrol were different as to their foundation, nature, purpose, and effects: in fact, the Conference's opinion was required by ordinary law, while the autonomous entities of Trentino-South Tyrol are regulated by the rules implementing the regional statute. Also, while the first was expressed by an assembly composed of all regions, the second was expressed by only one region. Moreover, the first one is a generic opinion, while the second specifically relates to its compatibility with the regional special statute and the pertinent implementing rules. Finally, when it is negative in content, only the opinion regulated by the rules implementing the regional statute may temporarily limit the effectiveness of the measure within the regional or provincial territory.

A fourth element of weakness of the Conference consists in its legitimation, which is a law and not the Constitution: as a result, its existence depends upon the unilateral intent of the State, which is revocable at any time. Also the ItCC, in judgement 408/1998, held that the unified Conference is not a constitutionally required body, and referred to it as a "non-constitutionally binding option". However, a suppression of the State-Regions Conference is merely hypothetical and hardly feasible: if the principle of loyal cooperation has found constitutional validation, it is not clear how such principle could be adequately implemented in the absence of the Conference (Ruggiu, 2006, 277).

Several critical comments have been made on the fact that these bodies have a limited ability to represent relevant interests: this argument is particularly appropriate in regard to the State-Regions-Local Autonomies Conference considering its heterogeneous composition. In addition, a number of commentators noted that if regions inhabited by 50 per cent of the population can count on less than one-fourth of the votes, this could affect the validity of approved resolutions. However, an equal representation of the subunits represents a typical feature of decentralised states, in which representation is not linked to the population's numerical consistency, but to the single territorial units (D'Atena, 2001, 129; but *contra* Mor, 1997, 513).

Above all, many opinions have highlighted the absolute uniqueness, from a comparative point of view, of the Italian situation, in light of the simultaneous participation of local entities and of the regional community within such bodies. Even if the ItCC upheld the absolute legality of this legal option, this three-part representation model remains quite unusual. Composite legal orders have a tendency to subordinate the local level to the regional level: as a consequence, introducing local autonomies within the representation system significantly subverts this assumption. At the same time, it emphasises the fact that the municipal dimension has always influenced the Italian institutional history. This combination may weaken the regional system, as any conflict between regions and local autonomies would come to the Government's advantage.

B. ...and elements of success of the system

It is appropriate at this point to consider also the successful aspects that characterise the system of Conferences in Italy. First of all, it is unquestionable that the permanent Conference represents an essential structure of the Italian regional system. In spite of its many weaknesses, to this day the Conference represents the only place where regions and the central government can meet to talk, share opinions, even ignore each other, but nevertheless meet. Should the Conference be dissolved, or its role reduced, regions would be left without an adequate means of negotiation.

Besides, the mere fact that a similar body exists within a composite order is in itself a factor of great importance, and it contributes to a shift that many different legal systems are progressively operating. The gradual acknowledgement of the principles of *cooperative government* has eased the way towards the establishment of similar organs, in which the highest ranks of both central and local governments are represented. In so doing, local communities strengthen their standing before the state, and this allows them to balance the state-gravitating inclination that may have shaped the institutional system in different periods of time. Furthermore, considering that the Italian regional system does not have a representative assembly, the existence of an institution such as the Conference partially makes up for its absence, considering that it does not simultaneously act as an instrument of alternative participation or capable of excluding the territorial second Chamber.

Another positive element is the fact that the presence of local executives within the Conference ensures that all members are competent; consequently, also their decisions – at least in theory – are properly elaborated and expressed, especially when they are technical in content.

Many commentators have also argued that the introduction of the Conference in the decision-making process constitutes another positive element that has eventually changed the Italian form of government. However, this opinion – which is aimed at providing substance to Regional involvement in this process – cannot be fully embraced. Unquestionably, the creation of the Conference had an effect on the decision-making process of the central state: in fact, in the past it has contributed to draft several fundamental state legislative measures, such as the Finance Act's supplemental act or the economic-financial program. All in all, local autonomies have taken part, to various degrees, in the law-making process. The opinions expressed by regional representatives within the Conference could truly have a bearing on the central law-making process if only their dissent could be considered as a parameter for review of the validity of the State law: only in this circumstance can the previously stated opinion, according to which local autonomies have substantially shaped the Italian system of government, gain some favour. On the contrary, as we have already mentioned, such ability has not been granted to the Conference: more so, Law n.131/2003 has expressly provided that certain types of agreements[6] promoted by the Government within the State-Regions Conference or within the unified Conference can be implemented in spite of

6 These are the agreements provided for by article 8(6) of Law 131/2003, promoted by the Government in order to harmonise existing laws, to attain a common opinion or to achieve shared objectives.

regional dissent, and the Government does not even have the duty to state the reasons for its diverging opinion.

Despite this profile, the Conference has certainly expanded its role. The original intent of the legislature was to create an advisory body, but eventually it extended its functions to embrace a decision-making competence, even if the ItCC expressly ruled that the legislative process is not connected to the loyal cooperation process (judgements 65/2016 and 43/2016 but, as a partial overruling, see judgement 251/2016).

It is also worth mentioning the role played by the Conference in relation to EU integration (see Baraggia in this volume). Overall, the process of worldwide economic globalisation is deeply affecting the distribution of competence between the central state and territorial autonomies. In particular, given the current propensity to create international organisations operating in areas usually reserved to local entities, this causes the point of attraction to move in favour of central authorities. In a way, this is the reason why many devolved systems are diverting from the guidelines defined by Constitutions.

Another beneficial element consists in the fact that the Italian system felt the need to provide an instrument of multilateral cooperation. Only such instruments can operationalise the principle of equal ranking of decentralised entities and the state, and allow territorial autonomies to come together as a united front. The most immediate and obvious positive consequence of these instruments of cooperation has in fact been the identification of a single forum for debate, in which the most "autonomist" opinions are balanced during negotiation in order to protect the entire system. It seems fruitful to establish a single speaker advocating the reasons of all regions before the state, rather than promote and uphold bilateral relations between the state and each single region. While this method can be significantly more effective, a fragmented negotiation does not benefit the entire system, as it is restricted to its functioning and favours only certain territorial entities among other regions, as they possess a stronger standing before the state. Unquestionably, a system of bilateral relations serves the purposes of more dynamic territorial entities only: its diffusion increases the recognition and the strengthening of distinct realities, thus intensifying the differences and the competition between territorial autonomies.

Literature

Umberto Allegretti, 'Per una Camera territoriale: problemi e scelte' (1996) *Le Regioni* 431

Sergio Bartole, 'Collaborazione e sussidiarietà nel nuovo ordine regionale' (2004) *Le Regioni* 578

Raffaele Bifulco, *La cooperazione nello stato unitario composto* (Cedam, 1995)

Piero Alberto Capotosti, 'Regione IV) Conferenza Stato-regioni' (1991) XXVI *Enciclopedia giuridica* 1

Guido Carpani, *La Conferenza Stato-Regioni* (Il Mulino, 2006)

Paolo Carrozza, 'Principio di collaborazione e sistema delle garanzie procedurali (la via italiana al regionalismo cooperativo)' (1989) *Le Regioni* 473

Alberto Carzaniga, 'Una sintesi su cosa dovrebbe essere la Cabina di regia nazionale' (1998) *Istituzioni del federalismo* 105

Matilde Castiello and Gianliborio Mazzola 'L'evoluzione del Sistema delle Conferenze' (2014) *Amministrazione in cammino* 1

Giovanni Coinu, 'Il SUAP nel riparto delle competenze legislative tra stato e Regioni nella sentenza Corte cost. n. 15 del 2010: la semplificazione come nuova materia trasversale?' (2010) *Le Regioni* 960

Matteo Cosulich, 'Le altre Conferenze. L'esperienza delle Conferenze permanenti Regione-autonomie locali' (1998) *Istituzioni del federalismo* 67

Antonio D'Atena, *L'Italia verso il "federalismo"* (Giuffrè, 2001)

Francesco Del Prete 'L'attuazione del principio di leale collaborazione nella prassi della Conferenza Stato-Regioni' (2020) *Istituzioni del federalismo* 69

Carlo Desideri and Luisa Torchia, *I raccordi tra Stato e Regioni. Un'indagine per casi su organi e procedimenti* (Giuffrè, 1986)

Giovanni Di Cosimo, 'Dalla Conferenza Stato-Regioni alla Conferenza unificata (passando per lo Stato-Città)' (1998) *Istituzioni del federalismo* 11

Oscar Gaspari, 'L'attività della Conferenza Stato-Città ed autonomie locali. Una scheda informativa' (1998) *Istituzioni del federalismo* 105

Edoardo López Aranguren, *Relaciones intergubernamentales en los estados autonómico y federal: estudio sobre los Estados Unidos, el Estado español y el País Vasco* (Instituto Vasco de Administración Pública, 2002)

Francesco Saverio Marini, 'La "pseudocollaborazione" di tipo organizzativo: il caso della Conferenza Stato-Regioni', in Antonio D'Atena, Pierfrancesco Grossi (eds.) *Diritto, diritti e autonomia. Tra Unione europea e riforme costituzionali* (Giuffrè, 2003) 339

Giorgio Mor, 'Tra Stato-Regioni e Stato-città' (1997) *Le Regioni* 513

Francesco Palermo, 'Beyond Second Chambers: Alternative Representation of Territorial Interests and their Reasons' (2018) *Perspectives of Federalism*, vol. 10, 2, 50

Stefania Pedrabissi, 'La nuova Conferenza di servizi' (2018) *Amministrare* 489

Johanne Poirier and Cheryl Saunders, 'Comparative experiences of intergovernmental relations in federal systems', in Johanne Poirier, Cheryl Saunders, and John Kincaid (eds.) *Intergovernmental Relations in Federal systems: Comparative Structures and Dynamics* (Oxford University Press, 2015) 440

Giancarlo Rolla, 'Lineamenti del regionalismo nei sistemi costituzionali multilivello. Un approccio di diritto comparato', in Guerino D'Ignazio (ed.) *Multilevel constitutionalism tra integrazione europea e riforme degli ordinamenti decentrati* (Giuffrè, 2011) 143

Ilenia Ruggiu, 'Conferenza Stato-Regioni: un istituto del "federalismo" sommerso' (2000) *Le Regioni* 853

Ilenia Ruggiu, *Contro la Camera delle Regioni* (Jovene, 2006)

Maria Alessandra Sandulli (ed.), *Le nuove regole della semplificazione amministrativa: la legge n. 241/1990 nei decreti attuativi della riforma Madia: trasparenza e anticorruzione, poterei sostitutivi, silenzio assenso* (Giuffrè, 2016)

Giuseppe Sorrente, 'Il sistema delle Cabine di regia' (1998) *Le istituzioni del federalismo* 87

5 Financial relations in the Italian regional system

Alice Valdesalici[1]

I. The rationale for reform and the significance of a legal investigation

The 2001 reform of the Constitution has started a process for reshaping financial relations in the Italian regional system.[2] Prior to 2001 the system of subnational financing was entirely grounded on central state transfers, which mostly came with strings attached. Besides that, resources were negotiated on a yearly basis with no chance of long-term planning from the part of the single subnational entity. Despite the fact that Italian regions have been progressively vested with relevant – mostly administrative – competences and as such significant spending responsibilities (50 per cent of overall public spending was in charge of territorial entities),[3] financial autonomy of subnational entities has remained untouched for years. Only in 2000 a partially different financing system was envisaged on paper (Law no. 56/2000) and certain taxes were assigned to the regions (i.e. a tax on business – the IRAP).

One of the major problems herein lies with the fact that subnational entities were not facing any responsibility in their financing. Giving rise to a large vertical fiscal gap, such a system failed to make territorial entities accountable for their decisions. This pattern brought over time to a duplication of administrative structures (and costs) together with an expansion in personnel spending. To this regard criticism can be drawn from the growing gap between decentralised public spending and the employees per level of government. It would be optimal if public employees were matched with the tier of government in charge for a specific public function. On the contrary, dating back to 1995, 54.3 percent of the public employees were hired by the State and the percentage has grown up to 57.4 percent in 2009, when the State was in charge of less than 50 percent of public spending (Palermo, 2011).

1 Senior Researcher, Institute for Comparative Federalism, Eurac Research.

2 On the concept of fiscal federalism in Italy, see among the many: Antonini, 2009; Antonini 2013; Bertolissi, 1997; Bertolissi, 2007.

3 In fact, from the late 1990s an incremental decentralisation process was started, culminating in 1999 and 2001 with two major constitutional amendments that considerably increased the political autonomy of ordinary regions.

DOI: 10.4324/9781003104469-6

It is not by chance that one of the main drivers for reform was the enhancement of financial and political accountability. A new financial setting had to be envisaged which prompted a better match between the spheres of those who benefit, who decide, and who vote, in order to ensure democratic control and inject efficiency into the system. With this purpose in mind, the previous system mostly based on State grants had to be reshaped, as the recognition of autonomy on the revenue side was perceived to be conducive to more accountability for the regions. At the same time, the socio-economic cleavage between the northern and the southern part of the country made it impossible to opt for a genuinely competitive model of fiscal federalism. The recognition of a certain margin of autonomy on tax matters had to coexist with a wide-ranging system of equalisation (Antonini, 2014).

After the enactment of the 2001 constitutional reform, the federalism debate has been increasingly captured by the financial dimension of intergovernmental relations. The allocation of powers and the design of intergovernmental relations in fiscal and financial matters are pivotal for the very existence of every federal system. Nevertheless, in Italy the debate on 'fiscal federalism' has monopolized every aspect of the federalizing process. While the 2001 reform intended to comprehensively address the institutional design of a (quasi-) federal State, afterwards political attention was paid predominantly to the financial dimension.

This is all the more so since the outbreak of the economic and financial crisis, which has exacerbated the situation, due to the poor conditions the Italian system of public finance was facing. The need to comply with the EU-driven economic constraints has added an additional level of complexity in the management of public finance, dealing a severe blow to the subnational autonomy in general and to financial autonomy in particular. Consequently, the new pattern is at present far from being translated into practice and the current Covid-19 emergency represents another stress-test for financial relations and subnational autonomy.

This complex picture adds to the need to investigate financial relations from a legal standpoint. The subject is topical in the political agenda and in the academic debate of every federal system. Despite that, the interest of legal scholars has shifted to the topic only in the last two decades thanks to the emergence of a broad understanding of fiscal federalism.[4] Even though there is no unanimous agreement on a common definition, over time an expanded understanding of the phenomenon has taken hold, as referred to 'the division of policy responsibilities among different levels of government and with the fiscal interactions among these governments' (Wildasin, 2008, 405). All in all, the investigation shall include the allocation of taxing and spending powers, as well as of regulatory and revenue responsibilities and shall be integrated by a dynamic understanding of the rules at work through intergovernmental relations.

4 With a few exceptions of a non-comparative nature, e.g., Dam, 1977.

This holds particularly true within the European context, and it is not by chance that the scholarly interest has recorded an expansive trend after the outbreak of the economic crisis and the hardening of the EU obligations. The idea that fiscal federalism is essential in determining the way a federal system functions has steadily taken root. Not only the financial endowment of the different levels of government is instrumental for the discharge of their powers, but also, there exists a mutual interdependence between financial and institutional components (Carboni, 2014, 8). On the one hand, financial arrangements are conditioned by the institutional structure of the federal system as a whole. On the other hand, the allocation of powers in financial and fiscal matters is instrumental for the discharge of legislative and administrative responsibilities, as it ensures that subnational entities can make use of their constitutionally assigned margin of autonomy. As such, financial rules have frequently impacted the institutional components and their functioning, and in some cases can be considered responsible for their formal or informal change (Palermo, 2012, 2, 10).

Against this background, the chapter pieces together the legal frame of reference of the 'Italian financial constitution'. The notion of a *financial constitution* is the literal translation of the term *Finanzverfassung*, coined by Austrian (Pernthaler, 1984) and German (Hellermann, 2010) scholars and referring to those constitutional provisions that establish the principles and rules of the system of public finance, and having particular regard to the determination, distribution, and use made of financial resources by the different levels of government (Valdesalici [b], 2018).[5]

After that the constitutional frame of reference is illustrated and the principles of the 'financial constitution' are investigated (par. 2); an overview of the implementing process (par. 3) and its specific regulations on paper (par. 4) and in motion (par. 5) are also provided. This is done going through the case law of the Italian Constitutional Court (hereinafter ItCC) in its evolution over time and paying exclusive attention to the subnational level of government, i.e. the regions. Against this composite legal scenario, the conclusive paragraph (par. 6) will try to make a balance and look at the way forward.

II. Framing the Italian financial constitution

The constitutional point of reference for outlining 'fiscal federalism in Italy' is Article 119. Accordingly, all territorial entities shall have financial autonomy both on the revenue and expenditure side. At the same time, autonomy has to be balanced with solidarity, cohesion and coordination as the Constitution provides for the overall coordination of public finance and for an equalisation mechanism, in order to ensure equality among all territories.

The provision further defines financial autonomy on the revenue side by setting the principle of self-sufficiency of territorial entities. As such regions – as well as

5 This is the terminology used, with little variation, by Italian and Spanish scholars as well. Among others, Salerno, 2007; Medina Guerrero, 2008, 98. The latter, indeed, makes specific reference to the 'territorial financial constitution'.

local entities – have to base their financing on 'autonomous resources', that is mainly through tax revenue linked to the territorial fiscal capacity [Art. 119(2) Const.].

It also provides for a taxonomy of the sources subnational financing shall rest upon by enumerating the different possible types (Bassanini, 2006). In sum, these include own and territorially shared taxes, plus non-earmarked equalisation transfers [Art. 119(2) and 119(3) Const]. Territorial entities can set and levy taxes and collect revenues of their own, in compliance with the Constitution and according to the principles of co-ordination of State finances and the tax system. They are also entitled to a share in the tax revenues related to their respective territories. For the sake of cohesion, solidarity mechanisms are also foreseen. State legislation shall provide for an equalisation fund – with no strings attached – for the territories with a lower per-capita fiscal capacity. The other State transfers shall be abolished.

Revenues raised from the above-mentioned sources shall enable entities to fully finance the public functions assigned to them (Art. 119(4) Const.). In searching for a balance between autonomy and solidarity, this provision is central in constraining the margin of manoeuvre of the legislature and imposing a system with a strong solidarity blueprint: if self-sufficiency cannot be reached with 'territorially-generated' resources, the State must guarantee an adequate financial endowment through equalisation.

This financing scheme is meant to cope with the physiologic functioning of the system. Additionally, specific-purpose grants can be reserved to single entities in extraordinary circumstances. Article 119(5) Const. explicitly lists some of these exceptional conditions, but it also introduces a general clause allowing a State intervention in all cases that go beyond the ordinary.

In 2012, the Parliament has amended several constitutional provisions (Articles 81, 97, 117, 119), constitutionalizing the principle of balanced budget as imposed by the so-called EU fiscal compact (const. law no. 1/2012). Taking into account the economic cycle, the State shall ensure the balance between revenue and spending, as well as the sustainability of the public debt (Art. 81 Const.). Territorial entities shall also contribute. As such, they have financial autonomy, while ensuring the equilibrium of their budgets and concurring to the enforcement of EU obligations [Art. 119(1) Const.]. The new rules impose limits to deficits and to the possibility to incur debts and, at the same time, they set strict limitations to regional overspending. Deviations from the equilibrium could occur, although entities may indebt only for investment expenditure and under the condition that the equilibrium is anyway reached by taking into account all territorial entities within the regional territory of reference (Ciolli, 2014).

For a proper understanding of fiscal relations, however, the analysis of the financial constitution shall also incorporate the entire block of constitutional provisions set forth by the 2001 revision of Title V of the Constitution to the extent that these are related to financial and fiscal issues (Groppi, 2008; Salerno, 2007). For a fully-fledged analysis, the reading of Article 119 must be integrated at best with Article 118 (distribution of administrative competences) as well as Article

117 (allocation of legislative competences).[6] These are of relevance as long as they stipulate on the allocation of legislative powers and administrative responsibilities in fiscal- and financial-related matters.

In defining the principles that guide the allocation of administrative competences, Article 118 ends up affecting the spending autonomy of territorial entities. In fact, the latter is only mandated as a principle, but it is not explicitly regulated either in the Constitution, or in the implementing regulation (see below par. 4). As such, spending responsibilities can be only implicitly inferred from the combined scope of the legislative and, mainly, administrative responsibilities vested with the subnational entities.

The distribution of legislative competences is even more central in understanding the new system in its functioning. While subnational entities have been vested with financial autonomy and solidarity duties (Art. 119), the State holds the exclusive legislative power over the State tax system, the equalisation mechanism and the 'harmonisation of budgets of all public entities'[7] [Art. 117(2), lit. e.], as well as over the 'determination of the essential levels of public services to be ensured in a uniform manner across the country' [Art. 117(2), lit. m.].

The centre is also responsible for the enforcement of 'the principle of balanced budget', that can be considered as a *sui generis* State competence. The latter is not listed in Article 117 Const., but can be drawn from Article 81 Const. and Article 5, constitutional law 1/2012 (Salerno, 2011) and inevitably conditions financial autonomy of subnational entities as these are bound to ensure that their budgets are in balance and shall contribute to the enforcement of EU obligations pursuant to Articles 119(1) and 97 Const. (Servizio studi del Senato e della Camera, 2017).

Finally, the State is responsible for defining the 'fundamental principles of coordination of public finance and of the tax system' [Art. 117(3)] while regions are vested with the power to determine the detailed regulation in the field as this is a concurrent competence title.

Due to the use made by the State of these legislative powers, the actual operation of these competences – either individually considered or in their interrelation with one another – is central in understanding the genuine dimension of financial autonomy and the functioning of financial relations. In this respect, the ItCC has played (and is still playing) a key-role in shaping the new financial constitution, also due to the long-lasting lack of implementation of the constitutional framework. Indeed, the Court, on the one hand, has urged for many years the legislature to give effective implementation to Article 119 of the Constitution (*ex plurimis*, judgments no. 370/2003, no. 37/2004, no.193/2007), on the other hand, has intervened, setting the milestones to orient the future legislator in the

6 Other provisions come also to the fore to the extent that they provide fundamental principles and values that inspire the system of territorial organisation in general (e.g., Article 5 Const.) and the tax system in particular (e.g., Article 23 and Article 53 Const.).

7 This title is included in the list of exclusive State competences only after 2012 (const. law no. 1/2012). Before 2012 it was included in the concurrent State-region enumeration.

implementation process (e.g., judgments no. 296/2003; no. 37/2004; no. 102/2008). In this respect, the Court has stated that the effective exercise of certain powers (such as the taxing powers) undergoes several limitations due to the lack of a prior legislative intervention of the State.

III. The implementation process and its main trajectories

The new financial constitution has remained on paper for eight years (2001–2009) and the model of State grants has been *de facto* confirmed. The delay has worsened the existing asymmetry between expenditure and revenue responsibilities, further deteriorating the condition of unaccountability of territorial autonomies.[8] Moreover, it has put under strain a proper interaction of the constitutional principles. In fact, pending the implementation of the reform, the central government has adopted ordinary legal acts that have undermined the financial autonomy of subnational entities.

Only in 2009 the national Parliament adopted the framework law no. 42/2009 providing for a new order of intergovernmental financial relations. The law innovates the subnational financing scheme with the aim to foster territorial accountability and to boost democratic control.

The recognition to the subnational entities of enhanced autonomy, especially on the revenue side, is conceived as instrumental in this respect. As such, one of the main pillars of the reform is the disabling of the 'State-transfer-based' system in favour of a 'tax-revenue-based' model.

In addition, the law prescribes the gradual dismantling of the current funding scheme, which grounds the transfers on the resources spent in the previous financial exercise (so-called historic spending). A set of criteria (so-called standard costs and needs) linked to pre-defined benchmarks as well as generally applied and neutral indicators should be introduced in its place with the aim to standardise territorial financing and foster efficiency and accountability (Antonini, 2009).

Major problems herein lie with the fact that law 42/2009 turned out to be rather ineffective in giving implementation to the new principles. Indeed, the law is nothing else than a delegation from the Parliament to the Executive of the power to adopt in two-year time several bylaws (i.e. enactment decrees), in order to allow the concrete functioning of fiscal federalism (Scuto, 2010).

First, the law basically replicates the constitutional principles and sets only very general criteria that shall regulate the new financial regime, further postponing the actual implementation. Second, with the legislative act the Executive is vested with the task to delineate the concrete functioning of 'fiscal federalism'. Due to the undetermined nature of both the constitutional framework and of law no. 42/2009, the setting in motion of the system remains the responsibility of the political

8 The deterioration of public finance is extensively described in: Italian Government, Report on Fiscal Federalism, June 30, 2010. http://www.astrid-online.it/static/upload/protected/Rela/Relazione-Federalismo-fiscale_30_06_10.pdf (accessed August 4, 2020).

majority (Scuto, 2010), although the need to reach a broader consensus would have been expected for a matter of constitutional relevance. From a comparative perspective this is quite unusual. In European federal systems, the financial settings are typically either designed in detail in the Constitution (e.g., in Germany and Switzerland) or in a normative act vested with constitutional (Austria) or quasi-constitutional (e.g., in Spain and Belgium) binding force (Parolari, 2018). Third, the involvement of territorial entities has been marginal and not assisted with adequate guarantees: the approval of the enactment decrees must follow a complex and derogating procedure, which aims at guaranteeing a minimum involvement of territorial forces. A prior agreement with territorial entities is prescribed, however no consequence is connected to the failure of the negotiations, apart from the need to motivate the dissent.

Finally, the decrees as a source of law have turned out to be rather inadequate for the purpose. The result has been a series of uncoordinated measures, providing for fragmented and desultory regulation of the new system, lacking the necessary comprehensiveness and consistency. It is not by chance then that key aspects, such as the regulation of the new equalisation system, have been almost overlooked, further delaying the concrete regulation and above all its successful entry in force.

As such, doubts are expressed about the prescriptive force of the enactment decrees. Most of these bylaws are not self-executing: either they need further integration by means of administrative rules, or they postpone the definition of essential aspects. Regarding the first point, other decrees were expected to correct possible malfunctioning or to integrate deficiencies, while the second problem can be traced back to the existing normative gaps. The Executive failed in effectively coordinating the adopted measures, and they turned out to be rather inadequate and ineffective in reorganizing the system in a comprehensive and rational way. This is for instance the case of the new equalisation concept based on standard criteria. The Government provided only a fragmented regulative scheme and did not tackle core elements: it failed to calculate the new financing criteria, but also to define the methodology to be applied.

IV. The rules from paper to practice

A. Ordinary regions

A comprehensive analysis of the implementing regulations discloses that the reform resulted at most in the design of a new scheme of subnational financing, which rests on two main trajectories: the national legislator retains almost exclusively the legislative power to tax, and a wide-scope equalisation system is confirmed, though according to a new 'standardized' concept.

Having regard to financial autonomy on the revenue side, the most significant change concerns the abolition of all central transfers, with the sole exception of non-earmarked equalisation transfers and specific-purpose-grants for extraordinary circumstances (Art. 119(5) Const). Pursuant to Article 119(4) Const, territorial entities shall have to fully finance their functions by means of own-tax sources, shared taxes and equalisation transfers.

Despite linking regional financing to the tax revenue generated from the territory of reference (eventually and substantially corrected by means of equalisation transfers for the entities with lower fiscal capacity), no other dramatic change has taken place.

Under the new scheme, territorial entities keep most of the tax-revenue they had under the previous system (Muraro, 2011). As to ordinary regions, 'regional' taxes can be classified in three categories. First, 'devolved taxes' that are set by a national law, but both the revenue and a limited varying power are devolved to the regions. Second, 'regional surtaxes' that are on top of those national taxes in relation to which regions can impose an extra charge, within the limits set forth by the State law. Third, 'own-taxes' that are set by a regional law on a tax-base not pre-empted by the State. Against this classification, the most relevant regional sources belong to the first and second groups and include the revenue from a tax on business (IRAP – i.e. regional tax on productive activities) and the surtax on the Individual Income Tax (IRPEF). The latter consists of a basic rate of 1.23 per cent (since 2011), plus an optional rate (up to 2.1 per cent as of 2015) to be applied within certain limits. Regions may also vary the tax rate of the IRAP and eventually reduce it to zero. Instead, own-taxes are very few (e.g., the special tax for the landfill of waste) and the yields are marginal.

Though taxing powers of the regions have been somehow reinforced, the tax system remains mostly centralized. The State holds the power to set and levy the most significant taxes, while own-taxes of the regions remain an exception (Buglione and Jorio, 2011; Immordino, 2011). Even though regions would in theory be vested with exclusive competence in those tax matters not expressively reserved to the State and with reference to tax-bases linked to the regional territory.

The persistent non-implementation of the reform, together with the fact that the national legislator has frozen the regional powers to apply surtaxes or vary the rates for years (with minor exceptions, e.g., the tourism tax), have been decisive in this respect. On top of that, the established doctrine of the ItCC has further limited the scope of regional autonomy in tax matters. On the one hand, regional taxes are only those set and regulated by a regional law, i.e. very few, as the tax room is almost entirely pre-empted by the State (judgments no. 296/2003, 297/2003; 216/2009). On the other hand, the regional power to tax may be exerted only in compliance with the principles of financial and fiscal coordination set forth by the national legislature. Furthermore, the Constitutional Court has upheld an extensive interpretation of the State competence to define the basic principles of coordination of the tax system. The way the centre can make use of this power has *de facto* nullified the regional room in tax matters (e.g., judgments no. 37/2004, 199/2016). The constitutional adjudications have stretched out the State interference on sub-national autonomy and, at present, it is mainly the centre that sets a tax and then decides on the powers and shares to be conferred to the regions. As such, tax autonomy of the regions remains a declared principle, but far from operating in practice.

Despite these criticisms, over time regional fiscal autonomy has been somehow strengthened and tax flexibility has been reinforced. In 2016, regional taxes considered as a whole (i.e. autonomous and devolved) amounted to 45 per cent of the regional budget, while only to 14.8 per cent in 1990 (Istat, 2016).[9] Although tax competition is low, the territorial differentiation in terms of tax pressure is becoming somehow noticeable, though limited to the devolved taxes, such as the regional tax on productive activities and the regional surtax on individual income. As to the latter, regions have exercised the varying power over the tax rate in different ways, in certain cases introducing a single rate for all income levels, while in others opting for a progressive tax rate. As to the first, differences are even more significant, as regions have the option to intervene on the tax rate, but also the authority to differentiate it because of the involved sector or taxpayers' category, as well as to introduce tax benefits (Court of Auditors, 2019).

Besides own- and devolved taxes, regional finance includes a share of tax revenue on a territorial base. This is the case of the VAT: ordinary regions are entitled to 67.07 per cent (2018), and the revenues thereof are then distributed according to the statistical data of the final consumptions of families, calculated on average on a regional base. *De facto*, the related revenues are not assigned to the single region, but they finance the healthcare equalisation fund that is still in place, despite the reform. Accordingly, at a first stage, the revenues are calculated based on the derivation principle but are then corrected in accordance with the prescribed equalising formula. Depending on the region at stake, the share of VAT covers between 65 and 92 per cent of the regional spending for healthcare (Bordignon and Ambrosanio, 2020).

The other trajectory of the new funding scheme consists in the gradual overcoming of the criterion of the 'historical spending', which grounds the transfers on the resources spent by a specific administration in the previous financial exercise. The equalisation parameter shall be progressively replaced by a set of objective criteria linked to predefined benchmarks and to generally applied and neutral indicators. The so-called 'standard costs and needs' approach should be applied to the redistribution of regional resources so as to ensure the full coverage of the 'essential levels of public services' in the field of healthcare, education, social assistance, and public transport (for capital spending only). These types of services shall be fully financed at the levels defined by the national legislator (pursuant to Art. 117(2), lit. e. Const., the State has the exclusive legislative jurisdiction to stipulate on that). However, this results *de facto* in a partial equalisation as the related transfers shall not be based on the effective needs, but on the standard needs, i.e. based on efficiency and not on actual spending. Put differently, inefficiency-related cost in the management of functions shall not be equalized.

The new concept should allow a standardisation of territorial financing, while fostering efficiency and accountability and correcting the drawbacks of the 'historic spending' approach: as a parameter, the latter enhanced inefficient and irresponsible spending, as the more a region spent and accumulated debt, the more

9 This result is also due to the fact that in the last decade the resources of subnational entities have been cut by the State in order to comply with EU obligations in time of crisis.

the State allocated to its funding the following year (Jorio, Gambino, and D'Ignazio, 2009).

In addition, the new solidarity mechanism is complemented by a second pillar that applies to all other (residual) regional functions. In this case, the single region decides on the level of services to be provided: no common standard is prescribed by the centre and the transfers are designed so to guarantee only a partial equalisation. In fact, the parameter is the per capita fiscal capacity and the related differences are reduced up to 75 per cent.

The complete implementation of both schemes is still pending and the previous 'transfer-based' system is still to a great extent in force. This is mainly due to the delayed implementation of the 2001 constitutional reform and foremost to the fragmentation and uncompletedness of the implementing legislation adopted insofar: neither have the standard costs and needs been calculated yet, nor has the national legislature completely determined the essential levels of services to be guaranteed throughout the country, with the partial exception of the healthcare sector (Bordignon and Ambrosanio, 2020). The economic crisis is frequently spotlighted as the responsible of the stalemate, neglecting the fact that the new equalisation concept should be considered as part of the solution to the Italian problems rather than the cause of them.

By contrast, the implementation process is concluded on the side of fiscal discipline. At present, all territorial entities are bound to respect the principle of balanced budget. Law no. 243/2012 (as amended by law no. 164/2016) imposes limits to deficits and to the possibility to incur debts for all territorial entities. At the same time, it sets strict limitations to overspending. Hence, deviations from the equilibrium could occur, although each region must ensure the recovery of the deficit through the adoption of a loan repayment plan. Surpluses shall be used either to cover the existing debts or for investment expenditure. To this end, an agreement between the region and the centre should be reached, to ensure the balance between revenue and expenditure, considering all entities within the region (including the region itself). For guaranteeing the enforcement of the principle as well as the transparency and the comparability of the different budgetary documents, the State has also adopted the rules for the harmonisation of the budgets of all public entities (decree no. 118/2011).

B. Special regions

The asymmetrical design of Italian regionalism is particularly evident when it comes to financial relations and related rules and procedures (see Palermo in this volume). As a rule, the two-track asymmetry – ordinary and special regions – is confirmed, though the 2001 reform introduced important changes concerning the distribution of legislative and administrative powers between State and regions. Indeed, the reform aimed also at reducing institutional disparities between special and ordinary entities, offering the latter powers similar to those enjoyed by the special regions from the 1950s onwards. However, the political aim of progressive 'assimilation' failed, largely due to non-implementation of the 2001 reform of financial relations, but also due to the coexistence of different systems of financing for special regions. In fact, the new financial rules do not apply to special regions, but they have been asked to reform their systems according to the same basic principles.

The specific regulations thereof have to be agreed between the single region and the State in bilateral negotiations. As such, every special region has its own financial constitution that is entrenched in the statute of autonomy and can be changed only after agreement with the interested parties.

All in all, special regions enjoy a higher degree of financial autonomy, but their systems differ from one another. Each entity has developed the scope of its self-government in a different way on the basis of territorial peculiarities and this impacts the degree of spending and revenue autonomy. This notwithstanding, a few common features can be identified and are outlined below.

Their financing systems are based mainly on a share of State taxes referable to the territory. The main differences among them concern the sharing percentage and the type of taxes that are shared. As a matter of fact, the percentage varies from a minimum of 25 per cent (e.g., Friuli-Venezia Giulia) to a maximum of 90 per cent (Trentino-South Tyrol and Aosta Valley), while for certain taxes some entities receive the entire amount of revenue referable to its territory.

The tax-combination can potentially encompass all State taxes. Usually, these are explicitly listed in a specific provision of the statute of autonomy. As a rule, the share is higher for those special regions which have been vested with major spending responsibilities – such as Trentino-South Tyrol and Aosta Valley (Valdesalici [a], 2018).

In addition to the prominent role vested by shared taxes, own sources of special regions encompass both devolved and autonomous own-taxes. As for ordinary regions, 'autonomous' own-taxes are residual, even though the constitutional case-law has accorded them a more extensive taxing power (judgment no. 102/2008). Furthermore, they receive the whole amount of a few other taxes (so-called devolved taxes), including the regional tax on productive activities (IRAP). Interestingly, most of the special regions have a rather extensive tax-varying power, enhancing fiscal flexibility. As such, they have been vested with the power to increase or decrease the rate over several State taxes (i.e. devolved taxes and surtaxes). Within the maximum tax-rate set by the State, they can introduce exemptions, deductions, tax reliefs or whatsoever alteration. Contrary to what happened for ordinary regions, the ItCC has accepted an extensive interpretation of their tax varying power, opening the way to regionally differentiated fiscal policies (judgments no. 357/2010; no. 323/2011; no. 2/2012).

State grants tend to be generally less consistent in special regions than in ordinary regions. Nevertheless, even in this case, regional discrepancies can be profound. In general terms, while the special regions of the North rely much more on revenue linked to taxation, the two islands (Sicily and Sardinia) tend to depend more on State transfers. To a certain extent, the varying relevance of these different components seems to reflect the existing cleavage in the respective economic performance (Cerea, 2010).

Although the reform does not directly apply to special regions, it had an impact on their system. In fact, law no. 42/2009 (Art. 27) mandates that each special entity agrees with the State upon its contribution to equalisation and to the recovery of public finance (including obligations imposed by the EU). Even in this case no 'one solution fits all' is possible. Though all of them have entered into agreement with the State for defining their contribution to EU obligations and the recovery of public finance (i.e. have reduced the revenue at disposal), only a few (Trentino-South Tyrol and Aosta Valley) have seized the opportunity to consolidate their political and financial autonomy further on (e.g., expanding their administrative and legislative jurisdiction as well as their overall financial autonomy).

V. The financial constitution in motion

Besides the complexity resulting from the openness of the constitutional framework and the piecemeal implementing legislation, unexpected economic and political drawbacks have challenged the very essence of the reform. As a result, at present it is still rather difficult to give evidence of the *status quo* of its (non-)implementation.

In this respect, the examination of the above-illustrated legal framework provides for a partial insight only. Among the many, the advancements of the new system have been marked by the grinding economic crisis and the stringent EU constraints to national finances, the rocketed spread (that made interests on State's debts more expensive than in the past), and the financial markets' pressures. These factors have indirectly impacted subnational budgets and strangled subnational autonomy, dismantling the progresses made insofar towards a comprehensive implementation of the new financial constitution.

Since 2010 the national Government has approved several measures aiming to rationalize public finance. The main driver has been the economic and financial crisis, and the efforts have predominantly targeted the balancing of the budget (Palermo and Valdesalici, 2014).

In challenging the constitutional guarantees of autonomy, the result has been a counter-wave of recentralisation. To understand the impact of these State 'austerity' measures on the 'regional system of public finance to-be', it is necessary to go through the case-law of the ItCC.

One of the major constraints to financial autonomy can be traced back to the concurrent State-region competence on the coordination of public finance. In the Italian Constitution the concurrency-ratio recognizes to the State the power to legislate on the fundamental principles, while the regions provide for the detailed regulation.

On this point, especially as of 2010, the intervention of the national legislator has often gone beyond the determination of the fundamental principles by introducing detailed regulations. This behavior has given rise to plentiful conflicts in front of the ItCC, which has mostly given an extensive interpretation of the State powers in the field at the expense of both financial and political autonomy of the regions (among the many, judgments no. 198/2012, 262/2012, 236/2013, 23/2014, 38/2016, 69/2016, 154/2017).

The main arguments upholding the constitutional validity of the State acts are linked to the acknowledgement that this is not to be considered a 'competence-title' in the traditional understanding. Instead, the Court has recognized that public finance coordination is a purpose-oriented task (among the many, judgments no. 8/2013, 38/2016; no. 69/2016). This approach has allowed for the increasing expansion of the margin of State intervention to the detriment to subnational autonomy, with a trend that further consolidated after the constitutional entrenchment of the principle of balanced budget (e.g., judgment no. 188/2014). Whenever the State legislation has forced the boundaries of the decentralized competences, the Court has gone along with this trend, legitimating such interferences in the light of the contingency moment (Di Marco, 2011).

If any, a safeguard to protect subnational autonomy could be found in the principle of loyal cooperation (see Woelk in this volume). Accordingly, the State must make all possible efforts to reach an agreement with subnational entities, when a decision affects their (financial) interests (e.g., judgments no. 88/2014 and no. 129/2016). Despite the settled case-law, the involvement of territorial interests in the decision-making process is still at an embryonic stage, suffering from the procedural limits inherent in the Italian system of intergovernmental Conferences.

Over time the case law has also developed a set of criteria that under certain conditions worked in holding off the State interference on subnational autonomy. In sum, the Court deems the constitutionality of the austerity decrees only if they pursue the rationalisation of public finance by means of merely transitional and time-limited measures and set the overall objectives alone, leaving to subnational entities a margin of choice on both the instruments and the way of proceeding (judgments no. 193/2012; 232/2011; 43/2016; 141/2016). Another restriction refers to the need to ensure an adequate correspondence between revenues and functions. The State measure is not valid if it severely impairs this ratio or make it impossible for the region to carry on the assigned functions (e.g., judgments no. 10/2016; 188/2015).

The exclusive State power as to 'the determination of the essential levels of public services to be guaranteed throughout the national territory' [Art. 117(2), lit. m. Const] exemplifies another emblematic restraint to subnational autonomy. Also in this case the ItCC has upheld an extensive reading of the State margins of action, reflecting the acknowledgment of the cross-cutting nature of this competence. As such the compliance with the standards set by the national law for well-determined essential rights must be ensured, even if the matter falls within the regional competence. Therefore, whenever the case for guaranteeing a uniform (minimum) level of public functions and services throughout the national territory is at stake, the State law is valid even if it interferes with areas of regional responsibility. An additional expansion of this clause has been later acknowledged by the Court in the light of 'the exceptional socio-economic circumstances' (i.e. the economic and financial crisis the country was facing) the State had to cope with (e.g., judgment no. 62/2013).

It is not by chance, then, that the situation has been further exacerbated with the constitutionalizing of the principle of balanced budget back in 2012. From that moment, the State powers and responsibilities to enact the principle and to ensure the sustainability of public debt have increasingly precipitated their impact on intergovernmental financial relations. Again, the decisions of the ItCC are crucial in understanding how and to what extent this principle intersects with subnational autonomy. In a landmark judgement (no. 88/2014), the Court explains that the regulation thereof is inseparably interwoven with the other central competences in the field of financial coordination as well as of harmonisation of public budgets. This occurs as the latter two competence-titles are conceived by the Court as instrumental to prevent budget deficits, to preserve the economic-financial balance and to guarantee the economic unity of the Republic (judgment no. 175/2014).

In addition to that, the fact that the rules are meant to give implementation to EU obligations further strengthens the State supremacy in the field. The result is a wide margin of maneuver from the part of the centre, strengthened by the Court's assumption that the 'homogeneity of the rules is inherent to the logic of the reform', otherwise the State could fall short of the goals pursued (Valdesalici, 2019).

Special regions embody a partial exception to this pattern. According to law no. 42/2009 and their statutes of autonomy, conditions and rules for ensuring the coordination of their financial systems with the national system of public finance have to be negotiated with the State on a bilateral basis. Put simply, all State acts, which apply to ordinary regions, do not apply to special entities. Between the State and each special region an agreement has to be reached, which identifies the specific obligations and limits the single region shall comply with.

Nevertheless, when as of 2011 the situation of public finance further deteriorated, the State austerity measures have anyhow addressed special regions, tightening up their obligations. In this regard the ItCC argues that special regions shall give their contribution to the recovery of public finance, even though as a rule the State has to respect the very essence of their autonomy by defining their constraints and contributions in bilateral agreements (among others, judgments no. 82/2007; no. 133/2010; no. 193/2012; no. 198/2012). This trend has been amplified since the constitutionalizing of the principle of balanced budget in 2012. The Court argues in this respect that the constitutional amendment legitimizes the State to introduce common and detailed rules for all autonomies (including special entities), even if these are more rigorous than the ones of the respective statute of autonomy. A different conclusion would contradict the very rationale of the reform (judgment no. 88/2014). After all, for the Court these measures are lawful, even if in relation to special regions the agreement should be favoured as a solution. In exceptional cases, however, the State may derogate from the principle of bilateral cooperation and determine unilaterally but provisionally the related contribution to the financial recovery, if it proves that this is indefectible to ensure the success of the financial measures of concern (e.g., judgment no. 19/2015).

VI. Making a balance: recent trends and emerging challenges ahead

Despite the process of decentralisation going on for three decades, the centre is not ready to give up its dirigiste approach. The evolution of financial relations between the State and the regions is telling in this respect. Except for special regions, the State ultimately determines the degree of financial autonomy, and regions have almost no guarantee in this respect. A counter-wave of recentralisation has been in place for ten years and the current Covid-19 emergency will probably exacerbate this trend further.

The wind of change has been blowing for too long a time and seems to be running out of strength. In the past years, several revisions of title V of the Constitution have been initiated but all have failed.

The story of the so-called 'differentiated regionalism' also points in the same direction. Right after the failure of the 2016 constitutional reform that intended to reduce the overall scope of regional autonomy, some regions have opted to start the process provided by Article 116(3) Const. (see chapter by Palermo). If certain budget criteria are met, an ordinary region can negotiate with the State an additional scope of legislative autonomy. The transfer of legislative competences can cover up to 23 subject matters including matters like education, environment, energy, and transport, and the related intergovernmental agreement has to be approved by absolute majority in Parliament. While keeping the basic distinction between ordinary and special regions, this provision allows, at least on paper, an additional layer of constitutional asymmetry, from here the term 'differentiated regionalism'.

So far, no agreement has been reached, though several regions have already started the negotiations three years ago. Among other things, the discussions have reached a stalemate precisely on financial matters.

The logic of fiscal federalism is reflected in the assumption that finance has to follow functions. Beyond being essential to political autonomy, the financial dimension plays an instrumental role making it possible for a subnational entity to carry on its constitutionally assigned competences. In the Italian case, however, this rationale suffers from the deficient implementation of the reform of financial relations, having particular regard to the new equalisation mechanism. The uncertainty associated to one of the backbones of any financial regime makes it impossible to reach an agreement for additional autonomy and the entire process is doomed to be frozen for an indefinite period of time.

In addition, in the Italian debate the distortive narratives on fiscal federalism are putting the entire process of decentralisation more and more at risk, financial relations included. All too frequently, the concept of fiscal federalism is considered equal to that of a competitive model of federalism, in which subnational entities would make use of their financial powers to compete with each other. As a result, there are many opponents to the new system, considered the profound socio-economic cleavage that characterizes the country: indeed, in Italy only a few regions (mainly of the North) stand out for their socio-economic performance.

Beyond the absence of any real understanding of the theory and practice of fiscal federalism, the regional panorama reflects a widespread lack of a truly federal culture, or at least of a 'culture of autonomy' (Palermo, 2018). If the implementation of fiscal federalism has not been within the political priorities of the national governments (indeed, rather the opposite is true), also the regional governments have not pressed for reaching this objective.

Finally, there is another criticism that has emerged in a striking way during the Covid-19 emergency, but it was already palpable during the past years of economic and financial crisis. Italian regionalism is lacking effective instruments of shared rule if regional interests are at stake: institutions providing for the involvement of territorial entities in the decision making at central level are very weak, and there are no mechanisms of participation to the constitutional reform processes. The lack of an institutional dimension of federalism shows all the weaknesses of the decentralizing process, as it results not only in serious difficulties in the implementing process but also in frequent intergovernmental conflicts when decisions are unilaterally imposed by the centre, especially if they determine a reduction of resources. The consequence is a general lack of guarantees for subnational autonomy and an effect of de-responsibilisation of the subnational entities, as it is always and ever the State that responds to the European Union for the compliance of the obligations originated by the EU system economic governance.

In view of this situation it is arduous to make an optimistic prognosis. Anyway, once the current pandemic is over, a reflection on the status of Italian regionalism will be urgent and should not be further extended. This notwithstanding, if a concrete project providing for a systemic review of financial relations (and beyond) will not be able to reach a broad political consensus, federalism will again be doomed to become a political flag, instead of being intended as an instrument for governing the territorial pluralism that characterizes Italy.

Literature

Luca Antonini, 'Federalismo fiscale: La manovrabilità dei tributi propri' (2009) *Astrid*

Luca Antonini, *La rivincita della responsabilità. A proposito della nuova Legge sul federalismo fiscale*, online publication (I quaderni della sussidiarietà, 2009)

Luca Antonini, *Federalismo all'italiana. Dietro le quinte della grande incompiuta* (Marsilio, 2013)

Luca Antonini, 'L'autonomia finanziaria delle regioni tra riforme tentate, crisi economica e prospettive' (2014) 4 *Rivista dell'Associazione Italiana dei Costituzionalisti*

Franco Bassanini, 'Principi e vincoli costituzionali in materia di finanza regionale e locale nel nuovo articolo 119 della Costituzione' (2006) *Astrid*

Mario Bertolissi, *'Rivolta fiscale', federalismo, riforme istituzionali* (Cedam, 1997)

Mario Bertolissi, 'Federalismo fiscale. Una nozione giuridica' (2007) 1 *Federalismo Fiscale*, 9–37

Massimo Bordignon and Maria Flavia Ambrosanio, 'Il nodo (irrisolto?) della perequazione regionale in Italia', in Francesco Palermo, Sara Parolari, and Alice Valdesalici (eds.), *Italia e Spagna: costituzioni finanziarie a confronto. Un bilancio a 10 anni dalle riforme* (Edizioni Scientifiche Italiane, 2020)

Enrico Buglione and Ettore Jorio, 'Schema di decreto legislativo in materia di autonomia di entrata delle regioni a statuto ordinario e delle province, nonché di determinazione dei costi e dei fabbisogni standard nel settore sanitario', in Antonio Ferrara and Giulio M. Salerno (eds.), *Il federalismo fiscale. Commento alla legge n. 42 del 2009* (Jovene, 2011)

Giuliana G. Carboni, 'Fiscal Federalism and Comparative Law' (2014) 5 *Comparative Law Review*, 1–20

Gianfranco Cerea, 'La finanza delle autonomie speciali: le previsioni originarie, la realtà e le prospettive del federalismo', in Jens Woelk (ed.), *Federalismo fiscale tra differenziazione e solidarietà: Profili giuridici italiani e comparati* (Eurac research, 2010)

Ines Ciolli, 'The balanced budget rule in the Italian Constitution: it ain't necessarily so… useful?' (2014) *Rivista dell'Associazione Italiana dei Costituzionalisti*

Court of Auditors, 'Rapporto sul coordinamento della finanza pubblica' (2019) https://www.corteconti.it/Home/Documenti/RapportoCoordinamentoFP

Kenneth W. Dam, 'The American Fiscal Constitution' (1977) 44 *The University of Chicago Law Review*, 271–320

Carlo Di Marco, 'La stabilizzazione finanziaria 2011 alle prese con il sistema delle autonomie territoriali' (2011) *Amministrazione in cammino*

Tania Groppi, 'Il federalismo fiscale nel quadro costituzionale' (2008) *federalismi.it*

Joachim Hellermann, 'Artikel 104a', in Christian Starck, Friedrich Klein, and Hermann von Mangoldt (eds.), *Kommentar zum Grundgesetz* (Vahlen, 2010)

Dario Immordino, 'L'autonomia finanziaria a dieci anni dalla riforma costituzionale' (2011) 2-3 *Le Regioni*, 415–454

Istat, 'I bilanci consuntivi delle regioni e province autonome' (2016) https://www.istat.it/it/archivio/214338

Ettore Jorio, Silvio Gambino, and Guerino D'Ignazio, *Il federalismo fiscale. Commento articolo per articolo alla legge 5 maggio 2009, n. 42* (Maggioli, 2009)

Manuel Medina Guerrero, 'Financiación autonómica y control de constitucionalidad (algunas reflexiones sobre la STC 13/2007)' (2008) 6 *Revista d'Estudis Autonòmics i Federals*, 92–124

Gilberto Muraro, 'Federalismo regionale: La rivoluzione può attendere' (2011) *Lavoce.info*

Francesco Palermo, 'Fiscalità locale: I nodi irrisolti' (2011) *nel Merito*

Francesco Palermo, 'Comparare il federalismo fiscale: cosa, come, perché', in Francesco Palermo and Matteo Nicolini (eds.), *Federalismo fiscale in Europa: Esperienze straniere e spunti per il caso italiano* (Edizioni Scientifiche Italiane, 2012)

Francesco Palermo, 'La cultura dell'autonomia. Riflessioni giuridiche su un concetto non solo intuitivo', in Roberto Toniatti (ed.), *La cultura dell'autonomia. Le condizioni pre-giuridiche per un'efficace autonomia regionale* (Università di Trento, 2018) http://liatn.eu/images/ebook/LIA-eBook-Cultura-dellautonomia.pdf, 69–83

Francesco Palermo and Alice Valdesalici, 'Italy: Autonomism, Decentralization, Federalism, or What Else?', in Jaime Lluch (ed.), *Constitutionalism and the Politics of Accommodation in Multinational Democracies* (Palgrave Macmillan, 2014)

Sara Parolari, 'From a Formal to a Substantial Approach: Sources of Law and Fiscal Federalism', in Alice Valdesalici and Francesco Palermo (eds.), *Comparing fiscal federalism* (Brill Nijhoff, 2018)

Peter Pernthaler, *Österreichische Finanzverfassung: Theorie—Praxis—Reform* (Wilhelm Braumüller, 1984)

Giulio M. Salerno, 'Alcune riflessioni sulla nuova Costituzione finanziaria della Repubblica' (2007) 1 *Federalismo Fiscale* 119–138

Giulio M. Salerno, 'Equilibrio di bilancio, coordinamento finanziario e autonomie territoriali', in Vincenzo Lippoliset al. (eds.), *Costituzione e pareggio di bilancio*, online publication (Il Filangieri, 2011)

Filippo Scuto, 'The Italian Parliament paves the way to fiscal federalism' (2010) 2 (1) *Perspectives on Federalism* 67

Servizio studi del Senato e della Camera, 'Aspetti di rilievo costituzionale del federalismo fiscale' (2017) https://www.senato.it/service/PDF/PDFServer/BGT/01008590.pdf

Alice Valdesalici [a], 'Autonomia finanziaria e specialità: un modello per sei sistemi ad alto tasso di differenziazione', in Francesco Palermo and Sara Parolari (eds.), *Le variabili della specialità: Evidenze e riscontri tra soluzioni istituzionali e politiche settoriali* (Edizioni Scientifiche Italiane, 2018)

Alice Valdesalici [b], 'Defining Fiscal Federalism', in Alice Valdesalici and Francesco Palermo (eds.), *Comparing Fiscal Federalism* (Brill, 2018)

Alice Valdesalici, 'L'impatto delle governance economica sull'autonomia finanziaria' in Walter Obwexer, Esther Happacher, and Stefania Baroncelli (eds.), *EU-Mitgliedschaft und Südtirols Autonomie II: Die Auswirkungen der EU-Mitgliedschaft auf die Autonomie des Landes Südtirol am Beispiel ausgewählter Gesetzgebungs- und Verwaltungskompetenzen–eine Fortsetzung Handbuch* (Verlag Österreich, 2019)

D.E. Wildasin, 'Fiscal Federalism' in S.N. Durlauf and L.E. Blume, (eds.), *The New Palgrave Dictionary of Economics* (Palgrave Macmillan, 2008) 405

6 Party systems in the Italian regions

Alex Wilson[1]

I. Introduction

This chapter analyses the evolution of regional party systems in Italy, where direct elections began in the 5 'special status' regions (1947–1964) and later extended to the 15 'ordinary status' regions (1970) covering most of mainland Italy. Whereas special regions displayed certain objective differences including strong ethno-regionalist parties, party competition in the ordinary regions was initially very similar and largely subordinate to the national party system. In 1995, a new electoral system was applied to all ordinary regions at a time of radical transformation in the party system and related processes of state decentralisation and constitutional reform. This new system involved the direct election of regional presidents and soon led to the development of more distinctive regional party systems. These shared many similarities with the national level, notably in terms of strong competing centre-left and centre-right coalitions, but were also an arena for varied forms of political leadership and are now characterised by rather different patterns of alternation in government.

The past decade has seen the bipolar dynamics of the national party system give way to a more multipolar competition, with the rise of powerful populist parties like Beppe Grillo's Five Star Movement (M5S) and Matteo Salvini's Lega, and a consequent weakening of the centre-left Democratic Party (PD) and the centre-right Forza Italia (FI). This development has undermined the logic of bipolar competition at national level, where government formation has proven increasingly difficult, and so more experimental and unstable governing coalitions have been formed. In contrast, regional party systems have survived the rise of populism and multipolarism almost intact. Whereas the M5S proved unable to win control of any regional government, largely because of its objections to forming pre-electoral coalitions, the Lega has simply displaced FI from the leadership of most regional centre-right coalitions, while continuing to form pre-electoral coalitions and governing together at sub-national levels. Over the past year, both the Lega and FI have lost votes to the far-right Brothers of Italy (led by Giorgia Meloni),

1 Alex Wilson is a Senior Policy Analyst in the Members Research Service of the European Parliament.

DOI: 10.4324/9781003104469-7

which competes as part of the same centre-right coalition. Regional elections are increasingly characterised by the salience of territorial issues and have seen a rising number of personal lists linked to local politicians, but no new regionalist parties have consolidated beyond the ones that existed historically in the special regions, while the Lega has becoming increasingly nationalist in its political orientation and organisation. Regional presidents have faced varying fortunes, often able to build up a strong territorial powerbase but later brought down by implication in corruption scandals. Like other subnational elites (e.g. directly elected mayors), they have been unable to force any lasting change in the centralised patterns of national decision-making, which are characteristic of a highly centralised political culture (Palermo and Wilson, 2014).

II. Development of regional party systems in Italy, 1947–1995

Regional party systems in Italy originated at different moments in time. Direct elections took place much earlier in the special regions of Sicily (1947), Trentino-Alto Adige (1948), Sardegna (1949), Aosta Valley (1949), and Friuli-Venezia Giulia (1964). The same parties competed as in national elections, with the Christian Democrats (DC) maintaining a strong presence throughout the special regions, while the Italian Communist Party (PCI) became the main opposition party. From an early stage though, ethno-regionalist parties began to consolidate into dominant positions in Val d'Aosta and the autonomous province of Bolzano.[2] The Union Valdotaine (UV) and the South Tyrolean People's Party (SVP) in Bolzano both collaborated closely with the DC. The 15 ordinary regions only held their first regional elections in 1970. While such regions were foreseen by the 1948 Constitution, it was not until the 1960s that the main Italian parties agreed to set up elected regional governments, and it was not until the mid-1970s that ordinary regions were actually delegated policy competences and financial resources. Even so, they remained heavily constrained by the national government and public administration in terms of what they could do, and had access to very limited financial resources of their own, being largely dependent on fiscal transfers from the national government (Hine, 1996). Nevertheless, the PCI saw elected regional governments as an opportunity to showcase its governing capacity by building on a successful municipal tradition in the 'red belt' regions of central-northern Italy (Tuscany, Emilia-Romagna, Umbria), where it was electorally dominant. The DC meanwhile used regionalisation to provide more governing opportunities for its growing political class and took advantage of its electoral position to dominate this nascent level of government.

2 The autonomous provinces of Trentino and Bolzano together constitute the region of Trentino-Alto Adige. Although a regional government still exists, most of its functions have passed to the provinces. Bolzano (also known as South Tyrol) has a majority of native German speakers whereas Trentino has a majority of native Italian speakers. Their party systems are also different with strong German-speaking regionalist parties present in Bolzano and mainly national parties competing in Trentino.

In this initial phase, party competition in the ordinary regions simply copied the main features of the national party system. This was a system of 'polarised pluralism' (Sartori, 1976) characterised by a dominant but heavily factionalised DC organisation, which always came first in national elections and remained at the heart of government by forming variable coalitions with smaller parties, the largest of these being the Italian Socialist Party (PSI). The PCI was the main opposition to this system of power but not considered suitable for national government by others because of its links with the Soviet Union. Italian Social Movement (MSI) was a right-wing party, excluded from power for its clear fascist sympathies. These parties and others competed in regional elections in much the same way as in national elections. While most Italian parties had to adapt their organisational structures to incorporate a regional level, the latter remained loosely structured and dominated by provincial party branches, which remained the key territorial units. This organisational continuity was encouraged by regional electoral systems, which adapted the national system of 'perfect' proportional representation (PR) with preference voting, with no legal threshold for entering parliament. Regional legislators were elected in provincial constituencies. The regional government (executive) was led by a regional president, who was nominated and could be replaced in office by the legislature. The regional president and his/her executive had to be drawn from among elected members of the legislature and serve both functions simultaneously (Vassallo, 2013). Elections took place every five years and early elections were not possible, so changes in government often took place between elections, a pattern that was also characteristic of the national party system. Governing coalitions at regional level shared the instability and reflected the strategies of their national counterparts (Vassallo and Baldini, 2000).[3]

While turnout in regional elections was initially very high (over 90 per cent in 1970), this had nothing to do with the salience of regional government or public awareness about regional politics.[4] Instead simultaneous regional elections constituted an important 'national test' for voters and politicians alike on their relative party strength. Ordinary regions were less visible than municipal governments, and had little political or institutional autonomy, contrasting with the special regions that had clearer policy competences as well as their own financial resources. Despite these limitations, regional party systems proved useful 'testing grounds' for potential coalitions that could be adopted at national level. The geographical concentration of electoral support for the main parties meant that regions had different partisan characteristics. PCI was historically strong in the central-northern 'red belt' regions, where it always came first in national and regional elections.

3 The average duration of regional governments in Italy (1947–1992) was a mere 542 days. Regions dominated by a single party (whether DC or PCI) tended to have longer lasting governments, whereas those characterised by more intense party competition tended to last even shorter than average (Vassallo and Baldini, 2000).

4 There has always been a low awareness among Italian citizens about the composition and preferences of the regional political class. This remains broadly true today, with the notable difference that regional presidents have become far more visible and well known among voters (Vassallo, 2013).

PCI assumed leadership of these regional governments by forming coalitions with other leftist parties, including the PSI. Such coalitions existed at municipal levels but had no precedent at national level. PCI was strong in several other regions but most regions became dominated by the DC, which governed in coalition with various smaller parties. The DC was a complex beast that showed different sides according to the territory in which it competed. Whereas in northern Italy the DC was at the heart of an entrepreneurial Catholic 'subculture' founded on small and medium sized enterprises in industrial districts, in southern Italy the party was characterised by a more personalised and clientelist form of politics whose priority was the redistribution of state resources. As the DC fell apart, its northern constituencies became the object of intense competition between Umberto Bossi's Northern League (LN) and Silvio Berlusconi's Forza Italia (Cento Bull and Gilbert, 2001). In southern Italy meanwhile, the DC fragmented into splinter parties composed of local powerbrokers, opportunistically allied to both coalitions, whose behaviour was characterised by clientelism sometimes verging on outright corruption (Allum and Allum, 2008). Although LN campaigned heavily to put the question of regional autonomy onto the national agenda (Cento Bull and Gilbert, 2001), it was not at all evident that ordinary regions would assume the important institutional position they have today, let alone become the focus of successive constitutional reforms. There was little sense that regional party systems differed materially from their national counterparts, that they were capable of developing new governing solutions or forms of political leadership, and that most voters identified closely with the regional level of government.

III. Electoral system reform and regional party system change, 1995–2010

A. Electoral system reform

The 1995 elections across the 15 ordinary regions marked the start of a radical and lasting change in their party systems, which affected their institutional visibility and forms of political leadership. National legislators crafted a distinct electoral system for the Italian regions that aligned with their own preferences for a more majoritarian form of government. The new rules of the game contained a powerful bipolarising logic that would go on to shape the structures of party competition at regional level.[5] Ordinary regions were among the last democratic institutions in

5 The regional electoral system differs significantly from the mixed electoral system used in the 1994, 1996, and 2001 national elections, although they shared a common bipolarising logic that incentivised the formation of pre-electoral coalitions. In 2005, the national electoral system was changed to model it on the regional system, including a majoritarian bonus for the winning coalition and parliamentary seats allocated on a PR basis. However, the national system differed from the regional one in two important ways. Whereas the majoritarian bonus was distributed nationally in the Chamber of Deputies, the bonus was distributed on a regional basis in the Senate. This made it hard to form a viable governing coalition

Italy to undergo radical changes resulting from the collapse and realignment of the national party system in the early 1990s. The governing parties (DC, PSI, and smaller allies) had been broken by the weight of the *Tangentopoli* political corruption scandals; the PCI had split into a majority Party of the Democratic Left (PDS, later DS and now PD) and a minority Party of Refounded Communists (PRC); and new parties such as LN and FI were filling much of the electoral void. The regional councils elected in 1990 under the 'old' party system were completely at odds with this new landscape, with many of their legislators also caught up in corruption scandals. Two general elections in 1992 and 1994 shifted Italy towards a more majoritarian system of bipolar party competition, helped by an electoral system change that saw the 'perfect proportional representation' (PR) system of the 1948–1992 period replaced by a mixed system with a majority of seats allocated via single-member constituencies. Italy still had numerous parties though – rather than two large parties as in the classic Westminster model – so bipolarism necessarily took the more unstable form of competing pre-electoral coalitions (Bartolini et al., 2004). National legislators nevertheless clung to the hope that this form of inter-coalitional bipolarism would increase accountability by allowing voters a more direct input into the election of the government. This also explains the related decision to introduce the direct election of mayors in 1993, under a new two round electoral system that made parties form into coalitions for the purposes of electing their mayoral candidate. Directly elected mayors had proven immediately popular with voters, prompting national legislators to devise a similar system for the regions, a less salient level of government whose representatives were little known (Fabbrini and Brunazzo, 2003).

The new electoral system for the ordinary regions was approved by the Italian Parliament only a few months before the 1995 regional elections (Law no. 43/1995). Known commonly as the Tatarella Law, this retained features of the old electoral system but was far more majoritarian in its allocation of seats and provided for the direct election of regional presidents. It represents the basis for most regional electoral systems today, although regions are now free to change their system entirely. Voters are asked to cast two ballots in a single round of voting. The first ballot is for a candidate for regional president, and the other ballot is for party lists to elect members of the regional council on a PR basis. Parties can form into coalitions fielding multiple lists supporting a joint candidate for regional president. The parties represented in the 'winning coalition' (decided by a plurality of votes) receive a 'majoritarian bonus' of additional seats in the regional council (around 20 per cent), to ensure the regional president has an inbuilt majority. The precise number of seats allocated by the 'majoritarian bonus' varies because the system is designed to ensure the winning coalition has a guaranteed majority of at

---

as the regional bonuses often cancelled each other out, leading to no clear majority in the Senate. The second difference is that the national electoral system contained no preference voting, with all seats allocated on the basis of closed lists chosen by party leaders. This system was used in the 2006, 2008, and 2013 national elections. After many political deliberations, it was eventually replaced by a mixed electoral system with mainly proportional features that was used in the 2018 national election.

least 55 per cent of seats (Vassallo, 2013). The electoral system allows split ticketing, so the first vote can be cast for a regional president while the second vote can support a party in opposition to that regional president. However, the winning coalition (and thus the majoritarian bonus) is determined by the vote for regional president and not the vote for party lists, so there is no possibility that the regional president will lack a governing majority. His/her position is further strengthened by the possibility to choose councillors elected under the 'majoritarian bonus', by means of a closed list tied to his/her candidature (known as the *listino*). After direct election, the president chooses members of the regional government (executive) either from among elected members of the regional council or from outside this body. In practice, regional presidents do not have the political strength to make these choices by themselves. Representation on the *listino* and membership of the regional executive are the subject of inter-party bargaining, with regional presidents having some input but never sole discretion over what are deemed to be coalitional choices (Vassallo and Baldini, 2000).

The Tatarella Law did not change an important and controversial feature of regional party systems, namely that seats allocated to parties in the regional council are determined by preference voting. The continuation of preference voting at regional level means certain practices of the 'old' party system continue today, including electoral clientelism and strong intra-party competition for votes (Vassallo, 2013). Local powerbrokers have the possibility to draw on a large number of preference votes in a territorial constituency, and use this to bargain their way into control of party structures and a prominent position in the regional government (Wilson, 2016). The Tatarella Law also could not guarantee regional presidents would not be replaced mid-legislature by parties or groups of councillors seeking new opportunities for advancement. These *ribaltoni* were an endemic feature of the old national and regional party systems, and soon made a comeback in three southern regions where presidents were replaced by their councils in 1998 and 1999. This loophole was closed by the 1999 constitutional reform, which enshrined the direct election of regional presidents and tied the terms of presidents and councils together so that a resignation of the regional president would lead automatically to fresh elections (Vassallo, 2013). However, the constitutional reform did not end the practice of *trasformismo* at regional level, as councillors can still change parties or coalitions after election to suit their career advancement and re-election prospects.

B. Party competition and coalition formation

The 1995 regional elections began to shape regional party systems in a more majoritarian direction, with the main centre-left and centre-right parties forming into larger coalitions supporting joint candidates for regional president. These elections took place simultaneously across the 15 ordinary regions, making them an important national test for Italian parties and their new coalitions. The choice of presidential candidates was negotiated entirely by national party elites, with the advantage of incumbency yet to be a major consideration in regional elections. The shift to bipolarism was incomplete though. Firstly, the LN had recently brought down the first Berlusconi government (1994–95) and so fielded its own presidential candidates outside the main coalitions. Secondly, the PRC chose to stand outside the centre-left coalition in many regions. This led to an inadvertent process of 'coalition testing' that simply confirmed the bipolarising logic underlying the new regional electoral system, which gives no discernible benefit to parties standing outside the main coalitions. The centre-left coalition won nine regions – four in the centre-north where it was historically dominant (Emilia-Romagna, Tuscany, Umbria, Marche), four in southern Italy (Basilicata, Lazio, Abruzzo, Molise), plus the northern region of Liguria. The centre-right coalition won in three northern regions where the DC had once been powerful (Veneto, Lombardy, Piemonte), as well as three southern regions that also used to be dominated by the DC (Campania, Puglia, Calabria). LN and PRC gained next to nothing by standing outside the main coalitions, having no 'blackmail potential' over regional legislatures because the winning coalition could secure a comfortable majority without them. The centre-left coalition would probably have won more regions (including Veneto and Piemonte) if it had included PRC. The centre-right coalition would have been electorally impregnable in northern Italy (and won control of Liguria) if LN was part of its coalition. Yet coalitional choices were made by national leaders whose priority then was not necessarily winning regional elections. In the 1996 national election, LN and PRC again stood apart from the main coalitions. Nevertheless, the later rapprochement between the centre-right coalition and LN, and between the centre-left coalition and PRC, meant the 2000 regional elections saw an *almost perfect system of coalitional bipolarism* in the Italian regions.

In the 2000 regional elections, LN backed the centre-right coalition in every northern region but did not compete in central-northern regions (except for Emilia-Romagna) or in southern Italy. PRC joined the centre-left coalition in every region except Tuscany, where the centre-left coalition was dominant anyway. The result was that the centre-right coalition made a clean sweep of all four northern regions, the centre-left coalition retained control of all four central-northern regions, and the most intense electoral competition took place in southern Italy where four regions were won by the centre-right and three by the centre-left. The 2005 election saw similarly broad coalitions fielded with no strong third parties, but resulted in a much bigger victory for the centre-left coalition (13 out of 15 regions), with the centre-right only holding onto its strongholds in Veneto and Lombardy. The centre-right coalition proved more competitive in the 2010 regional elections, where it won 6 of the 13 regions (against 7 for the centre-left). Although some parties or individual politicians did compete outside the main coalitions, including a nascent Five Star Movement (M5S) that fielded lists in five regions in 2010, their support was generally very low. The main coalitions were bolstered by an array of personal lists, which competed as part of the coalition in specific regions and were usually associated directly with the presidential candidate or another prominent regional politician. The use of presidential lists has grown in every set of regional elections.[6] While personal lists can help pre-electoral coalitions be more competitive, they also reflect a growing trend towards personalisation of electoral politics that can ultimately be detrimental to established parties. Their use is consistent with a broader trend in regional elections towards heavily candidate-centred campaigns (Vassallo, 2013).

Regional party systems are now also characterised by different patterns of alternation in government, a key indicator for party system change (Mair, 1997). Before 1995, the regions were characterised by partial alternation in government and post-electoral coalition formation, as some parties remained in office by forming variable coalitions on the basis of election results.[7] After 1995, most regions became characterised by wholesale alternation in government and pre-electoral coalition formation, with voters determining which coalition of parties won office. However, the new regional party systems inherited the geographically uneven concentration of electoral support of their predecessors, making particular coalitions dominant in regions that thereafter saw no alternation in government (Wilson, 2009). Party systems in central-northern Italy (Tuscany, Emilia-Romagna, Umbria, Marche) became dominated by the main leftist party (PCI, PDS, DS, now PD), which formed coalitions with other groups close to the leftist DC tradition, in order to cement its hold on power. Party systems in the large northern regions of Veneto and Lombardy saw the DC vote taken over and extended by the centre-right coalition, which has never lost power in either region. Other ordinary regions have seen wholesale alternation in government as the strength of the competing coalitions is more evenly balanced. This includes some northern regions (Liguria, Piemonte) and all central-southern regions except Basilicata (a centre-left stronghold). The 1999 constitutional reform extended the possibility of direct election to all 'special status' regions that wanted it. Friuli-Venezia Giulia, Sardegna, Sicily, and the province of Trentino took up this possibility and their party systems are now similarly characterised by intense competition and wholesale alternation in government between competing coalitions. The small region of Aosta Valley and the autonomous province of Bolzano have stuck to more proportional electoral systems, reflecting their consensual systems of government as well as the continued dominance of ethno-regionalist parties in their territory (Palermo, 2020).

6 An occasional feature of the 2000 regional elections, presidential lists became far more common in 2005 (nine lists in six regions) and 2010 (eight lists in six regions). The 2013–2015 electoral cycle saw 15 presidential lists fielded in eleven regions, albeit with varying degrees of success (from 1.6 per cent to 23.1 per cent) (Tronconi, 2015). In addition, non-party lists backing the main coalitions (or standing outside them) compete in many regions. These are linked to local politicians or local issues and reflect the growing territorial dimension of regional politics.

7 Usually the largest party in each region (DC or PCI) remained in office by forming different coalitions with smaller parties. However, in some regions DC and PCI alternated in government after elections. In such cases, smaller parties like PSI could remain in office by forming opportunistic coalitions with either PCI or DC.

C. *Multi-level party organisations*

In many ways, state regionalisation and direct election of regional presidents further reinforced the territorial imbalances within Italian parties, encouraging them to focus on areas where they are dominant or have good chances of winning elections, and neglecting large areas of the country where they are historically uncompetitive. The Democratic Party (PD), in line with its predecessors, remains organisationally and electorally weak in much of northern Italy, so has focused its efforts on retaining control of the 'red belt' and competing more effectively in southern Italy. Forza Italia and its predecessors put in little effort in the 'red belt' regions dominated by the PD, focusing on their northern strongholds and in southern Italy. Italian parties have become more 'stratarchical', with each level of party organisation relatively autonomous and focused on managing their respective level of government (Wilson, 2016). This is consistent with a 'cartel party' model where parties increasingly rely on state resources and legitimacy through governing (Katz and Mair, 1995), and partly a question of necessity as Italian parties now lack the financial resources (due to party fissions and falling membership revenue) to sustain large organisations and party bureaucracies (Ignazi et al., 2010). Parties have therefore allowed some of their prominent institutional leaders at sub-national level, such as directly elected regional presidents or mayors, considerable leeway in their style of governing and the alliances they make to retain power (Wilson, 2016). This includes the possibility to bypass party bureaucracies at sub-national levels and govern more informally through powerful personal networks (Vassallo, 2013). Regional presidents have a strong electoral advantage due to incumbency, with increased voter salience making parties reluctant to change them between elections, a feature that increases their bargaining power. The office of regional president has become far more appealing for national politicians because of direct election and the increased powers of regional governments. Career paths of politicians between national and regional levels are now more bidirectional, whereas before 1995 they were largely unidirectional as ambitious politicians sought to use the region as a stepping stone to national office (Grimaldi and Vercesi, 2018). Control over regional government has given new institutional resources and political visibility to Italian parties, but this reliance on the state means they face huge difficulties mobilising support in regions where they are out of power. Stratarchy also led to a high toleration of clientelist practices that sometimes verges on outright corruption, leading to a voter backlash that ultimately drained support for established parties and boosted populist movements such as the M5S or the Lega. Interestingly, the Lega is the only party in Italy that never relinquished the centralised mass party model, and continues to be characterised by strong local activism and processes of party socialisation combined with centralisation of power around the party leader (Albertazzi et al., 2018), allowing it to profit from growing divisions within the moderate centre-right parties.

IV. Populist challenges and regional party systems, 2011–2020

A. Another party system change?

The past decade has seen a substantial change in regional party systems, with the rise of M5S as a 'third pole' that has weakened both centre-left and centre-right coalitions. This is especially true in electoral terms (Tronconi, 2015; Massetti, 2018). Yet whereas multipolar competition has transformed national politics in Italy and made it very difficult for either centre-left or centre-right coalitions to form stable governments, it has had only a transitory impact on regional party systems that remain underpinned by electoral systems that force bipolar competition. This explains one of the paradoxes of party systems in the Italian regions, which is the (still) prominent role of the PD and FI, even as their vote shares in regional elections have suffered. FI has been steadily losing support across the country to the Lega, which has surmounted it as the leading party in the centre-right coalition. More recently, Brothers of Italy (FdI) has taken votes from the Lega and relegated FI to third place in the centre-right coalition. Nevertheless, most centre-right challengers for regional president have been affiliated to FI, not only in southern Italy (where the Lega remains organisationally weak) but also in some northern regions where the Lega has become by far the larger party in electoral terms (Liguria, Piemonte). Strong bipolar competition at regional level means that presidential candidates must appeal to the centre ground, and FI candidates can be useful for targeting 'moderate' voters that might otherwise abstain or support the centre-left coalition. Having said that, the FI vote share fell to single digits in most regions that held elections in 2020, and a sustained decline of this magnitude will ultimately consign the party to a marginal role. There is also considerable evidence that the Lega can spearhead opposition to the centre-left in the 'red belt' more effectively than FI ever managed, wrestling control of Umbria (2019) and Marche (2020), and coming a strong second in the larger regions of Emilia-Romagna and Tuscany (2020).

The PD has maintained a position of centrality in the Italian party system despite numerous party fissions, largely because the splinter parties formed to the centre or left of it have not endured in organisational terms. This is also true at the regional level, even if the last set of regional elections (2017–2020) saw PD support fall in every single region compared to the previous round. The PD vote share is now below 20 per cent in all of southern Italy, falling to single digits where the PD has been closely implicated in corruption scandals. This includes the former stronghold of Basilicata, where the centre-left lost power for the first time in 2018. PD support also fell in Lazio (from 30 per cent in 2013 to 21 per cent in 2018), even as the regional president Nicola Zingaretti became PD party leader. Party support in northern regions has fallen to 25 per cent or well below, with the notable exception of the remaining PD strongholds in Emilia-Romagna and Tuscany (35 per cent in 2020). For the first time ever, the PD lost control of Umbria (2019) and Marche (2020) to centre-right coalitions led by populist candidates for regional president (Lega in Umbria, FdI in Marche). PD performance in regional elections is difficult to compare with other levels of election in Italy because of the prevalence of personal lists linked to the PD candidate for regional president, which serve to boost the coalition but diminish the electoral performance of the party itself. Yet the steady decline has been hard to mask, with the PD becoming electorally uncompetitive in northern Italy and directly implicated in corruption scandals in southern Italy. Nevertheless, the PD controls key regions and may profit from declining electoral support for the M5S, its current governing partner at national level. The PD also benefits from the popularity of certain regional presidents affiliated to the party. This was evident in the 2020 regional elections, where the centre-left secured victory in Puglia and Campania thanks to the popularity of its incumbents. The price to pay is that such regional presidents are taking an increasingly independent approach towards the party line and are often at odds with the party leadership in Rome.

Part of the reason why PD and FI struggled so much in the 2010s was a series of corruption scandals that engulfed the Italian regions, contributing to an increasingly negative perception of regional governments as the new locus of political corruption in Italy. On several occasions, these scandals caused regional presidents to resign, leading to fresh elections where the governing coalitions were heavily punished by voters. The peak of corruption scandals in the Italian regions coincided with a difficult period when regional governments had to make significant reductions in public expenditure as part of the national austerity drive of the Monti and Letta governments (2011–2014). Whereas centre-right regional governments pursued stronger austerity measures than their centre-left counterparts (Toubeau and Vampa, 2020), the toxic combination of austerity and corruption contributed to a further decline in turnout in regional elections to well below 60 per cent in the 2012–2015 electoral cycle (Tronconi, 2015; Massetti, 2018). While declining turnout is a general feature of the Italian political system, the relative decline in regional elections has been greater than in comparable national or European elections (Massetti, 2018), and at odds with the expectation that more powers and resources for regional governments would increase levels of political participation. Quite the opposite seems to have happened in the Italian case, although turnout levels improved in the 2020 regional elections. Over time, regional elections have also lost their value as a 'barometer test' for Italian parties in view of impending national elections (Massetti, 2018). Only a minority of ordinary regions now hold their elections on the same day (seven in 2015, six in 2020), in sharp contrast with the preceding decades when (almost) all ordinary regions held their election at the same time, less than a year before national elections. Since 2008, national elections have taken place a few years after the bulk of regional elections, and have tended to coincide with only a handful of elections in ordinary and special regions. As a result, the impact of regional elections on the national party system is now less pronounced and the same is generally true vice versa.

B. Limited impact of the Five Star Movement

The rise of the M5S contributed to tensions within the main centre-left and centre-right coalitions and made them less electorally competitive. In 2015, the centre-right coalition fielded more than one presidential candidate in Puglia, Tuscany, and Marche. It lost comprehensively in all three regions. At the same time, an independent leftist candidate in Liguria split the centre-left vote so badly that the centre-right won back control of the region. These exceptions ultimately helped to remind Italian parties about the basic rule that broad centre-left or centre-right coalitions are the only means of securing government office at regional level.[8] Recent regional elections (2018–2020) have seen the return of two broad coalitions, as well as the demise of third parties including M5S. The M5S policy of rejecting pre-electoral coalitions with other parties made it unable to win regional elections, even at the height of its electoral appeal. Only twice the M5S came close to winning regional elections on its own, winning 35 per cent of the vote in Sicily (2017) and 39 per cent in Molise (2018). On both occasions, it ultimately lost out to the centre-right coalition. The M5S has secured more than 20 per cent of the regional vote share on only four other occasions: Abruzzo and Piemonte in 2014 (21 per cent), Liguria in 2015 (25 per cent), and Lazio in 2018 (27 per cent). Its failure at regional level could be linked to its lack of political organisation at that level. The M5S is a highly centralised party that relies heavily on voluntary local activists, but its only regional organisation are the elected councillors (Tronconi, 2015). M5S has also been ambivalent about decentralisation in Italy, with considerable hostility towards regional governments, associated in the minds of its activists with the corruption of governing parties. While readily capitalising on local issues, including opposition to unpopular infrastructure decisions taken at national level (e.g. the TAV railway line in Piemonte or the TAP gas pipeline in Puglia), M5S has been unwilling to advance autonomist demands or form regional alliances that could secure the changes it would like to see in regional government. In 2019, M5S formed an unexpected governing coalition at national level with the PD, replacing the outgoing populist coalition with the Lega. This led many in the M5S movement to question the value of avoiding pre-electoral alliances, especially in a context of declining electoral support for the movement. While M5S still usually stands outside both main coalitions in regional and local elections, this approach is no longer set in stone and the M5S agreed terms to join the centre-left coalition in Umbria (2019) and Liguria (2020). However, this did not significantly strengthen the centre-left coalition (which lost

8 This feature now contrasts the Italian regions with the national party system, where unusual alliances have been formed that cut across the left-right political divide. The Monti, Letta, and Renzi governments (2011–2018) were all backed by the centre-left coalition together with a varying number of centre-right dissidents. The Conte I government was backed by a controversial populist alliance of LN and M5S, while the current Conte II government is the fruit of a governing coalition of M5S and the PD. Meanwhile, the traditional centre-left and centre-right coalitions continue to dominate regional elections and monopolise regional government formation.

both regions), nor did it improve support for the M5S (7 per cent in Umbria, 8 per cent in Liguria). The 2020 regional elections saw M5S support fall to single digits in every region where elections were held, regardless of its particular coalitional choices in that region.

C. *Dominance of the Lega*

The failure of the M5S as a movement to leave lasting change on regional party systems stands in marked contrast to the Lega, which has adopted a far-right populist discourse founded on hostility to immigration and the EU; retained an active mass party organisation in northern regions; and grown its electoral presence across the rest of the country through the personal appeal and distinct message of its leader Matteo Salvini. The latter increasingly ignores the question of regional autonomy and focuses on protectionist, anti-immigrant, and nationalist positions. Lega regional presidents are instead the ones primarily responsible for advancing the autonomist narratives that have shaped the movement since its origins (Albertazzi et al., 2018; Vampa and Scantamburlo, 2020). The party has further defied political science stereotypes by moving from being an ethnoregionalist party that only competed in northern regions (1991–2010) to becoming the main centre-right party across the country (Massetti, 2018). This change of strategy was exemplified by the decision to abandon the Lega Nord label and compete as the Lega (for Salvini premier) since 2018, and by a change of party organisation that has seen the old Lega Nord gradually replaced by a new Lega party. However, this nationalised approach continues to rely very heavily on the Lega's electoral dominance in northern Italy. The Lega dominates the regions of Lombardy and Veneto (>30 per cent vote), and has now eclipsed FI in the neighbouring regions of Piemonte and Liguria. The 2015 regional elections saw the Lega surpass FI in the 'red belt' regions, where it has become the main challenger to the PD. Between 2018 and 2020, support for the Lega was greater than FI even in many central-southern regions (Lazio, Abruzzo, Basilicata, Sardegna, Campania, Puglia). The Lega has also become the main party for Italian speakers in the special regions of Trentino-Alto Adige, Friuli-Venezia Giulia, and Aosta Valley.[9] The 2020 regional elections indicate that its main rival within the centre-right coalition is now FdI, which performed strongly in central-northern and southern Italy.

D. *Is the regional electoral system still democratic?*

Twelve regional elections that took place between 2012 and 2015 saw the winning coalition secure the support of just 15–25 per cent of registered voters, due

9 The Lega currently controls the regional presidencies of Veneto, Lombardy, Umbria, Friuli-Venezia Giulia, and the autonomous province of Trentino. Between 2010 and 2014, the Lega also controlled the regional presidency of Piemonte, where it is currently the largest party (37 per cent vote share in 2019).

to the high rate of abstention and the strong performance of M5S outside both main coalitions (Massetti, 2018). Although turnout improved in the 2020 regional elections, which saw winning coalitions secure more convincing victories than usual (48–78 per cent of the vote), there remain concerns about the legitimacy of directly elected regional presidents under the 'PR with majoritarian bonus' electoral system, and the way this can exaggerate the performance of the winning coalition. Although regions are free to change their electoral systems to a more proportional system and even abandon the direct election of presidents altogether, no region has gone down this path because direct election remains very popular with the general public. Most regions have amended their electoral laws but the changes have been relatively modest (Massetti, 2018). Many have changed the method of allocating the 'majoritarian bonus' by scrapping the *listino* and replacing it with a greater number of seats allocated to parties in the winning coalition. Several regions have abolished split ticketing in regional elections (i.e. voting for different coalitions in the presidential and party ballots) and have raised electoral thresholds for parties or coalitions to secure seats. Some regions have addressed concerns about the weakness of regional opposition by capping the number of seats that the winning coalition can receive, or guaranteeing a minimum number of seats for opposition parties. Preference voting remains a feature of all regional electoral systems, although the number of preference votes now varies by region and several have introduced gender balance requirements. The only region to abolish preference voting was Tuscany in 2005. However, a broader reform of the Tuscan electoral system in 2014 saw preference voting restored, together with other changes including a second round of voting if no party or coalition secures at least 40 per cent in the first round. No other region foresees the possibility of a second round of voting,[10] even if such a system is widely used in local elections in Italy. Umbria and Sardegna have set minimum electoral thresholds (respectively 34 per cent and 25 per cent) that the winning coalition must secure to obtain a majoritarian bonus at all, while other regions have reduced the size of the majoritarian bonus. It is now theoretically possible that in some future regional elections, winning coalitions will not be guaranteed a governing majority.

V. Concluding remarks

This chapter has sought to describe the various transformations over time in regional party systems, driven by broader changes in party politics, electoral system

10 Aosta Valley adopted an electoral system for the 2013 regional election with the possibility of a second round of voting if the winning coalition secured less than half of votes or seats in the first round. On this occasion, the winning coalition secured a majority of seats anyway and the second round never took place. A new electoral system introduced for the 2018 regional election involved a single round of voting and seats allocated by PR without forming coalitions. However, if a single party could secure at least 42 per cent of the vote share then it would receive 21 of the 35 seats in the regional council. While experimenting with majoritarian bonuses, Aosta Valley has never envisaged the direct election of regional presidents, the latter always nominated by the legislature.

design, and regionalisation of the state. The conclusions are perhaps then a good moment to reflect in comparative perspective on what has *not* really changed in regional party systems. The first point to note is that regional party systems in Italy have tended to reinforce (rather than undermine) the core dynamics of party competition at national level. Regional party systems are underpinned by electoral systems that encourage broad coalitions to form for the purposes of winning elections and governing together afterwards. They are characterised by bipolar competition and wholesale alternation in government, and any attempts at third poles (including the M5S) have ultimately failed. This contrasts with the national level, where more innovative coalitions have been pursued because the very notion of bipolarism has come under strain, being no longer able to deliver viable governments. Whereas national governments are now characterised by unusual alliances that diverge from patterns of bipolarism, the regions serve to remind the centre-left and centre-right parties and voters of their 'true' positioning in the party system. Due to electoral volatility and declining turnout, as well as the unpredictable impact of 'third pole' challengers, regional party systems have also become *more competitive*, with wholesale alternation even in some regions historically dominated by a particular coalition. This tendency has rather been to the detriment of the centre-left coalition, which has lost control of former 'red' regions such as Basilicata, Umbria, and Marche, as processes of party fission and poor governing records continue to weaken support for the PD.

It is also somewhat surprising that over 50 years of party competition in the ordinary regions has delivered no new regionalist parties, or at least none that have endured. If anything, Italian politics is becoming more nationalised as the Lega has evolved from ethno-regionalism to a more state-wide organisation. Classic ethno-regionalist parties remain strong only in Bolzano (South Tyrol) and Aosta Valley, but even these are starting to lose their dominant position in the party system. The South Tyrolean People's Party (SVP) is contending simultaneously with far-right challengers in the German speaking community and a powerful Lega that is coalescing the votes of Italian speakers in the province (Vampa and Scantamburlo, 2020). Union Valdotaine meanwhile has undergone a series of organisational splits and recent corruption scandals that threaten its historic control over the region, with the Lega winning regional elections there in 2020. The only other enduring regionalist party is the historic Partito Sardo d'Azione (PSdA), now at the head of a centre-right coalition governing in Sardegna, but with little over one-tenth of regional votes. Regionalism in institutional terms has not led to regionalism in party political terms, distinguishing Italy from other devolved states in Europe (Spain, UK), but making it quite similar to federal systems with a strong national political culture (Germany, Austria).

Directly elected regional presidents have been able to build up strong territorial powerbases in Italy, but these are personalised and do not outlive their stay in office. National party elites have been willing to accommodate powerful presidents but reluctant to develop genuinely federal party organisations, even if these could help to compensate their weak implantation in many parts of the country. Regional party branches and their leaders have sometimes gained *de facto* autonomy through a stratarchical party organisation, but this comes with limited influence over the decision-making of national elites. Regional presidents in Italy never came to wield the power of regional 'party barons' in Spain or even state minister-presidents in Germany. Their lack of influence over national decision-making extends to leadership selection for regional elections, where candidates for regional president are still the subject of coalitional bargaining between parties at national level, with only incumbent regional presidents having a strong claim for re-election. Their lack of national influence is also evident in broader processes of constitutional reform and state decentralisation, where regional presidents have generally been unable to shape the content of competing reform proposals and only played a modest role in referendum campaigns (Palermo and Wilson, 2014). Centre-right regional presidents have been more successful in pushing the issues of 'fiscal federalism' and 'regional asymmetry' onto the national agenda, through concrete reform proposals as well as regional autonomy referendums. This process owes much to Lega leaders that want to keep the autonomist issue burning in its electoral heartlands and compensate for the nationalist drive of Salvini (Giovannini and Vampa, 2019).

2020 will always be remembered as the year that Coronavirus uprooted our daily lives. It has also had a distinct effect on political leadership. One common effect has been to strengthen the visibility and autonomy of executives, in particular executive leaders (presidents or prime ministers), at the expense of legislatures that have struggled to function and retain visibility during a time of social distancing and crisis decision-making. The Italian regions are no different in this respect, with regional presidents making a political comeback and gaining increased visibility during a national crisis. This is sometimes because they are at the helm of an effective response to dealing with the virus in a highly exposed region, such as Luca Zaia (LN) in Veneto, or because they developed a popular regional narrative on lockdown measures, such as the centre-left PD regional presidents in Campania (Enzo De Luca) and Puglia (Michele Emiliano). This contributed to the re-election of all three presidents in 2020 with convincing majorities (70 per cent in Campania, 78 per cent in Veneto, 47 per cent in Puglia). In other cases, regional presidents have been slow off the mark and associated with broader failures of regional governance in the healthcare system, notably in Lombardy where Attilio Fontana (Lega) is widely viewed as indecisive and self-interested. Only time will tell if the pandemic will give regions and regional presidents a more prominent position in national political life, or whether it will induce further doubts about the merits of having regionally differentiated healthcare and welfare systems managed by a costly political class that is still too prone to corruption.

Literature

Daniele Albertazzi, Arianna Giovannini, and Antonella Seddone 'No regionalism please, we are Leghisti!' The transformation of the Italian Lega Nord under the leadership of Matteo Salvini' (2018), 28 *Regional and Federal Studies*, 645

Felia Allum and Percy Allum, 'Revisiting Naples: Clientelism and organized crime' (2008), 13 *Journal of Modern Italian Studies*, 340

Stefano Bartolini, Alessandro Chiaramonte, and Roberto D'Alimonte 'The Italian party system between parties and coalitions' (2004), 27 *West European Politics* 1

Anna Cento Bull and Mark Gilbert, *The Lega Nord and the Northern Question in Italian Politics* (Palgrave Macmillan, 2001)

Sergio Fabbrini and Marco Brunazzo, 'Federalizing Italy: the convergent effects of Europeanization and domestic mobilization' (2003), 13 *Regional and Federal Studies* 100

Arianna Giovannini and Davide Vampa, 'Towards a new era of regionalism in Italy? A comparative perspective on autonomy referendums' (2019), *Territory, Politics, Governance* (online advance access)

Selena Grimaldi and Michelangelo Vercesi, 'Political careers in multi-level systems: Regional chief executives in Italy, 1970–2015' (2018), 28 *Regional and Federal Studies* 125

David Hine, 'Federalism, Regionalism and the Unitary State: Contemporary regional pressures in historical perspective' in Carl Levy (ed.), *Italian Regionalism: History, Identity and Politics* (Berg Publishers, 1996)

Piero Ignazi, Luciano Bardi, and Oreste Massari, 'Party organisational change in Italy (1991–2006)' (2010), 15 *Modern Italy* 197

Richard S. Katz and Peter Mair, 'Changing models of party organisation and party democracy: the emergence of the cartel party' (1995), 1 *Party Politics* 5

Peter Mair, *Party system change: approaches and interpretations* (Oxford University Press, 1997)

Emanuele Massetti, 'Regional elections in Italy (2012–15): Low turnout, tri-polar competition and Democratic Party's (multi-level) dominance' (2018), 28 *Regional and Federal Studies* 325

Francesco Palermo, 'La forma di governo regionale a vent'anni dalla riforma: cosa resta della specialità?', *Osservatorio sulle fonti*, n. 2/2020. See http://www.osservatoriosullefonti.it

Francesco Palermo and Alex Wilson, 'The Multi-level Dynamics of State Decentralisation in Italy' (2014), 12 *Comparative European Politics* 510

Giovanni Sartori, *Parties and Party Systems: A Framework for Analysis* (Cambridge University Press, 1976)

Simon Toubeau and Davide Vampa, 'Adjusting to austerity: the public spending responses of regional governments to the budget constraint in Spain and Italy' (2020), *Journal of Public Policy* (online advance access)

Filippo Tronconi, 'Bye-Bye Bipolarism: The 2015 Regional Elections and the New Shape of Regional Party Systems in Italy' (2015), 20 *South European Society and Politics* 553

Davide Vampa and Matthias Scantamburlo, 'The 'Alpine region' and political change: Lessons from Bavaria and South Tyrol (1946–2018)' (2020), *Regional and Federal Studies* (online advance access)

Salvatore Vassallo (ed.) *Il Divario Incolmabile: Rappresentanza politica e rendimento istituzionale nelle regioni italiane* (Il Mulino, 2013)

Salvatore Vassallo and Gianfranco Baldini, 'Elezioni, assemblee e governi regionali, 1947–2000' (2000), 3-4 *Le Istituzioni del Federalismo*, monograph

Alex Wilson, 'Coalition Formation and Party Systems in the Italian Regions' (2009), 19 *Regional and Federal Studies* 57

Alex Wilson, 'Regional Presidents, Multi-Level Parties and Organizational Stratarchy: The Case of Italy' in Ferdinand Muller-Rommel and Fernando Casal Bertoa (eds.), *Party Politics And Democracy in Europe: Essays in Honour of Peter Mair* (Routledge, 2016)

Part II

Italy's major contributions to the global discussion

Italian regionalism in the global debate

7 The Italian regions in the European Union

Story of an unaccomplished relationship

Antonia Baraggia[1]

I. Introduction

The role of sub-national entities in the European Union is one of the most fascinating but also ambiguous and debated issues in the EU integration process.

The place of sub-national levels of government in EU Member States lies at the crossroads of several lines of tensions in the EU: the tension between the original international nature of the EU and its subsequent "constitutional" path; the tension between the general "pan-European" landscape and the particular identities expressed not only at the national but even more at regional level; the tension between a supranational federalizing process and the national trends of decentralization and regionalization; and, lastly, the never-resolved tension between different forms of legitimacy (input, output, messianic) of the EU (Scharpf, 1999; Weiler, 2012).

More generally, the place of the regions in the EU – and Italian regions are no exception – lies at the core of the persistent tension between global forces and the renewal of particular identities. As Hirschl argues, "the general trend towards political convergence, globalism and supranationalism have spawned an array of localist counter-movements that profess to represent a given polity's, region's or community's 'genuine' identity" (Hirschl, 2016, 35).

Despite being different phenomena, the EU integration process and the "regionalization" in Member States exercised a degree of mutual influence on each other, since the latter influenced the development of the EU and vice versa, and the development of the EU profoundly influenced the regional dimension in Member States.[2]

This "osmotic" and bidirectional relationship is at the core of the construction of the EU constitutional order as a composite state (Bifulco, 1995), characterized

1 Assistant Professor of Comparative Law, University of Milan.
2 Political scientists have described such mutual influence, on the one hand, in terms of "Europeanization", referring to the influence of the EU in fostering the creation of new regions or stimulating regionalization processes already in place. On the other hand, especially in case of well-established regional institutions with legislative powers, the extension of EU powers in areas of regional competences has often eroded regional power in favour of the national level (see Featherstone and Radaelli, 2003).

DOI: 10.4324/9781003104469-8

by a kind of "porosity", which "reflects that the borders dividing these various levels of public authority are permeable so that ideas and norms leak from one level to another, giving rise to a creative process of cross-fertilization" (Finck, 2015, 7).

In such a complex intertwining, assessing the role and the relevance of sub-national units in the EU is a complex task, without definitive answers. On the one hand, the regional presence in the EU could be a complementary resource that fills the democratic gap the EU is experiencing, to concretely apply the principle of subsidiarity and proximity, and to increase the efficacy of EU policy implementation. On the other hand, however, strong regional identities may also create a challenge for the EU, fostering fragmentation, weakening the role of Member States vis-à-vis regional belongings, and even endangering the creation of an even closer European Union, as in the case of secessionist claims (Hirschl, 2016, 27).

The topic is undoubtedly complex, but since it can also be studied from different methodological angles, it is possible to reach different – even contradictory – assessments of the role of sub-national entities in the EU. Hence, not one but many different stories can be told about the regions and the EU: the tale of regions as institutional actors in a multilevel constitutional space; the development of the regions as instrumental actors to implement EU policies and to achieve EU goals; the regions as "political" actors, representatives of a given historical community; and the regions as artificial constructs built under the influence of EU conditionality merely for economic purposes.

The literature which has tried to capture the nature of this relationship has often focused on specific key "moments" of the European path of the regions: the initial EU blindness to the regions (Ipsen, 1966, 256; D'Atena, 1998, 1401; Weatherill, 2005, 1); the rise (or the hope) of the "Europe of Regions" in the wake of the innovation introduced by the Maastricht Treaty; and the decline of the regional dimension, especially in the aftermath of the economic crisis in 2008 and the rise of neo-centralism in many Member States.

Although these accounts do have the merit of shedding light on core aspects of the development of this complicated relationship, my aim in this chapter is to offer a more nuanced story of the place of the regions in the EU, exploring the path taken by the Italian regions.

I will consider the role of regions in the EU in two different, but strictly related perspectives: the institutional perspective, which looks at regions as constitutional actors; and the "functionalist" perspective, which considers regions as key economic actors for the implementation of EU policies (Poggi, 2018, 4). Despite sub-national institutions and economic areas not necessarily being the same, I argue these two dimensions must be considered as interconnected in order to better understand the complexity and the role of the European path of sub-national entities. Indeed, these two dimensions are two different forms of representation of regional interests in the EU: the institutional dimension gives voice to the "identitarian" representation and it may reinforce the input legitimacy of the EU, while the functional approach highlights the expression of interests and may act as a source of "output legitimacy" (Scharpf, 1999).

Adopting this perspective, the chapter will look neither at the case law of the Constitutional Court in this area, nor at the numerous specific policies (except for a short reference towards the end on the use of structural funds).

In the analysis that follows I argue that despite movement towards the recognition of the regional level in the multilevel EU architecture, sub-national units are not yet perceived as full institutional actors in a multitiered system, as the involvement of the regions in EU affairs remains dependent on the rules determined at State level.

On one hand, while the EU does now "see" the regions, it does not speak directly to them, since the EU legal order is still based on the dialectic between the supranational and the national level. On the other hand, the Italian experience is also characterized by what has been called the "blindness" of the national level towards the European dimension of the regions. Indeed, even though the constitutional provision introduced in 2001 clearly "constitutionalized" the European relevance of regions, the subsequent implementation of this role has been weak and incapable of giving effectiveness to the constitutional text.

This chapter is divided into three parts: first, I will discuss in general terms the issue of the regional dimension in the EU, highlighting the dualism between the "institutional" and the "functional" approach. Second, I will analyse the situation in Italy, focusing on the European dimension of the regions in light of the 2001 constitutional reform. Finally, I will conclude this study with a critical assessment how effective regional actors are in the EU 20 years on from the new path being adopted by the reform of Article 117 of the Italian Constitution.

II. Sub-national actors at the beginning of the EU integration process: "institutional blindness" vs "functionalist sight"

One of the most successful accounts of the role of the sub-national units in the EU has been the thesis of the "regional blindness" of the EU.

Looking at the institutional dimension of regions, one finds clear evidence of that "blindness" as little attention was paid to the role of sub-national units in the EEC framework in the early days of the European Community.

This is hardly surprising since Germany was the only EEC founding member with a fully-fledged federal system. Italy had only established the five special regions. The other Member States – France, the Netherlands, Luxemburg, and Belgium – had a unitary form of State with no recognition of sub-national units with legislative powers. Moreover, the internal organization of Member States – unitary, regional, or federal – was considered a constitutional matter of the Member States, towards which the EEC, like any other international organization, was "indifferent" (Cartabia and Weiler, 2000, 199).

However, could adopting a functionalist approach uncover an awareness, at the very beginning of the EU experience, of the critical role played by the regional level for the creation of the Common Market and the Community economic goals? It is fair to say the European Community was not blind towards the regional dimension per se, but it was unable to see the regions as something other than economic units. In other words "the EU takes for granted the existence of a regional level within the member states, since it is functional to the Community's regional policy" (Palermo and Santini, 2004, 6).

The Treaty of Rome definitely contains the seeds of this attention for regional dimensions, albeit only in economic terms. For example, Article 87 of the EC Treaty accepted "aid to promote the economic development of areas where the standard of living is abnormally low or where there is serious underemployment" as compatible with the Common Market because of the need to promote social cohesion in Europe.

At this time, Italy was facing the problems caused by the economic divide between North and South, so it is no surprise it played a fundamental role in this recognition of the importance of the regional dimension. As early as the 1956 Conference of Messina and in the "Spaak report", the Italian delegation pushed for the creation of a European fund to promote the development of particularly deprived and underdeveloped regions in the Community. In particular, the Italian delegation argued the presence of underdeveloped regions – like the regions of southern Italy – could endanger the creation of the Common Market as a whole, and it pushed for the formation of financial instruments to help regional development (Fauri, 2001, 126).

The attention paid by Italy to the "regional" dimension favoured the creation of two key instruments for the future regional policy of the EU: the European Social Fund (ESF) and the European Bank of Investment.[3] This paved the way for the realization of the EU regional policy, one of the most successful chapters of the EU integration story and the "bright" side of the European dimension of regional entities.

In this first phase of EU integration, regions were merely recipients of EU policy, mediated through the national level. There were no channels for regional participation in the definition of policies and they were not seen as institutional interlocutors of the EU, but just passive recipients of decisions taken without them (Falcon, 2001, 329).

In the 1970s, this functionalist conception had to cope with the rise of the institutional dimension of the regions. Both Italy and Belgium embarked on institutional reforms in the direction of the regionalization and even federalization of their internal structures. Italy eventually completed its process of regionalization with the creation of the ordinary regions. Belgium divided its territory into three cultural communities, reflecting the language divisions in the country and forging the bases for the creation of the three regions that would be established with the 1980 constitutional reform.

Moreover, the accession of the United Kingdom and Ireland in 1973 boosted the formation of a more structured EU regional policy as, during the accession negotiations, the UK obtained assurances the European regional policy would be set up. As a consequence, in 1975, the European Regional Development Fund

3 Art. 129–130 EC Treaty. In particular, Art. 130 lett. a).

(ERDF) was created to assist the economic development of the most disadvantaged regions in Europe.

Once regional policies had entered the framework, the 1980s became the golden decade for the institutional emersion of the regional dimension. When Spain entered the EU, it had already adopted a regional structure in the aftermath of regime change; likewise Austria, a traditional federal state, joined the EU, bringing new strength to the recognition of the federal dimension in the EU.

The regional presence was also prompted by the creation of "European regions", the so-called "NUTS"[4], based on the already existing sub-national units in the Member States, in order to manage and allocate regional policy funds. Interestingly, in the case of absence of a sub-national division in a Member State, the establishment of a sub-national level is "imposed as a matter of fact or of political 'persuasion' (benefits deriving from the regional policy, whose functional raison d'être factually prevails over the policy of regional-blindness)" (Palermo and Santini, 2004, 6–7).

The institutional dimension of regions perfectly matched the growing relevance of the Community's regional policy. The presence of regional/sub-national units in the Community was no longer the exception, but a common feature – even though with peculiarities, asymmetries and profound differences – of EU Member States.

The success of such relations led to a new phase of the regionalization of EU policy, as can be seen by looking at the implementation of the Integrated Mediterranean Programme (IMP) and the reform of the structural fund in 1988.

These marked a turning point since, for the first time, the regions were given a "voice" vis-à-vis the EU and Member States. In particular, with specific regard to the IMP, Council Regulation no. 2088 of 23 July 1985 provided for the effective involvement of sub-national entities in the elaboration and implementation of European decisions, thus establishing a direct relationship between the regions and the Commission, without the State level playing an intermediary role (Chieffi, 2004). Along similar participative lines, in 1988 the structural funds[5] were reformed making "partnership" a pillar of fund governance. This meant a form of trilateral cooperation between the Commission, the Member States and the regions to design, manage, and implement structural funds.

Needs related to the implementation of the structural funds have fostered major change in Member States encouraging decentralization and regionalization (Scott, 1999, 639). In some cases, the socio-economic areas, identified for statistical purposes for the execution of European policies, the already mentioned NUTS, evolved into regional political entities (Palermo and Santini, 2004).

4 Reg. CE n. 1059/2003 May 26, 2003. The term NUTS refers to "Nomenclature of Territorial Units for Statistic". NUTS is a territorial unit identified for statistical purposes. In particular NUTS serves for the collection and development of EU regional statistic, for socio-economic analysis of the regions and for framing EU regional policies.

5 Council n. 2052/88, 24 June 1988.

This process of "Europeanization" is even more evident with the accession of the Eastern countries. Despite the fact that the provision of regional or sub-national entities was not part of the Copenhagen criteria – confirming the indifference of the EU towards the internal organization of power (of its Member States) – sub-national levels of government have been established in Hungary, Poland, and the Czech Republic (Palermo and Parolari, 2013). This process of decentralization has been driven by the need to comply with the financial and statistical criteria dictated by the governance of the structural funds. As has been argued, "the imperative of finding appropriate organizational forms to meet the requirements for EU regional and cohesion policies has been a catalyst for the reform of local and regional government in the CEECs" (Hughes, Sasse, and Gordon, 2004, 13). In other words, "regional government was the 'golden key' to the structural funds" (Hughes, Sasse, and Gordon, 2002, 13).

As Savino argued, the described evolution demonstrates how functional needs linked with the correct implementation of Community policies can prevail over the original regional-blindness of the EU (Savino, 2007, 443). Indeed, the Community first and later the EU were able to penetrate the internal structure of Member States by means of establishing, even indirectly, implementation tasks for the European programme, thus promoting, even indirectly, the decentralization process or even forcing change from a unitary structure towards a decentralized one (Savino, 2007, 443).

III. From Maastricht to Lisbon: from "blindness" to "imaginary"

In parallel with the functional development, the regionalization of the EU was finally recognized with the treaty reform. More specifically, the Single European Act in 1986 opened the path to the recognition of the institutional dimension of the region, confirmed by the Maastricht Treaty which introduced several changes on this issue: the creation of the Committee of Regions, building a channel for the direct participation of the regions in EU affairs; the introduction of mechanisms of indirect involvement of the regions via national governments; and the "constitutionalization" of the principle of subsidiarity (Article 5.2 TEU), which is the key concept for the multilevel governance of the EU.

This process of openness towards the regional dimension continued with the Treaty of Amsterdam (which strengthened the powers of the Committee of Regions) and the White Paper on EU governance, where the Commission acknowledged

> there needs to be a stronger interaction with regional and local governments and civil society. Member States bear the principal responsibility for achieving this. But the Commission for its part will: establish a more systematic dialogue with representatives of regional and local governments through national and European associations at an early stage in shaping policy. Bring greater flexibility into how Community legislation can be implemented in a way which takes account of regional and local conditions.

The EU institutional steps towards a more inclusive framework for sub-national entities in EU policies is reflected in the parallel functional development of new instruments under the regional policy of the EU, such as the cross-border cooperation area, with programmes like Interreg and the European Grouping of Territorial Cooperation (EGCT).[6] The latter in particular was developed in the light of the principle of subsidiarity (Recital (15) Regulation (EU) No 1082/2006) and provided a comprehensive institutional framework for cross-border cooperation based on institutional flexibility which allowed "the creation of innovative and place-based territorial cooperation structures" (Csizmadia 2020, 4).

The commitment to broader openness and involvement of the regional level reached its apex in the Lisbon Treaty, where major emphasis was placed on regional participation in EU governance.

The first mention of the regional level of governance within the EU can be found in Article 4 TEU: "The Union shall respect the equality of the Member States before the treaties as well as their national identities, inherent in their fundamental structures, political and constitutional, inclusive of regional and self-government."

The Lisbon Treaty also included territorial cohesion as core objective of the EU and formalized the place of cohesion policy as a territorial policy of the EU.

Moreover, the Lisbon Treaty introduced express recognition of the role of the regional legislative assemblies in European affairs. In particular, the Protocol on the application of the principles of subsidiarity and proportionality in Article 6 provides for the consultation of regional assemblies by national parliaments:

> Any national Parliament or any chamber of a national Parliament may, within eight weeks from the date of transmission of a draft legislative act, in the official languages of the Union, send to the Presidents of the European Parliament, the Council and the Commission a reasoned opinion stating why it considers that the draft in question does not comply with the principle of subsidiarity. It will be for each national Parliament or each chamber of a national Parliament to consult, where appropriate, regional parliaments with legislative powers.

This broad recognition of regional participation should not be overstated. As is often the case, the devil is in the details and this is the case of regional status in the EU. Looking carefully at the procedure envisaged by Protocol 2, it is clear regional authorities are excluded from any direct involvement in the Early Warning System (EWS), with the exception of the regional parliaments with legislative powers, which may be involved in the control mechanism of a national Parliament.

The literature on this topic has often proven to be quite critical of the real effects of this openness, with the entire procedure of the subsidiarity mechanism seen to remain "firmly attached to bi-centricity. It safeguards the monolithic

6 Regulation (EC) no 1082/2006 of the European Parliament and of the Council of 5 July 2006.

nature of the Member State in assuming that any action originating within the State is that of the State" (Finck, 2015, 16). In other words, "Protocol 2 is a state-centric process of subsidiarity review whose objective is to improve the accountability of, and inject democratic legitimacy into, what continues to be an equally state-centric legislative process" (Cygan, 2014, 268). Moreover, Olivetti argues that

> as single entities, the regions remain formally invisible for the European Union, although some avenues are opened to make them visible through the Member State to which they belong. And they are visible through the Committee of Regions and, informally, in consultation procedures, on the same footing of other subjects and organized interests.
>
> (Olivetti, 2013, 330)

There has also been discussion as to whether the involvement of regional parliaments with legislative powers is mandatory or merely optional, and this has been left to the discretion of the national level. As for Italy, a combined reading of Article 6 of the Protocol and the set of provisions of Article 117 Const., has led to the recognition of the right of regional entities to participate in monitoring compliance with the principle of subsidiarity (Fasone, 2009, 409; Olivetti, 2013, 329).

However, determining the procedural rules for the participation of regional legislatures is entirely left to the national level. Regional instances, with the exception of a few cases with a strong federal tradition[7], continue to be filtered by the state level, which remains the true gatekeeper of the European projection of the regions. The lack of effective participation of the regions in EU affairs adds to the weakness of the so-called input legitimacy that the EU suffers from so chronically.

Even if the EU has overcome its blindness towards the regional dimension, which has emerged as a tangible reality within the EU legal space, the advent of the "Europe of Regions" or the realization of a "federal union" has remained a kind of "imaginative reality", a road never taken by the EU.

IV. The European path of the Italian regions: the institutional perspective

Thus far, the focus has been solely on one side of the story, because the other side of the story is the national side, i.e. how the national legal and political environment (in Italy) has shaped – favouring or hindering - the role of the regions in the EU. The European framework gives the national legislator broad discretion to design the procedures and determine the intensity and effectiveness of regional involvement in EU affairs.

7 In the case of Germany and Austria, the *Länder* are represented in the second chamber of the Parliament, so they have access to the subsidiarity control mechanism directly, falling within the notion of "national parliament".

Member States have taken several "internal" paths to regulate the involvement of sub-state entities in the European decision-making process. In such a perspective, there are no specific substantial or procedural constraints; or, in other words, the script is outlined but the actors have plenty of room to decide how it is interpreted. The focus now will shift to looking at precisely how it has been "interpreted" by the Italian actors.

As has been argued, Italian regions have suffered not only from the blindness of the EU, but also, domestically, from the blindness of the Italian public powers (Fasone, 2013, 126).

Although some weak forms of participation of the regions in EU affairs can be traced back to the 1970s and 80s, and some regions did open offices, following Law no. 52/1996, in Brussels. It was only with the 2001 constitutional reform that the relationship between the EU and the regions entered the constitutional sphere. Until 2001, no reference to EU legal order was actually made in the Italian Constitution. Thus, the 2001 constitutional reform marked a turning point, since it touched upon both the place (the primacy) of EU law in Italy and the place of the regions in the domestic and in the multilevel constitutional contexts.

However, even after the constitutional reform, the regions struggled to carve out spaces in the European decision-making process, and even when they did, their involvement was vague, incomplete, and ultimately rather ineffective.

Article 117(5) Const., introduced in 2001, is particularly important to the analysis that follows and so it is worth including it here:

> the Regions and the Autonomous Provinces of Trento and Bolzano take part in preparatory decision-making processes of EU legislative acts in the areas that fall within their responsibilities. They are also responsible for the implementation of international agreements and EU measures, subject to the rules set out in State law which regulate the exercise of subsidiary powers by the State in the case of non-performance by the Regions and autonomous provinces.

The new Article 117(5) constitutionally introduced both the "ascendant" and "descendant" phase of regional participation in the EU. The constitutional discipline is quite poor, with it left to the State to define the role of regional involvement in practice. Most of the power to do this lies in the hands of the ordinary legislature, which has to set the procedures, bodies, and mechanisms for regional participation – in the broad sense – in the EU. Despite the pivotal role played by regions in shaping participation in EU affairs, the Italian Parliament has been characterized by a sort of apathy towards the regional councils and their competences (Fasone, 2013, 128) and it has often kept on legislating as if the constitutional amendments had not been approved. Conversely, the regions often adopted laws and introduced procedures to regulate their participation in EU affairs, anticipating national action.

At a national level, three main steps were taken to implement the constitutional provisions, making them operational (Law no. 131/ 2003, Law no. 11/2005), and to implement the change introduced by the Lisbon Treaty (Law no. 234/2012).

Law no. 131/2003 governs direct participation of Italian regions in EU affairs. The law makes it possible to designate regional representatives in government delegations involved in the procedure for the adoption of the final act at EU level. The methods for selecting regional representatives in government delegations were defined by the State-Regions Conference, in the General Agreement of cooperation between the government and the regions for the participation of the latter in the formation of EU acts (Act no. 2537/2006 CSR).

However, even in this form of direct participation, the regions are not representative of regional interests but must express the unitary position of the State (Cannizzaro, 2003, 4).

Looking at the "indirect" ascendant phase – i.e. the participation of the regions in the formation of the national position in EU affairs – the procedures are set out by Law no. 234/2012, which was adopted four years after the entry into force of the Lisbon Treaty and which repealed Law no. 11/2005.

The whole of chapter IV (Articles 22–27) of Law no. 234/2012 is about the participation of the regions in the EU. The most relevant provision, which was actually introduced in 2005, is a special European session of the Permanent Conference for relations between the State, the regions, and the autonomous provinces of Trento and Bolzano. This special European session must be convened at least once every four months, or at the request of the regions and autonomous provinces. Such sessions are designed to align the national policy in the drafting of EU acts, with needs represented by the regions and the autonomous provinces, for matters they are competent for.

In more general terms, the legislation requires EU law initiatives for matters of regional competence to be sent by the President of the Council of Ministers to the Conference of Regions and Autonomous Provinces and to the Conference of the Presidents of the Legislative Assemblies of the Regions and of the Autonomous Provinces, so they can be forwarded to the councils of the regions and autonomous provinces. Then, for matters that are their competence, the regions and the autonomous provinces can send observations, within 30 days from the date of receipt of the documents, to the President of the Council of Ministers or to the Minister for European Affairs (Article 24).

The regions made (and make?) limited used of this process, thus indirectly confirming the complexity and long-windedness of the procedure (Ninatti, 2014, 318). Indeed, it is at the same time complex and vague, as the law only contains some generic references to regional parliamentary participation (Article 24), but does not identify a specific procedure for interparliamentary cooperation between the regional councils and the chambers, or even just a term by which the former must send their observations to the latter.

The provision governing regional participation in the EWS is also rather disappointing. In fact, Article 25 of Law 234/2012 does not provide a detailed procedure, stating only that for the purposes of verifying compliance with the principle of subsidiarity, regional assemblies can send their observations to the Chambers in *due time* for parliamentary examination, informing the Conference of Presidents of the Legislative Assemblies of the Regions at the same time. The absence of a precise term is a shortcoming that could well make the mechanism less effective as each chamber has a total of eight weeks to send its reasoned opinions on subsidiarity to the Commission. In truth, a term for the regional assembly is needed in order to allow the regional councils a minimum amount of time to examine the draft European act and to ensure the Chambers have time to examine and take into account regional opinions. In general, partly due to the uncertainty of the procedure, the Italian regional assemblies are in a weak position both in the EWS and in "political dialogue".

Last but not least, the constitutional reform also constitutionalized the "descendant phase", concerning the implementation of EU norms and the fulfilment of the obligations deriving from Italy's membership of the European Union. In this regard, Law no. 234/2012 requires the regions and autonomous provinces, in matters of their own legislative competence, to transpose the European directives, without prejudice to the substitutive powers that the State can use in the event of any inaction by the regions themselves (Articles 29, 40, and 41). This State substitution power, codified in Article 120 (2) Const., represents another interesting change introduced by the 2001 constitutional reform. In the new formulation, the government can act for bodies of the regions if the latter fail to comply with international rules and treaties or EU legislation (Martinico, 2012, 369). This constitutionalization follows the interpretation adopted by the Constitutional Court in several important decisions – above all no. 126/1996 – about the responsibility of the State in the case of non-compliance of the regions and finally put an end to the contrasting interpretation which had flourished up until then due to the lack of a normative provision.

The overall discipline of the participation of the regions in EU affairs is still quite weak, and the EU seems to consider regional consultation more as a burden rather than a positive contribution to enhance decision-making at EU level. As Caretti observed, even the most recent regulation of the matter confirms "the irrepressible tendency of our legislator to build procedures characterized by an exasperated Baroque taste with all the risks that this entails of jeopardizing functionality a priori" (Caretti, 2012, 844).

In the end, even the most recent legislative intervention in 2012 confirmed that the Italian regions, at EU level, remain in the shadows of national institutions and sometimes even get lost within the tortuous procedural pathways. This also needs to be seen in the broader context of Italian regionalism, characterized by centripetal forces that tend to limit the constitutional space given to the regions by the reform. It would go beyond the scope of this chapter to delve into the discussion of the constitutional division of competences introduced in 2001; however, some awareness of this general trend is necessary to really understand the limitations and constraints on Italian regions at European level.

V. The Italian regions in Europe: the relevance of functional integration

The regulatory and implementation framework certainly is not favourable for the development of regional projection in Europe. Despite this, the regions have been able to find functional alternative channels, spaces, and methods of interfacing in Europe, despite the lack of institutional options.

This is hardly surprising since the regions are responsible for implementing 70 per cent of European policies, thus finding themselves invested in a flow of policies and resources that emanate from the supranational level. While the regions have not yet found an effective bottom-up channel of representation, they are still the final – and important – terminal for numerous European policies. Some regions are aware of this pivotal position and have distinguished themselves by a certain activism designed to make the implementation of European law more effective and to efficiently manage the resources of European funds. At times, this has even meant anticipating, in regional regulations, legislative measures emanating at the central level. This context of regional development policies provides a number of interesting examples.

The development of the structural fund is deeply rooted in the development of regional autonomy. As early as the 1990s, thus even before the constitutional reform,

> European funds were an integral part of a process of redefining the relations between the centre and the periphery implemented by the centre-left government and aimed at permanently modifying the system of representation of interests by shifting its fulcrum from parties to institutions and from specific representation of the interests characteristic of the First Republic to the general one based on efficient, responsible local administrations with a leadership legitimized by direct election rather than by party legitimacy.
>
> (Fargion, Morlino, and Profeti, 2006, 121)

The recent dynamism of Emilia-Romagna and Tuscany are good examples of this. Both requested and obtained 30 million euros from the ERDF to help them cope with the coronavirus crisis. These two regions are the first to use the flexibilities provided for by the Coronavirus Response Investment Initiative (CRII).[8] Under this scheme, Emilia-Romagna will fund a call for projects for industries and research centres to finance short-term projects to develop and test innovative service and product solutions during the emergency and the gradual re-opening phases. Tuscany, on the other hand, will provide regional SMEs easier access to liquidity to keep their businesses running at times of economic uncertainty.

Even during the Eurozone crisis, the regions, albeit in the grip of the cuts in public spending decided by the central level, stood out for a certain efficiency in accessing and using EU structural funds in their recovery plans (Fabbris and Michielin, 2010, 12). Structural funds coming from both the ERDF and the ESF have financed the bulk of anti-crisis measures in many regions, granting, on

8 About the use of Cohesion Funds in the coronavirus emergency, see https://ec.europa.eu/regional_policy/en/newsroom/news/2020/03/16-03-2020-cohesion-policy-and-eu-solidarity-fund-contribute-to-the-coronavirus-response-investment-initiative.

average, twice the contribution of discretionary regional funds. In three regions (Calabria, Campania, and Apulia), structural funds have filled the gap left by limited regional budgets and central government funding (Fabbris and Michielin, 2010, 8).

These two examples illustrate the role financial instruments play in fostering the deep functional integration of the regions into the EU. More generally, they show the importance in EU governance of the exercise of power based on the use of financial resources, a kind of power labelled as "*potentia*" (Loughlin, 2001, 104), in opposition to the power of setting rules and coercive norms (*potestas*).

Besides functional integration, the activism of the regions in the European landscape has given rise to other functional forms of cooperation, especially inter-regional ones.

The treaties might provide for forms of cooperation between the national institutions of the different countries but they say nothing about cooperation at the level of sub-state bodies. However, despite the treaties, this cooperation has developed de facto through different forms of inter-regional cooperation. This is the case for CALRE (Conference of the Regional Assemblies with legislative competences), which represents an interesting example of the cooperation of regional parliaments with legislative powers on issues of shared relevance.

Other forms of cooperation have flourished in already established bodies, like the Committee of Regions (CoR). The Subsidiarity Monitoring Network, which is part of the CoR, is an interesting example as it counts analysing the territorial impact assessments of EU policies as one of its main functions, with these potentially becoming part of opinions addressed to the Commission. These functions are based on a flow of information and data sent via the Regpex electronic database, by sub-national bodies. These practices are interesting "side-effects" of the enhanced use of the principle of subsidiarity, which has fostered not only the development of relations between the EU and the Member States but also between regions themselves, even through informal channels (Toniatti, 2001, 927).

Over time, there have also been other forms of de facto "horizontal" integration of regions in EU affairs outside of the treaties.

As Weatherill (2005, 20) argues:

> More broadly these trends invite further reflection on how a simple hierarchical model of 'EU-State-regions' does not adequately capture the reality of complex cross-cutting alliances in Europe. And the more effective such associations are shown to be in driving forward regional interests the more one would wish to challenge the notion that the EU harms regional power. It may in fact provide an arena within which regions may go over their State's heads, individually (by opening offices in Brussels) or, probably more effectively, collectively, in so far as functionally comparable groups emerge.

In summary, the "horizontal activism" and functional activities found in some of the Italian regions seem to suggest that even if the "Europe of Regions" is far from a current reality, the "Europe with the Regions" is a factual reality of the EU's multitiered legal system.

VI. 2001–2021: what is the state of regional participation in EU affairs?

When the European dimension of Italian regions was constitutionalized in 2001, legal scholars were divided about the real impact of the new constitutional provisions. On the one side, part of the literature was quite sceptical, considering the constitutional amendment merely a (belated) ratification of something that already existed in practice, albeit regulated by ordinary law; on the other side, some scholars saw the new discipline as a decisive step, which heralded a new season for the importance of the regions in the EU.

Twenty years since the constitutional reform, the participation of Italian regions in Europe remains relatively weak, and the combined potential of the constitutional provisions and the Lisbon Treaty's focus on the regions has not been fully exploited.

Many reasons can be found for what could be defined as the "unaccomplished Europeanization of Italian regions." First, the situation in Italy described briefly above shows the regional dimension in the EU is still filtered by the national level, with few if any options available for their direct, non-mediated participation. In summary, even the most recent developments have demonstrated that "the Europe of regions is an attractive catch, but for the European Union the dominant legal and political paradigm remains a Europe of the States" (Weatherill, 2005, 2).

Second, the story of regional participation in EU processes shows how even constitutionalization is no guarantee of achieving effective participation. The constitutional provision gave the ordinary legislator the task to define the "*quantum*" of regional participation, leaving open several possible solutions. The implementation of the constitutional provision has not been able to establish a structured, efficient form of cooperation and integration between the national and regional levels.

Third, recent cases of Italian regionalism show the regions have suffered from a new centralism (Merloni, 2012, 786), at both national and supranational level, especially amid the economic crisis, which has led to a reduction of the autonomy of the sub-national entities in economic and social policies. The current health emergency is going to question the role of regions in the supranational sphere and it is an interesting field of research which could open up new opportunities and challenges for sub-national entities.

Despite Italy's shortcomings in relation to the Europeanization of the regions, focusing on functional integration leads to some interesting examples that show the regional dimension is key for the implementation of EU policies, even though the regional dimension in the EU appears to be quite faded.

The convergence of the EU federalizing process and the internal regionalization process in 2001, the so-called "double federal knot" (D'Atena, 1998, 1401), produced profound transformations in the exercise of power at all levels of governments. This redistribution of power needs to set procedures and rules to ensure the participation of all levels of governments in the decision-making process and the subsequent implementation of policy decisions. The Italian experience has proved to be quite ineffective in giving a voice to the regional level in the EU.

This "original sin" of the Italian approach to the "Europeanization" of the regions appears particularly problematic today, in the presence of profound structural changes in the EU as it faces crises that question its legitimacy and its future as a supranational integration project. In this context, then, today more than ever it is legitimate to ask whether there is still space for the regions in the EU (Pitruzzella, 2011, 1129) and if so, what should be their role in the future of EU integration.

Literature

Adele Anzon, 'La delimitazione delle competenze dell'Unione Europea' (2003) *Diritto pubblico* 787

Raffaele Bifulco, *La cooperazione dello Stato unitario composto. Le relazioni intergovernative di Belgio, Italia, Repubblica Federale di Germania e Spagna nell'Unione Europea* (CEDAM, 1995)

Angela K. Bourne, 'The Impact of European Integration on Regional Power' (2003) 41 (4) *Journal of Common Market Studies* 597

Fernando Bruno, *Stati membri e Unione Europea: il difficile cammino dell'integrazione* (Giappichelli, 2012)

Enzo Cannizzaro, 'Convenzione europea e Titolo V della Costituzione italiana: spunti critici', (2003) 8 *Il diritto dell'Unione Europea* 3–11

Paolo Caretti, 'La l. n. 234 del 2012 che disciplina la partecipazione dell'Italia alla formazione e all'attuazione della normativa e delle politiche dell'Unione Europea; un traguardo o ancora una tappa intermedia' (2012), 5-6 *Le Regioni* 837–844

Marta Cartabia and Lorenza Violini, 'Le norme generali sulla partecipazione dell'Italia al processo normativo dell'Unione Europea e sulle procedure di esecuzione degli obblighi comunitari. Commento alla legge 4 febbraio 2005, n. 11' (2005) 4 *Le Regioni* 475–512

Marta Cartabia and Joseph H.H. Weiler, *L'Italia in Europa. Profili istituzionali e costituzionali* (Il Mulino, 2000)

Lorenzo Chieffi, 'La nuova dimensione costituzionale del rapporto tra Regioni e Unione Europea' (2004) *Democrazia e Diritto* 87

Mario P. Chiti, 'Regioni e Unione europea dopo la riforma del Titolo V della Costituzione: l'influenza della giurisprudenza costituzionale' (2002) 6 *Le Regioni* 1401–1424

Bence Csizmadia, 'The European Grouping of Territorial Cooperation: An Innovative Advancement of Regional Cross-Border Governance but Still Far From Being a Panacea', European Diversity and Autonomy Papers, EDAP 01/2020

Adam Cygan, 'The Regions Within Multi-Level Governance: Enhanced Opportunities for Improved Accountability?' (2014) 21 (2) *The Maastricht Journal of European and Comparative Law* 265, 268

Antonio D'Atena (ed.), *Federalismo e regionalismo in Europa* (Giuffrè, 1994)

Antonio D'Atena, 'Il doppio intreccio federale: le Regioni nell'Unione europea' (1998) 6 *Le Regioni* 1401–1426

Antonio D'Atena (ed.), *L'Europa delle autonomie. Le Regioni e l'Unione Europea* (Giuffrè, 2003)

Enzo Di Salvatore, *L'identità costituzionale dell'Unione europea e degli Stati membri: il decentramento politico-istituzionale nel processo di integrazione* (Giappichelli, 2008)

Tiziana Fabbris and Francesca Michielin, 'The economy of the Italian regions: recent developments and responses to the economic crisis', in Eric Von Breska (ed.) Working

Paper – *A series of short papers on regional research and indicators produced by the Directorate-General for Regional Policy* (European Commission, Regional Policy, 2010)

Giandomenico Falcon, 'La "cittadinanza europea" delle Regioni' (2001) 2 *Le Regioni* 327–342

Valeria Fargion, Leonardo Morlino, and Stefania Profeti (eds.), *Europeizzazione e Rappresentanza Territoriale. Il caso Italiano* (Il Mulino, 2006)

Cristina Fasone, 'Le assemblee legislative regionali e i processi decisionali comunitari: un'analisi di diritto comparato' (2009) 3-4 *Le Istituzioni del Federalismo*

Cristina Fasone, 'Towards New Procedures between State and Regional Legislatures in Italy. Exploiting the Tool of the Early Warning Mechanism' (2013) *Perspectives on Federalism*

Francesca Fauri, *L'Italia e l'integrazione economica europea. 1947–2000* (Il Mulino, 2001)

Kevin Featherstone and Claudio M. Radaelli (eds.), *The Politics of Europeanization* (Oxford University Press, 2003)

Michèle Finck, 'Challenging the Subnational Dimension of Subsidiarity in EU Law' (2015) 8 *European Journal of Legal Studies*

Diane Fromage, 'Regional Parliaments and the Early Warning System: An Assessment Six Years after the Entry into Force of the Lisbon Treaty' (2016) Luiss School of Government, Working Paper Series, SOG-WP33

Tania Groppi, 'Regioni, Unione europea, obblighi internazionali', in Tania Groppi and Marco Olivetti (eds.), *La Repubblica delle autonomie. Regioni ed enti locali nel nuovo Titolo V* (Giappichelli, 2001) 139ff

Ran Hirschl, 'Secession and Nullification as a Global Trend' (2016) 2 *Constitutional Studies* 23–40

James Hughes, Gwendolyn Sasse, and Claire Gordon, 'Conditionality and Compliance in the EU's Eastward Enlargement: Regional Policy and the Reform of Sub-national Government' (2004) 42 (3) *Journal of Common Market Studies* 523–551

Antonio Iacoviello, 'La partecipazione delle autonomie territoriali alla fase ascendente del processo decisionale europeo: i modelli organizzativi delle Regioni italiane' (2018) *Diritti Regionali*

Hans Peter Ipsen, 'Als Bundesstaat in der Gemeinschaft', in Ernst von Caemmerer, Hans-Jürgen Schlochauer, and Ernst Steindorff (eds.) *Probleme des Europäischen Rechts. Festschrift für Walter Hallstein zu seinem 65. Geburtstag* (Vittorio Klostermann, 1966) 256

Giovanna Iurato, 'L'UE e la rappresentanza territoriale regionale' (2006) 4 *Le Regioni* 679–710

Martin Loughlin, *Foundations of Public Law* (Oxford University Press, 2001)

Nico Lupo, 'National and Regional Parliaments in the EU Decision-Making Process, after the Treaty of Lisbon and the Euro-Crisis' (2013) 5 (2) *Perspectives on Federalism*

Giuseppe Martinico 'The Impact of "Regional Blindness" on the Italian Regional State', in Elke Cloots, Geert De Baere, and Stefan Sottiaux (eds.), *Federalism in the European Union* (Hart Publishing, 2012) 362–380

Francesco Merloni, 'Alla ricerca di un nuovo senso per un regionalismo in crisi' (2012) 4 *Le Regioni* 783–790

Stefania Ninatti, 'La proiezione internazionale dell'autonomia regionale", in Lorenza Violini and Quirino Camerlengo (eds.), *Lineamenti di diritto costituzionale della Regione Lombardia* (Giappichelli, 2014) 307–333

Marco Olivetti, 'The Regions in the EU decision making processes', in Marta Cartabia, Nicola Lupo, and Andrea Simoncini (eds.), *Democracy and subsidiarity in the EU* (Il Mulino, 2013)

Francesco Palermo, *Il potere estero delle Regioni. Ricostruzione in chiave comparata di un potere interno alla Costituzione italiana* (CEDAM, 1999)

Francesco Palermo, 'The "New Nomos" of Cross-Border Cooperation', in Francesco Palermo, Giovanni Poggeschi, Guenther Rautz, and Jens Woelk (eds.), *Globalization, Technologies and Legal Revolution: The Impact of Global Changes on Territorial and Cultural Diversities, on Supranational Integration and Constitutional Theory* (Nomos, 2012) 71–91

Francesco Palermo and Sara Parolari (eds.), *Regional Dynamics in Central and Eastern Europe* (Brill, 2013)

Francesco Palermo and Alessandro Santini, 'From NUTS to Constitutional Regions: Addressing EU Regions in the EU Framework', in Roberto Toniatti, Francesco Palermo, and Marco Dani (eds.), *An Ever More Complex Union. The Regional Variable as a Missing Link in the EU Constitution?* (Nomos, 2004), 3–26

Cesare Pinelli, 'I limiti generali alla potestà legislativa statale e regionale e i rapporti con l'ordinamento internazionale e con l'ordinamento comunitario' (2001) 7-8 *Foro italiano* 194

Giovanni Pitruzzella, 'La crisi e l'Europa delle Regioni' (2011) 6 *Le Regioni* 1125–1130

Annamaria Poggi, 'Dove va il regionalismo in Europa?' (2018) 16 *Federalismi.it*. Available at https://www.federalismi.it/nv14/articolo-documento.cfm?Artid=36948

Anna Margherita Russo, 'I "Parlamenti regionali" nel Multilayered Parliamentary system europeo: le relazioni interparlamentari attraverso la "lente" del principio di sussidiarietà' (2019) 41 (4) *DPCE On Line*. Available at http://www.dpceonline.it/index.php/dpceonline/article/view/849

Mario Savino, 'Regioni e Unione europea: il mancato "aggiramento" dello Stato' (2007) 3–4 *Le Regioni* 433–472

Roberto Scarciglia (ed.), *Unione europea e autonomie regionali. Prospettive per una costituzione Europea* (Giappichelli, 2003)

Fritz Scharpf, *Governing in Europe. Effective and Democratic?* (Oxford University Press, 1999)

Vivien A. Schmidt, 'Democracy and Legitimacy in the European Union Revisited: Input, Output and "Throughput"' (2012) 61 (1) *Political Studies* 2–22

James Wesley Scott, 'Regional Policy: An Evolutionary Perspective', in Paul Craig and Gráinne de Búrca (eds.), *The Evolution of EU Law* (Oxford University Press, 1999) 639

Roberto Toniatti, 'Potere estero e politica economica delle Regioni: il nuovo assetto istituzionale e le ragioni dell'economia territoriale' (2001) 5 *Le Regioni* 917–942

Roberto Toniatti, Francesco Palermo, and Marco Dani (eds.), *An Ever More Complex Union. The Regional Variable as a Missing Link in the EU Constitution?* (Nomos Verlagsgesellschaft, 2004)

Lorenza Violini, 'Le Regioni italiane e l'Europa. Da Maastricht a Lisbona', in Stelio Mangiameli (ed.), *Il regionalismo italiano dall' Unità alla Costituzione e alla sua riforma* (Giuffrè, 2012) 463–528

Stephen Weatherill, 'The Challenge of the Regional Dimension in the European Union', in Stephen Weatherill and Ulf Bernitz (eds.), *The Role of Regions and Sub-National Actors in Europe* (Hart Publishing, 2005)

Joseph H. H. Weiler, 'Europe in Crisis—On "Political Messianism", "Legitimacy" and the "Rule of Law"' (2012) *Singapore Journal of Legal Studies* 248–268

Joseph H. H. Weiler, 'The Crumbling of European Democracy', in Mark A. Graber, Sanford Levinson, and Mark Tushnet (eds.), *Constitutional Democracy in Crisis?* (Oxford University Press, 2018) 629

8 Asymmetries in the Italian regional system and their role model

Francesco Palermo[1]

I. Introduction

The Italian regional system is not often referred to in comparative federal studies. The reason for this is not only the deliberate absence of any reference to federalism in the Italian constitution and its clear rejection in the case-law of the Constitutional Court,[2] but also and foremost the lack of a 'federal spirit' (Burgess 2012) in how the system operates and the limited 'culture of autonomy' in the political process (Toniatti 2018). Consequently, Italy is missing in the more traditional lists of federal or quasi-federal countries (see Watts 2008, 25), subjective as they might be. However, some institutional features of the Italian regional system are particularly relevant to the theory and practice of comparative federalism (Palermo and Kössler 2017, 6). This is the case, in particular, of asymmetry in constitutional status, institutions, powers, finances, and inter-governmental relations, making Italy one of the most differentiated countries in the world.

Asymmetry in Italy is not only *de facto*,[3] with the deep economic, political, social, cultural, geographic, historical, linguistic, and other differences among the various parts of a highly diverse country. It is also, and to a quite remarkable extent, *de jure*, with different rules as to most elements of governance. As asymmetry is becoming one of the most important features of contemporary federal systems (Tarlton 1965, Agranoff 1999, Council of Europe 2013, Sahadžić 2020), and Italy has not only the longest experience with it, but also a wide variety of reasons behind asymmetry, a lot can be learned and inferred from such experience when analysing federal phenomena.

This chapter explores the multidimensional, devolutionary asymmetry of Italian regionalism, both in terms of constitutional law and of powers transferred to (and

1 Full professor of comparative constitutional law, University of Verona and head of the Institute for comparative federalism, Eurac Research, Bolzano/Bozen.

2 See in particular judgment 365/2007, in which the Court adopts a very 'conservative' understanding of federalism, according to which federal countries are only those where a federal compact is stipulated by the constituent entities. Since this is not the case in Italy, as sovereignty is allocated in the Italian people and exercised primarily by the national Parliament, the country is not considered a federation. See Bartole 2007.

3 For the distinction between *de facto* (political) and *de jure* (legal) asymmetry see Watts 2008.

DOI: 10.4324/9781003104469-9

used by) the regions, with particular regard to the developments that took place after the constitutional reform of 2001. It starts by providing some essential information on the reasons behind asymmetry and on its evolution (II.), it then looks at the main instruments of constitutional (III.) as well as legislative, administrative, and financial asymmetry (IV.), and it concludes (V.) by showing the current trends and possible lessons that the Italian experience has to offer in this regard to the global debate on asymmetry in federal and regional systems.

II. Background and evolution of regional autonomy

Italy is a deeply diverse country, and regional diversity is not limited to the constitutional-legal framework. Widespread variations can be detected, inter alia, in geography,[4] in demographic factors,[5] in the economy,[6] in culture and identity, in the human capital,[7] as well as in the political landscape (Wilson in this volume). The enormous socio-economic divide between the northern and southern part of the country is just one out of many differential factors.

The drafters of the 1948 constitution were fully aware of such deep divides and at the same time they were afraid that reflecting them too much in the new constitutional framework could represent a threat for the national unity – which had yet to be achieved – and for the very territorial integrity of the country (Rolla 2015). Despite the prevailing reluctant attitude towards too strong a decentralization, the establishment of a strong sub-national level of government was inevitable in at least five areas: Trentino-Alto Adige/South Tyrol, Aosta Valley, Friuli-Venezia Giulia, Sicily, and Sardinia. In the case of Trentino-Alto Adige/South Tyrol it was inevitable, for Italy had to comply with the international obligations imposed by the Paris Peace Treaty (1947), which included the Gruber-De Gasperi Agreement (1946) on the protection of the German-speaking minority in

4 Geomorphological features differ significantly. Mountains form 100per cent of Trentino-South Tyrol but only 1.4 per cent of Apulia; flat areas cover around 50 per cent of Veneto, Lombardy, and Emilia-Romagna, but only the 23.2 per cent of the national territory.

5 Lombardy is the mostly populated region (>10 million inhabitants), while Aosta Valley is the smallest (<130,000). In size Lombardy is just the fourth region (<24,000 km2), while Sicily ranks first (around 26,000 km2) and Aosta Valley is the smallest (<3,300 km2). Discrepancy can be seen even in terms of population density, with a ratio ranging from Campania (427 inhabitants/km2) to Aosta Valley (39 inhabitants/km2).

6 The GDP per capita (nominal income) amounts on average to 36,000 euro in the Northwest and only to 19,000 euro in the South. On the other hand, the autonomous province of Bolzano (South Tyrol) is well above the average with 47,000 euro, while Calabria is last with 17,000 euro. Unemployment is on average 6.1 per cent in the North and 17.6 per cent in the South. Anyway, interesting exceptions to this pattern are represented by Basilicata in the South with a rate of 10.8 per cent, and Liguria in the North with 9.6 per cent. At either end of the territorial ranking are South Tyrol with 2.9 per cent and Calabria with 21.6 per cent; data from 2018 (ISTAT 2020).

7 See the big differences in performance by high school students in nationwide evaluations 2019: https://invalsi-areaprove.cineca.it/docs/2019/Rapporto_prove_INVALSI_2019.pdf.

South Tyrol, which was attributed a high degree of autonomy (Woelk, Palermo, and Marko eds., 2008). As for the other regions, threats of possible secession made the establishment of a sub-national level of government seem ever more pressing: Aosta Valley formalized in 1943 a proposal for greater autonomy, and Sicily drew in 1946 a constitution for a possible independent state, later adapted in 1948 as a special statute of autonomy (*statuto di autonomia*) under the new constitution. Furthermore, geographical remoteness had to be taken into account for the island of Sardinia, while special treatment for Friuli-Venezia Giulia was the result of its location at the border with the Iron Curtain and of the international regime for the area of Trieste until 1954, rather than of the presence of the Slovene minority.

Against this background, the republican constitution of 1948 provided for an innovative experiment with regionalization. Five – out of twenty – regions were provided with a 'special' status:[8] three in the Alpine arch in the North, inhabited by sizeable minority groups and all situated in the periphery (Aosta Valley, Trentino-South Tyrol – consisting of the autonomous provinces of Trento and Bolzano/Bozen[9] – and Friuli-Venezia Giulia), and the two main islands (Sicily and Sardinia). Each special region has a different system of powers due to bilateral negotiations with the central authority, which is guaranteed by a 'special statute', a basic law which has the rank of a national constitutional law. At the same time, the regionalization of the whole country, with the establishment of 'ordinary' regions, was supposed to avoid too strong an asymmetry between the five special regions and the rest of the territory, and to experiment with a 'third way' between a federal and a unitary system (Arban in this volume).

However, the early establishment of the 15 ordinary regions failed[10] and for at least 20 years regionalism was implemented in the special regions only. Ordinary

8 Terminology is telling of the understanding of autonomy by the drafters of the constitution. Article 116 Const. stipulates that "Friuli-Venezia Giulia, Sardinia, Sicily, Trentino-Alto Adige/*Südtirol* and Valle d'Aosta/*Vallée d'Aoste* enjoy special forms and conditions of autonomy pursuant to their respective special statutes adopted by constitutional law". While covering 25 per cent of the regions and over 20 per cent of the territory, these regions are considered 'exceptional'.

9 The two autonomous provinces are comparable to a special region as to their competence catalogue, and the region has no significant powers left.

10 The reasons were especially political in nature. The two main parties in the constitutional assembly which drafted the constitution in 1946–47 (the Christian-Democratic Party and the Italian Communist Party) had opposite views on regionalization: the Christian-Democrats, inspired by the social doctrine of the Catholic Church, advocated the principle of subsidiarity and promoted (moderate) decentralization; the Communists firmly opposed decentralization as a principle at odds with democratic centralism. The compromise produced a modest regionalization. However, just after the elections in 1948, when the Christian-Democrats won the majority and formed a government with the liberals pushing the Communists in the opposition, the attitude towards decentralization radically changed for political opportunism: the Christian-Democrats, ruling in Rome, opposed decentralization in order to preserve their power, and the Communists supported it for exactly the same reasons, as they were in the opposition in Rome but very strong in some parts of the country. Ordinary regions were set up

regions were established as late as in the 1970s. Since then, a permanent increase in the regional powers gradually narrowed the gap between ordinary and special regions. The path has been all but straightforward and coherent, influenced by shifting political priorities and very much determined by constitutional adjudication: as there still is no effective institutional representation of regional interests at central level, progress could often be achieved only through litigation by challenging national legislation before the Constitutional Court (Delledonne in this volume). These conflicts and a jurisdiction underlining the necessity of cooperation and consultation led to the gradual emancipation of ordinary regions and to the establishment of instruments aimed at improving intergovernmental cooperation (Ceccherini and Woelk in this volume).

In the 1990s, important legislative reforms have been adopted, especially on the pressure from the more active ordinary regions to develop their potential for self-government and thus increasing asymmetry in the exercise of autonomous powers. The political demand for more self-government became an absolute priority for the rich and industrialized northern regions and at the same time for the government in Rome. Also due to pressures by a federalist, and on occasions secessionist, political party, the issue of federal reform had to be dealt with politically and in more comprehensive and symbolic terms, thus requiring a constitutional reform (Fasone and Piccirilli in this volume). In 1999 and 2001, two major constitutional amendments were approved that considerably increased the autonomy of ordinary regions, with the political aim of reducing institutional disparities between special and ordinary regions, offering the latter powers similar to those enjoyed by the former. The two-track asymmetry – ordinary and special regions – is confirmed, though the distribution of legislative and administrative powers between the central authority and the sub-national entities has been substantially reviewed.

III. Constitutional asymmetries and their instruments

A. Special regions

While the constitutional reforms in 1999 and 2001 significantly reduced disparities between special and ordinary regions in terms of legislative powers, profound differences remain between the two types of regions. Four institutional (*de jure*) elements are particularly relevant: the rank of the statute of autonomy, the extent of legislative and administrative powers, the financial regime, and the intergovernmental relations. The varied implementation of these features among the special regions has not only increased the differences between special and ordinary regions, but also those among each special region.

The *statute of autonomy* is the basic law that outlines the structural elements of each region. The statutes of autonomy of special regions are adopted by the

only in 1970, when a center-left coalition was built (Christian-Democrats and the Italian Socialist Party) and some form of political cooperation with the Communist Party was started.

national parliament by constitutional law (article 116.1 of the constitution),[11] while those of ordinary regions are adopted by regional assemblies by a special procedure (art. 123.2 const.).[12] The entrenched process for the approval of autonomy statutes of special regions makes it harder to amend them. Thus, on the one hand, the special autonomy is more securely guaranteed, being regarded as a fundamental constitutional principle (D'Atena 2014, 10); on the other hand, such a strong guarantee can turn into a 'golden cage', making it highly difficult to update the statutes.[13] The only exception consists in the financial provisions, which may be amended by an ordinary national law, after an agreement between the central and the regional executives.[14] This procedure reflects the essence of the principle of bilateral cooperation, ensuring the parity of the parties involved during the negotiations. By no means can the central authority unilaterally revise the statute provisions regulating the financing regimes, as financial intergovernmental relations with special regions can only be defined bilaterally. At the same time, the approval of the financial agreement by the national parliament is meant to guarantee its sovereignty in budgetary affairs.

Under the constitutional framework prior to the 2001 reform, the special regions were entitled to much broader *legislative and administrative powers* than the ordinary regions. While the latter could legislate in a limited number of subjects, listed under article 117 of the constitution, and only within the framework outlined by a national law, the special regions had much broader jurisdiction, with their powers being listed in their respective statutes of autonomy and, in most cases, they could legislate without requiring prior state intervention. As of 2001, ordinary regions enjoy a quite similar legislative power, as the previous limitations were removed. The sources of law underlying the two types of regions, however, remain different: while the constitution outlines the rules for the distribution of powers between the centre and the ordinary regions, the powers of the special regions are laid down in both the constitution and each individual statute of

11 The process to adopt constitutional laws is laid down in article 138 const. It requires two votes by each of the two chambers of parliament, both by absolute majority of the members with an interval of at least three months. If in the second vote a two-thirds majority is reached, no referendum can take place. If only the absolute majority is in favour in the second reading, a nationwide referendum can take place.

12 Absolute majority of the members in two votes to be expressed with an interval of at least two months and possible confirmative referendum upon request of one-fiftieth of the voters in the region or one-fifth of the members of the regional assembly.

13 This is confirmed by the fact that none of the special statutes has been significantly amended since their adoption, with the exception of that of Trentino-Alto Adige/South Tyrol, which was extensively modified in 1972 following a long and complex agreement with the German speaking minority in Alto Adige/South Tyrol, resulting in the abolition in fact (but not formally) of the region and the transfer of nearly all legislative and administrative powers to the two autonomous provinces of Trento and Bolzano/Bozen. Conversely, the statutes of ordinary regions, all adopted in the 1970s, have all been replaced by new ones between 2002 and 2012. Attempts to reform the statutes of special regions after the constitutional reform from 2001 have been made but all failed so far.

14 This holds true in all special regions, with the partial exception of Sicily.

autonomy, thus making the framework rather complex and even contradictory at times, often requiring the final say by the Constitutional Court. In addition, competences from the national level can be transferred or delegated to special regions, either by law or, more frequently, by means of enactment decrees.[15]

As to *finances*, each special region has a different agreement with the centre, mostly regulated in its respective autonomy statute. In general, financial arrangements are quite generous towards the special regions compared to the others, although after the adoption of strict austerity measures as of 2010 the picture is more nuanced (Valdesalici in this volume).

Finally, one characteristic common to all special regions – perhaps the most important from an institutional standpoint – is that they may *negotiate* with the state, bilaterally and on equal footing, the development of their autonomy regime. For each special region a joint body (*commissione paritetica*) is established based on the principle of parity, that is with an equal number of representatives of the central government and of the region concerned.[16] The members are appointed half by the national government and half by the region, with different rules in each region as to the role of regional governments and parliaments in designating their members. The joint committees follow procedures resembling negotiations in the field of international relations: either there is consensus among the parties, or no agreement is reached. Put differently, the relationship between the central authority and the special regions is not based on hierarchy but on equality. These bodies draft the bylaws (*norme di attuazione*), implementing provisions of the respective autonomy statutes, which are submitted to the national government and approved in form of governmental decrees (Cosulich 2017). Joint committees are formally designed as consultative bodies of the national government, which means that they can be renewed each time the government changes, but they can substantially be considered as quasi-legislative organs, as the government is not allowed to unilaterally amend the drafted decree.[17]

The binding force of enactment decrees is superior to that of parliamentary statutes. According to the constitution, regular governmental decrees have the same force as the laws of parliament (article 77). This means that a subsequent law of parliament can abolish or amend a governmental decree and vice versa (*lex posterior derogat priori*). However, where the enactment decrees for the implementation of the autonomy statutes are concerned, they cannot be amended by a subsequent law of parliament. In simple words, enactment decrees enjoy a position higher than the ordinary laws of parliament and thus hold a status that is in between an ordinary law and a constitutional law.[18]

15 On the enactment decrees see below. Where this opportunity has more consistently been used is in Trentino and South Tyrol (in the latter even more), which have been granted jurisdiction, for example in the fields of land register, invalidity pensions, vehicle registration authority, energy, personnel of the Courts, shop opening times, and many others.
16 Aosta Valley wasn't entitled to use these instruments – at least formally – until 1993.
17 Constitutional Court, ruling no. 37/1989.
18 See Constitutional Court, judgements No. 20/1956, 22/1961, 151/1972, 180/1980, 237/1983, 212/1984, and 160/1985.

The rationale is to put state and special regions on an equal footing in negotiations. If a law of parliament could trump a piece of legislation negotiated bilaterally by the same number of representatives of the state and of the special region, the whole system would be impaired and, in sum, senseless. This is why, when it comes to the relations between the national level and the special regions (as well as to the protection of minority groups by means of special territorial autonomy, where relevant), the principle of democratic legitimacy is limited by the principle of parity. In fact, several aspects raise issues of compatibility with the democratic principle. It can be surprising, for instance, that decrees adopted by small, unelected bodies, in an untransparent manner (no public records exist of the work of the committees) and enacted by the government prevail over the laws of parliament. As the Constitutional Court noted, however, such derogation is justified by the constitutional requirement of protecting the special regions in the process of implementation of their autonomy statutes, that are constitutional laws of the state. And it is not by chance that the court never struck down an implementing decree, affirming that the peculiar, bilateral procedure for its approval is per se the guarantee of a joint will, which is enough to presume that this is respectful of the constitution.[19]

As to the scope, almost all the relevant contents of the autonomy statutes can be regulated by enactment decrees.[20] Originally, they were supposed to achieve two fundamental aims: on the one hand, the transfer of administrative functions from the state to the special regions (including finances and human resources); on the other hand, the adoption of detailed provisions in issues regulated in a general fashion by the autonomy statute.[21] However, given the privileged position of this kind of provision, the enactment decrees have been used by some special regions beyond the 'mere' implementation of the autonomy statutes. Some measures provide, for instance, the transfer of new competences beyond the division of legislative and administrative powers laid down in the autonomy statute or even substantially change the provisions of the autonomy statutes.[22] As a matter of fact, they have evolved from an instrument of implementation of the statute into an ordinary instrument of government. According to the constitutional jurisprudence these sources of law can 'integrate' the provisions of the statue of autonomy, provided that they do not betray the aim the statute is grounded upon.[23]

19 Judgement No. 213/1998.

20 As to the financial relations with the state, they are generally regulated by both enactment decrees and special laws of the Parliament. The latter require the consent of both the state and the special autonomy. Also in these laws, thus, the principle of parity clearly comes to the fore.

21 For example, regarding South Tyrol, practical rules on issues like the ethnic quota system in the administration, the use of languages, the school system, the census of language groups, etc., are to be found in enactment decrees.

22 This was the case, for example, for the enactment decree on the administrative court for South Tyrol, which provides for an entirely political appointment of judges, contrary to the general rule which would impose a selection based on merit (DPR 426/1984).

23 See Constitutional Court, judgements no. 20/1956, 212/1984, 341/2001.

Although in some areas the enactment decrees were probably abused, this instrument has proven to be the key to the establishment of a sound and legally guaranteed system of rules on delicate aspects of the autonomy regime, where it has been correctly exploited. Not all the regions have made the same use of the joint committees: as of summer 2020, the adopted enactment decrees for Trentino-South Tyrol were 189, almost 5 times those for Sicily and Sardinia (41 and 42) and 3 times more than for Aosta Valley (62 acts so far).[24]

All this confirms that in practice asymmetry is a feature characteristic not only of the relationship between special and ordinary regions, but also among the special regions themselves. After all, big differences equally exist among the ordinary regions, with very different degrees of development of self-government, of economic performance, and of political as well as administrative capacity (for the links between economic development and use of autonomy see Trigilia 2001).

B. Ordinary and (potentially) differentiated regions

With regard to the ordinary regions, the constitutional amendments of 1999 and 2001 provided for a relevant change of their status. In 1999, the direct election of the regional president was introduced (the only case in Europe), in order to enhance political stability (Fusaro 2004). It also strengthened their constitutional autonomy, as the basic laws of the ordinary regions are now adopted by the regions themselves – and no longer eventually approved by the national parliament as before.

The reform of 2001 completely reshaped the relations between the centre and the ordinary regions. The equality of all component units of the 'Republic' (state, regions, provinces, municipalities) was introduced, expressing the idea of (functional) 'spheres' rather than (hierarchical) levels of government. Most importantly, the reform drastically changed the distribution of legislative and administrative powers between state and regions. The constitution (article 117) now lists all legislative powers of the state as well as the fields of concurrent legislation (i.e. those in which regions can legislate only within the framework of general guidelines determined by a national law). Residual powers now lie with the regions, according to classic federal schemes. Administrative powers are no longer connected with the power to legislate, but distributed in a flexible manner according to the criteria of 'subsidiarity, differentiation and proportionality' (article 118). Financial autonomy of sub-national entities is enhanced (article 119) and regions have to establish a consultative body for the representation of local authorities within their territory (article 123.4). The elimination of preventive national control (before the reform, all regional laws had to be approved by the government before entering into force) marks the (formally) equal rank of regional and national legislation.

24 The number of implementing decrees approved greatly depends on the political climate between the concerned region and the national government: during the 1996–2001 legislative period, 27 bylaws were issued for Trentino- South Tyrol, 9 for Friuli-Venezia-Giulia, 8 for Aosta Valley, 6 for Sardinia and 4 for Sicily.

Moreover, the reform of 2001 provided for another form of constitutional asymmetry, taking into account the strong factual, economic, and political asymmetry among the ordinary regions. While keeping the basic distinction between ordinary and special regions, the constitution allows for further differentiation among the ordinary regions, based on the same principle of negotiation that informs the special regions. Those ordinary regions that fulfil certain budget criteria – the ones in the North are generally more interested in this opportunity due to their financial capacity – can negotiate with the national government the transfer of legislative competence up to 23 subject matters, most of them very significant,[25] and this agreement has to be approved by absolute majority in the national parliament (article 116.3). This provision introduces an additional layer of constitutional asymmetry covering significant areas, like education, environment, energy and transport. While so far no such agreement could be reached, Emilia-Romagna, Veneto, and Lombardy are in the process of completing negotiations, the last two after receiving a strong political mandate by regional referenda held in 2017[26] (Piccirilli 2018). Seven more ordinary regions have formally mandated their President to start the negotiations[27] and three have started initiatives in the same direction,[28] so that only two regions have not taken any action.[29] If this process will be concluded, the asymmetrical features of Italian regionalism will further increase.

It must be noted, however, that this process has been and still is confronted with enormous resistance, in some political circles and, above all, by several intellectuals, especially from the South, who consider the *de jure* differentiation among the ordinary regions a threat to national unity and solidarity as the equalizing role of the state would be reduced (Viesti 2019). Such reaction is indicative of the overall dominant attitude in the country vis-à-vis asymmetry (which is to be at best tolerated but possibly limited, covering up with formal equality the immense differences that exist in practice) and ultimately vis-à-vis autonomy as a whole, as autonomy means differentiation and the same rule for all is the opposite of autonomy (Bin 2016).

From a systematic point of view, a structural difference between 'special' and 'differentiated' autonomy will remain. While in both cases the degree of regional

25 They include, inter alia, education, security on workplace, disaster management, part of the pensions, research, airports, energy management, transport and navigation networks, environmental protection, cultural heritage, and others.

26 In Veneto, support for more autonomy in the referendum was a landslide 98.1 per cent of the votes cast (57.2 per cent turnout); in Lombardy 95.3 per cent (but turnout 38.3 per cent). In Emilia-Romagna no referendum was held. The three regions signed preliminary agreements in 2018; after the 2018 elections, negotiations restarted with the new government. After some stop and go, the government drafted a general bill on regional differentiation in 2019, whose discussion has been postponed due to the coronavirus emergency.

27 Campania, Liguria, Lazio, Marche, Piedmont, Tuscany, and Umbria.

28 Approving motions, resolutions, or recommendations; this is the case of Basilicata, Calabria, and Apulia.

29 Abruzzo and Molise.

autonomy is negotiated, only for special regions negotiation is based on parity and amounts to a fundamental principle of the constitutional order, whereas 'differentiated' ordinary regions negotiate based on the principle of loyal cooperation[30] (Woelk in this volume) but not on equal footing. And in fact, while special status is irrevocable (as a principle, not necessarily in all its manifestations), differentiation based on article 116.3 const. can be revoked unilaterally by the national legislator.

IV. Legislative, administrative, and financial asymmetry

As mentioned above, the 2001 constitutional reform provided the ordinary regions with much broader legislative and administrative powers than before, elevating them to a level quite similar to that of the special regions with regard to the scope of their legislative power. Yet, the sources of law underlying these two types of regions remain different: legislative powers of special regions are not regulated by the national constitution in the first place, but by their autonomy statutes, i.e. by national constitutional laws. However, where the 2001 reform has provided ordinary regions with a greater degree of autonomy, this automatically extends to special regions too, as long as their statutes are not updated (article 10, const. law no. 3/2001).[31]

Asymmetry results also from autonomous legislative choices by each region. In some case, the scope of such choice and graduation might depend on the nature (special or ordinary) of the regions, for example in the electoral legislation (Trucco and Bailo 2020). The special regions may regulate their system of government and the electoral rules in the so called 'statutory laws', that are regional laws adopted following a reinforced procedure and thus having a stronger binding force than regular regional laws. These laws have to comply with the constitution and must respect the fundamental principles of the legal system (including those set by national legislation). Ordinary regions can also choose their system of government (in the respective statute of autonomy), provided that the fundamental principles laid down in the national legislation are respected,[32] and can adopt their own

30 As confirmed by the department for legal affairs of the national government in an opinion issued on 19 June 2019.

31 In practice, there have been no significant cases of competences attributed to the ordinary regions that special regions did not have and that they therefore claimed. No single Constitutional Court ruling dealt with such case. However, this clause is systematically relevant since the reform established a powerful residual powers rule, establishing that regions (all of them) retain the residual legislative power in all subjects not specifically attributed to the exclusive competence of the central authority or to the shared competence (art. 117.4 Const.).

32 Some regions have tested the limits of such fundamental principles especially by trying to circumvent the national rule that allows the regions to opt either for a quasi-presidential system (popular election of the regional president and new elections if he/she is dismissed by the regional assembly) or for a parliamentary system (president elected by the assembly, that can freely dismiss him/her). In the case of Calabria, which tried to go for a middle-way between the two (the assembly could dismiss the president and

electoral laws, within the limits of a national framework law.[33] Consequently, very different electoral and institutional systems exist in the regions. In South Tyrol – a consociational, ethnic, proportional democracy – and in Aosta Valley there is a parliamentary system, with the executive elected by the regional Parliament. In all other (ordinary and special) regions, including Trentino governed by the same statute as South Tyrol, the system is presidential, i.e. the regional President is directly elected within a majoritarian, bipolar, competitive democracy. All ordinary regions except two have so far adopted their own electoral laws and quite remarkable differences exist despite the limits imposed by the national legislation (Camera dei Deputati 2020).

A wide-ranging regional asymmetry can be found with regard to the scope of administrative autonomy. The rules determining administrative competence after the reform from 2001 are different between special and ordinary regions. The principle of parallelism still applies to the former, i.e. the special regions hold administrative competence in the subject-matters they are attributed legislative power; in practice, they either (and more frequently) delegate it to local entities, or implement it directly making use of their offices. In ordinary regions, instead, administrative functions are vested in principle with the municipalities, except when larger entities (provinces/metropolitan cities, regions, or the state) better guarantee their exercise based on the principles of "subsidiarity, differentiation and appropriateness" (article 118.1 const. – Martinico in this volume). This means, in practice, that administrative functions are not assigned by the constitution – that only determines the criteria for their distribution – but by the national and the regional legislation (Carli 2018, 112). This means, in turn, that the same administrative function is not carried out by the same level of government in all regions, and that the degree of asymmetry in this area is, at least potentially, quite strong.

Asymmetry is very significant also with regard to financial autonomy. While both ordinary and special regions enjoy financial autonomy both on spending and revenue, the differences in quantitative and qualitative terms are huge, not only between the two categories of regions,[34] but also, in particular, among the special regions[35] (Valdesalici in this volume). These as well as the structural, procedural,

---

replace him/her by the vice president), the Constitutional Court struck down the regional provision (judgement 2/2004).

33 Law 165/2004.

34 The financing system of ordinary regions is rooted in the constitution (article 119) and most implementing regulation have been adopted between 2009 and 2011 by the national legislature. Financing is mainly tax-revenue linked to the territorial fiscal capacity. Special regions enjoy a wider autonomy within a financial regime set forth by the respective autonomy statute, whose specific regulations have to be agreed between each entity and the central authority in bilateral negotiations.

35 Most revenues for special regions come from a share of national taxes referable to the regional territory, but remarkable differences exist as to the sharing percentage, which varies from 30 per cent (Friuli-Venezia Giulia) to 90 per cent (Trentino-South Tyrol and Aosta Valley). Also the criteria for distribution are different. Furthermore, Sicily has a different mechanism of accounting, according to which tax-revenue coming from sharing schemes are accounted for own-taxes.

and numerical differences between and among the regions remain,[36] despite the austerity measures introduced by the national government in the aftermath of the financial crisis between 2008 and 2012 which have overall reduced regional financial autonomy for both categories of regions.[37] A number of further smaller asymmetric features also exist. For example, while special regions are in charge of their local government, in ordinary regions local government is mostly regulated by national legislation (Longo in this volume), and the capital city of Rome enjoys a further special regime different to that of any other city (article 114.3 const.; Orso 2020).

V. Concluding remarks: trends of asymmetry in theory and practice

Borrowing from Friedrich (1968), asymmetry, like other manifestations of federalism in broader sense, is a process. In the Italian context, this process is unfolding in waves, with regard to both the institutional and the political dimension.

Institutionally, the establishment of forms of asymmetry has normally been counteracted by more symmetric trends. This first happened in the very drafting process of the constitution, when ordinary regions were created primarily in order to limit the centrifugal dynamic of the special regions. In the early 1970s, when ordinary regions were eventually set up, a big step towards asymmetry was made in Trentino-South Tyrol, by de facto dismantling the region and creating a unique institutional configuration, with two autonomous provinces quite different from one another under the same statute of autonomy. The gradual emancipation of ordinary regions led to the constitutional reform in 2001, which aimed at reducing the gap between the two categories of regions. At the same time, the reform opened up to a further layer of differentiation, by allowing ordinary regions to take up additional powers in significant areas. While the attempts to do so were frustrated by limited implementation of the constitutional provisions, all ordinary regions were able to adopt their new autonomy statutes and so to strengthen their autonomy and ~~to~~ experiment with more differentiation. This was not the case for the special regions, whose statutes of autonomy remain old, as they do not take into account the constitutional reform of 2001 and are hence becoming obsolete in a number of areas, with overall negative consequences for their asymmetric potential. In parallel, two main constitutional reform projects, one aiming at increasing regional autonomy (2006) and the other at curtailing it (2016), have been rejected by popular vote after having been passed in Parliament.[38] In the

36 The Constitutional Court ruled that the national power to trump regional competences in time of emergency cannot circumvent the conventional principle underlying the relationships between the central authority and the special regions (judgements no. 182/2011, 262/2012, 104/2013, 229/2013, 19/2014, 26/2014).

37 According to the Constitutional Court, (economic) emergency justifies the action by the national government going beyond the formal allocation of powers (inter alia judgment no. 10/2010).

38 During the third government led by Silvio Berlusconi (2005–2006), a far-reaching constitutional amendment to overcome the reform of 2001 was presented, concerning

meantime, austerity measures after the economic crisis limited the margin of autonomy of both ordinary and special regions altogether, although with quite different impact on each region. Finally, when the process leading to differentiation among ordinary regions was almost completed, a change in government (2019) and the emergency prompted by the outbreak of the coronavirus pandemic (2020) stalled the process again.

Politically and practically, the attitude towards asymmetric autonomy has also been swinging. Some special regions abandoned quite early their 'autonomist consciousness': in particular, Sicily and Sardinia concentrated more on the creation of political ties with the central government and on benefiting from the considerable financial aids granted by the central authority rather than on taking advantage of the potential of their institutional autonomy. During the 1990s, autonomy and differentiation became popular and politically viable, up until the constitutional reform in 2001. Over the past 20 years, autonomy lost its political appeal: some scandals at regional level lowered support for regional autonomy, the budget cuts after the economic crisis made it even less popular, and overall the discourse about unity and solidarity dominates the political debate. Not least, the party that was campaigning for autonomy and differentiation (*Lega*, formerly *Lega Nord*) changed its political priorities and became a national/nationalistic rather than federalist party. The effects of the corona crisis are still to be evaluated, as on the one hand the calls against regional differentiation especially in health care became loud, but on the other hand the necessity of a differentiated approach to a very different impact of the virus in the various regions became evident, and the political role of some regional presidents during the crisis grew immensely (Delledonne and Padula 2020).

The pendulum is constantly shifting and so is the relevance of asymmetry in practice. Some trends, however, remain the same. The *first* is the overall growing degree of institutional and political asymmetry, despite several attempts to limit it. This is due to the mounting difference among the regions, which in one way or another finds avenues to be reflected, at least in part, in the institutional structure and, much more, in the management of policies. Paradoxically, the more the prevailing political discourse calls for unity, solidarity, and formal equality among the territories, the more the differentiation grows in practice. Differentiation does not necessarily mean more autonomy, it can also mean less. For example, the trajectory of the special regions shows that some have increased their autonomy over time, while in others it became less. Friuli-Venezia Giulia was created as late as

53 articles of the whole constitution and was finally adopted by the center-right coalition's majority in parliament in November 2005. However, its entry into force was prevented by a popular vote (61 per cent against) in a referendum held in June 2006. A second attempt was made during the government by Matteo Renzi (2014–2016). The proposal aimed at designing a different Senate in terms of composition, powers, and representation. Under the proposed reform, the Senate would have lost almost all its power; the senators would have no longer been elected directly but would have been selected by regional assemblies. Also in this case, a referendum was called in 2016 and rejected the reform (59 per cent against).

1963, only after the international monitoring phase of Trieste ended, and from the beginning had a narrower scope of autonomy compared to the other special regions, starting from the financial endowment. Sicily and Sardinia currently enjoy a degree of autonomy that resembles much more those of ordinary regions than those of other special ones. Thus, in practice, the only truly special regions are the two small alpine areas inhabited by sizeable minorities, Trentino-South Tyrol and Aosta Valley (Bin 2002), representing together less than 3 per cent of the Italian population and less than 4 per cent of the national territory. In fact, differences among special regions are so significant that it is questionable whether one can consider special autonomies as belonging to one single category or rather each special region as a case per se (Palermo and Parolari 2018). Furthermore, the likely start of the process of formal differentiation of the ordinary regions will further increase the degree of asymmetry in the Italian regional system.

The *second* common trend is the inevitable push for asymmetry that derives from an ineffective model of multilateral intergovernmental relations (Ceccherini in this volume). The Senate has not been designed as a territorial second chamber, and the numerous attempts and proposals to make it such not only failed (such as in the referenda in 2006 and 2016), but are also in vain (Ruggiu 2006). In fact, comparative analysis clearly shows that territorial second chambers are currently unfit to properly represent territorial interests, due to the inevitable prevalence of the political dimension, and this happens even in the case of the German *Bundesrat*, which is the only 'non-parliamentary' body in which the subnational governments are represented and vote as such and upon instruction by the respective governments (Palermo 2018). Therefore, alternative, executive bodies based on cooperation are established and are blooming everywhere, doing what second chambers are not able to do, i.e. negotiate issues of subnational interest with the national interlocutor, at the level where political power is allocated: the executive. In Italy, this task is performed by the conferences, notably the State-Regions Conference', but this also proves to be ineffective. It guarantees a formal consultation when regional interests are affected, but it lacks real decision-making power. Furthermore, even if it had more power, it remains structurally unfit to accommodate claims by individual regions, being a collective body working according to the majority principle. Whenever cooperative forms are not (perceived as) sufficient, or when certain territories present a strong (minority) identity or other factors that make them different from the rest of the country, multilateral fora are normally unfit to fulfil their claims for differential treatment. This is why in Italy, regions (especially those that are stronger in political or other terms) pursue bilateral forms of negotiation with the national level: the less effective the multilateral instruments or the more adversarial the political relations between individual regions and the center, the more bilateral channels are pursued and the multilateral ones ignored or bypassed. Joint committees in place for special regions and similar mechanisms that will be established for differentiated ordinary regions are and will be used to a growing extent, thus further enhancing bilateralism and the following asymmetry.

The *third* trend could be called the asymmetric development of asymmetry, or the shifting pendulum of asymmetry. Over 70 years, and even more over the past

20 years following the constitutional reform of 2001, the constitutional picture has become more complex and more asymmetric. The multidimensional constitutional asymmetry in Italy includes several categories of regions: the special ones (each one with a very different degree of autonomy in terms of form of government, distribution and use of legislative and administrative competences, and financial arrangements); the ordinary ones negotiating additional legislative powers with the central government, and the remaining ordinary regions.

Since 2001, a quasi-federal constitutional structure coexists with a weak federal culture and the pendulum oscillates wildly between (symmetric) centralization and (asymmetric) decentralization. Such oscillations have relatively little to do with the constitutional framework and much more with the political attitude[39] and the case-law of the Constitutional Court, which is the real umpire of asymmetry in practice: overall, devolution of powers and asymmetry have been very much supported by the Court before the 2001 reform, and were since then overall discouraged by the same Court. More recently, the pendulum of asymmetric regionalism has been put into motion again, right after the failure of a constitutional reform that intended to reduce the overall scope of regional autonomy, especially through the strong popular support for the initiatives of the northern regions to achieve differentiated degrees of autonomy.

In any case, asymmetry has been from the outset and continues to be the main feature of Italian regionalism, the only one making it possible to accommodate such a great deal of diversity within a common framework, in a difficult and never stable search for a new balance. Given the growing diversity and claims for its recognition in most countries of the world, a closer look at Italy's overall successful experience with asymmetric regionalism is highly advisable.

Literature

Robert Agranoff (ed.), *Accommodating Diversity: Asymmetry in Federal State* (Nomos, 1999)

Sergio Bartole, 'La Corte costituzionale chiude al "federalismo" dal basso' (2007) 6 *Giurisprudenza costituzionale* 4039

Roberto Bin, 'L'autonomia e i rapporti tra esecutivo, legislativo e le commissioni paritetiche', in Andrea Di Michele, Francesco Palermo, and Günther Pallaver (eds.), *1992: Fine di un conflitto. Dieci anni dalla chiusura della vicenda sudtirolese* (Il Mulino, 2002) 205

Roberto Bin, 'Chi ha paura delle autonomie?', in *Scritti in ricordo di Paolo Cavaleri* (ESI, 2016) 52

Michael Burgess, *In Search of the Federal Spirit* (Oxford Univ. Press, 2012)

Camera dei Deputati (Servizio Studi), 'Le leggi elettorali regionali. Quadro di sintesi', 3 August, n. 109 (2020), http://documenti.camera.it/leg18/dossier/pdf/AC0365.pdf?_1592119803131

Massimo Carli, *Diritto regionale* (Giappichelli, 2018)

Matteo Cosulich, *Il decreto legislativo di attuazione statutaria nelle regioni ad autonomia speciale* (Editoriale Scientifica, 2017)

39 The reform of 2001 was scarcely implemented also because several regions did not make use of the opportunities provided by the new constitutional framework and just some were proactive.

Council of Europe, Congress of Local and Regional Authorities, 'Regions and Territories with Special Status in Europe', Resolution and Study, CPR(25)2 (2013)

Antonio D'Atena, 'Passato, presente… e futuro delle autonomie regionali speciali' (2014) 4 *Rivista AIC*, https://www.rivistaaic.it/it/rivista/ultimi-contributi-pubblicati/antonio-d-atena/passato-presente-e-futuro-delle-autonomie-regionali-speciali

Giacomo Delledonne and Carlo Padula, 'Accentramento e differenziazione nella gestione dell'emergenza pandemica' (2020) 4 *Le Regioni* 753

Carl J. Friedrich, *Trends of Federalism in Theory and Practice* (Praeger, 1968)

Carlo Fusaro, 'La forma di governo regionale: pregi e difetti di una soluzione che funziona', in Stefano Ceccanti and Salvatore Vassallo (eds.), *Come chiudere la transizione* (Il Mulino, 2004) 167

ISTAT, 'Conti economici territoriali, 2016–2018' (2020), https://www.istat.it/it/files//2020/01/Conti-economici-territoriali.pdf

Federico Orso, 'Per il governo di Roma capitale: tra specialità e ordinarietà' (2020) 1 *Le Regioni* 75

Francesco Palermo, 'Beyond Second Chambers: Alternative Representation of Territorial Interests and their Reasons' (2018) 10 (2) *Perspectives of Federalism* 50

Francesco Palermo and Karl Kössler, *Comparative Federalism* (Hart, 2017)

Francesco Palermo and Sara Parolari (eds.), *Le variabili della specialità* (ESI, 2018)

Giovanni Piccirilli, 'Gli "Accordi preliminari" per la differenziazione regionale' (2018) 2 *Diritti regionali*, https://www.dirittiregionali.it/wp-content/uploads/2018/04/documento-integrale-5.pdf

Giancarlo Rolla, 'Alcune considerazioni in merito al fondamento costituzionale del regionalismo speciale. L'apporto del diritto comparato' (2015), 13 *federalismi.it*, https://www.federalismi.it/nv14/articolo-documento.cfm?Artid=29838&content=Alcune+considerazioni+in+merito+al+fondamento+costituzionale+del+regionalismo+speciale.+L%27apporto+del+Diritto+comparato&content_author=%3Cb%3EGiancarlo+Rolla%3C/b%3E

Ilenia Ruggiu, *Contro la Camera delle Regioni. Istituzioni e prassi della rappresentanza territoriale* (Jovene, 2006)

Maja Sahadžić, *Asymmetry, Multinationalism and Constitutional Law: Managing Legitimacy and Stability in Federalist States* (Taylor & Francis, 2020)

Charles D. Tarlton, 'Symmetry and asymmetry as elements of federalism: a theoretical speculation' (1965) 27 (4) *Journal of Politics* 861

Roberto Toniatti (ed.), *La cultura dell'autonomia: le condizioni pre-giuridiche per un'efficace autonomia regionale* (Università di Trento, 2018), e-book at https://iris.unitn.it/retrieve/handle/11572/202049/324873/LIA-eBook-Cultura-dellautonomia%20%282%29.pdf

Carlo Trigilia, 'Social Capital and Local Development' (2001) 4 (4) *European Journal of Social Theory* 427

Laura Trucco and Francesca Bailo, 'Forma di governo regionale e legislazione elettorale' (2020) 2 *Osservatorio sulle fonti* 1047, https://www.osservatoriosullefonti.it/archivi/archivio-saggi/speciali/speciale-la-forma-di-governo-regionale-a-vent-anni-dalla-legge-costituzionale-n-1-del-1999/1560-forma-di-governo-regionale-e-legislazione-elettorale/file)

Gianfranco Viesti, *Verso la secessione dei ricchi? Autonomie regionali e unità nazionale* (Laterza, 2019)

Ronald L. Watts, *Comparing Federal Systems* (McGill–Queen's University Press, 2008)

Jens Woelk, Francesco Palermo, and Joseph Marko (eds.), *Tolerance through Law. Self Governance and Group Rights in South Tyrol* (Brill-Nijhoff, 2008)

9 Local governments and metropolitan cities

The Italian experience and its comparative relevance

Erik Longo[1]

I. Introduction

The Italian system of local government derives from a variety of arrangements which were developed by Legislature implementing the principle of Autonomy established in Article 5 of the 1948 Constitution. The most recent developments in local government took place at the end of the twentieth century with the reforms of the Consolidated Act on Local Autonomies of 2000 and the reform of the Title V of the Constitution (Constitutional Law No. 3 of 2001), and in 2014 with the institutional reform of the Delrio Law (see Section II, B). Italy's case touches important nodes of the scholarly debates at the core of the legal and political transformation of local government. It deals with several problems regarding municipalities and other local authorities in both regional and federal systems, such as the issue of the constitutional entrenchment of local authorities, the problem of (over)regulation of municipalities (Palermo and Kössler, 2017), the issues of governing the development of urban areas (Graizbord, 2008), the questions of democracy and participation, and the need for socio-economic reforms in times of austerity.

The trajectory of Italy's constitutional and legislative reforms has clearly strengthened the powers of Regions and local government and, in general, increased their level of autonomy, but, at the same time, it has left some ambiguities. This path had its ground-breaking moment with the approval of Constitutional Law No. 3 of 2001, which transformed the institutional character of local government and metropolitan areas giving them a more defined 'constitutional guarantee' (Carrozza, 2007) and the role they deserve in the social and economic development of Italy.

The recent law introducing metropolitan cities shares with other countries in Western Europe the recurring idea of large cities as a stimulus for the needs of their local communities, but also – and above all – for national development, principally by activating relations and networks with other European institutions (Crivello and Staricco, 2017).

1 Associate professor of Constitutional law at the University of Florence (Italy). E-mail: erik.longo@unifi.it.

DOI: 10.4324/9781003104469-10

The trend towards the growing importance of local governance is assuming a greater significance in the current COVID-19 pandemic, since the way the virus is sweeping around the globe makes it clear that cities, with their high population density, are the places where public health protocols could make a difference.

This chapter, however, will not develop these issues in all their theoretical and practical details; it rather aims at proposing an informed overview of the Italian reform of local government and metropolitan cities in order to discuss both the limits and potentials of the current scenario and make a comparison with other Western European experiences.

This chapter is divided into three parts: the first concerns the legal history of Italian local government, the second discusses the introduction of a new legislation devoted to establishing metropolitan cities in Italy and then analyses the judgment of the Italian Constitutional Court (ItCC) on this reform, and the third focuses on the comparative relevance of the Italian experience on metropolitan cities.

II. The constitutional origin of local government in Italy

It is a commonplace in political history that Italy is a 'Country of cities.' Since the Middle Ages, every city represents a unique place with its rules, customs, and culture, which is relatively separate from other authorities (Martines, 1988). As Cattaneo (1858) wrote, the Roman Empire itself began within a city and then extended the government of a city over the territories surrounding the Mediterranean Sea and beyond. The struggle between localism and centralism is a key factor in understanding modern Italy, but it is also a good framework to use in the analysis of the evolution of Italian institutions (Amoretti, 2002, 129; Ziblatt, 2006).

The attempt to gain control over Italian local institutions has a long history. After the unification in 1860, the Piedmont-Sardinian king introduced a strong central government, and created a well-established network of decentralized ministerial bodies (*Prefetture*) devoted to controlling cities and territories (Putnam et al., 1994). The result was a highly centralized structure of government for such an urbanized country. The pre-republican territorial system was characterized by the simultaneous presence, at local level, of both state bodies and those of local authorities operating in the same fields, but before the enactment of the republican Constitution, the latter was not granted the power of self-government (Castelli, 2013, 360).

A. From the Constitution of 1948 to the reforms in the 1990s

Some aspects of the Piedmont-Sardinian laws were operative even after the ratification of the 1948 republican Constitution, which established local autonomy as a fundamental constitutional principle (Article 5). The adoption of the Constitution signalled a significant break with the past principles that had regulated local government. It granted legislative and administrative powers to ordinary regions (Articles 117 and 118), but this authority was not fully transferred nation-wide until 1970 (Arban in this volume).

The Constitution also provides for the presence of local and intermediate level of government between regional and local authorities. Municipalities, currently around 8,000 in Italy, have a large amount of autonomy in the Italian system; their administrative responsibilities cover fields such as social welfare, education, culture and recreation, spatial planning, and local police.

The powers of local and intermediate government depend on both constitutional rules and legislation developed in the 1990s and 2000s. The Constitution attributes to the State the power to determine the political organization of municipalities (*comuni*) and provinces (*province*), which is a district-type local authority of a larger geographical scope. Local charters (*statuti*) of provinces and municipalities can dictate only minor rules, and even then, the basic law is currently set forth by the 2000 legislation on local government.

With Law No. 142/1990, a new system of local autonomy was enacted. Between 1990 and 1997, a series of measures increased the financial autonomy of regions and local government. Another series of laws on municipalities and *province* adopted between 1993 and 1999 instituted majoritarian election systems for councils and introduced the direct election of the mayor and the president of the *provincia*. Other changes affected the regime of controls upon the administration. Just as important as the latter, were the changes in the regime of administrative functions. The most important innovation, provided by Law No. 59/1997 and implemented by a series of subsequent legislative decrees (the most important of which was legislative decree No. 112/1998), introduced for the first time into the Italian legal system the principle of (vertical) 'subsidiarity,' which provides that the administrative functions, generally attributed to municipalities, may be allocated to a higher level of government on the basis of the principles of subsidiarity, differentiation, and proportionality, in order to ensure their uniform exercise.

As territorial government rests on constitutional foundations, the reform of intermediate authorities is a tricky constitutional matter since it affects the strategies and equilibrium of the whole structure of the Republic (Longo and Mobilio, 2016). Local government is not just the lower level of the nation, but also a constitutive part of the constitutional design as it is also mentioned by the European Charter of Local Self-Government, an international treaty which was adopted in 1985 under the auspices of the Congress of Local and Regional Authorities of the Council of Europe (Boggero, 2018; Mehde, 2006).

B. From the 2001 constitutional amendment to the Delrio Law

With the 2001 constitutional amendment (Constitutional Law No. 3/2001), 'metropolitan cities' were entrenched for the first time into the Constitution and became, together with municipalities, provinces, regions, and the State, 'constitutive entities' of the Italian Republic (Article 114, para. 1) (Mobilio, 2017).

In theory, the arrangement of Article 114 of the Constitution seemed to signal the shift from a centralistic to a new 'regional-quasi-federal' structure of the Italian Republic (Palermo and Wilson, 2014; see also Const. Court judgment No. 274/2003 and 365/2007); Article 118, based on the subsidiarity principle, designed a brand-new collection of national administrative powers (Martinico in this volume; see also Const. Court judgment No. 303/2003); and Article 119 set up a new financial autonomy for regional and local governments. In reality, the implementation of the 2001 reform of regions and local governments has been inadequate and largely ineffective (Falcon, 2011; Caravita, 2013), due to the unclear and inconsistent drafting of the provisions devoted to the division of legislative competences between State and Regions.

Indeed, the political culture and party system has held back the 2001 reform and the necessity of creating intergovernmental coordination structures (Palermo and Wilson, 2014). After the general elections of 2001, the winning centre-right coalition decided to put obstacles in the way of implementing the 2001 constitutional reform. The centre-right coalition boasted about devolution – then the mantra of the Lega Nord party – but practised centralization. Therefore, after a period of strong momentum for local authorities and a dominant pro-decentralization approach in the 1990s, a trend reversal (centralization) occurred ten years later.

The implementation of the reform has produced an enormous amount of litigation brought before the Constitutional Court (Calzolaio, 2012). The Court rewrote the division of legislative and administrative powers laid down by the reform thus assuming a quasi-political role in the implementation of the reform instead of that of simply the arbiter among powers.

The story of 'metropolitan cities' is significant. Whereas the reform entrenched them into the Constitution for the first time (even though they were first laid down in a 1968 piece of legislation and then in the Consolidated Act on Local Autonomies of 2000), the legislature took almost 13 years to bring them into being amid the enactment of a controversial law with many legal and institutional flaws. During these years many attempts to create metropolitan entities have been made.

In accordance with Law No. 131/2003 – implementing article 2 of Constitutional Law No. 3/2001 – the government should have adopted, within two years of its coming into effect, one or more legislative decrees aimed at determining the essential functions for enabling the metropolitan cities, as well as the municipalities and the provinces, to operate in a way that would satisfy the primary needs of the community. Even Articles 23 and 24 of Law No. 42/2009 on 'fiscal federalism' enumerated the new self-governing entities. Yet, again, the creation of metropolitan cities was not pursued. The last attempt was made by the Government of Mario Monti with Law-Decree No. 95/2012, which was eventually struck down by the ItCC because it stated that a Law-Decree must be used only to tackle issues of an extraordinary or emergency nature, not as a law-making instrument to bring about organic and systemic reforms, and also because the principles of autonomy contained in the current Title V of the Constitution had been contravened.

Metropolitan cities were finally established with Law No. 56 of 2014, also known as 'Legge Delrio,' (after Graziano Delrio, the minister of regional affairs during the executive led by Enrico Letta) which contains also a general reform of provinces and municipalities in every aspect of their organization and powers (Sterpa, 2014; Pizzetti, 2015; Vandelli, 2014).

The 'Delrio Law' was prompted by the need to re-examine, among other major issues, the role of central, regional, and local authorities. An important part of this shift rests on the willingness to reshuffle intermediate government by abolishing the direct elections of Provincial presidents and councils. The main driver of these laws can be found in the governmental response to the Eurozone crisis affecting the European Union (EU) member states since 2009–10 (Bolgherini, 2014). The provinces were also targeted by the European Central Bank in its call for debt reform in 2011, and their abolition became emblematic of the rhetoric of cutting the 'costs of politics' (Bussu and Galanti, 2015).

The need to comply with EU agreements and the consequent austerity measures adopted by central governments inevitably impacted sub-national levels. Under the umbrella of austerity and the consequent resource cuts this entailed, many other measures have affected local governments (Mangiameli, 2013). The most stringent and pervasive reform has been that of Articles 81 (on budget law), 97 (on administrative organization), and 119 of the Constitution made by constitutional Law No. 1/2012, which added that all local governments are required to maintain a balanced budget (Fabbrini, 2013).

However, the phenomenon of local government transformation may not uniquely be related to the economic crises, since such a trend – in Italy as well as in other countries – appears to have been already underway. In the Italian case, as several scholars have highlighted (Piperata, 2012), the crisis revamped old prejudices against local government and introduced fiscal constraints on the 'debt state' (Streeck, 2017).

III. The Delrio Law

Hence, the Eurozone crisis prompted the shrinking of territorial government in order to cut state budgets and implement the European policy of austerity. The enactment of the Delrio Law marked the culmination of a controversial political campaign and much-debated passage of the bill through parliament. Parliament came to grips with these issues and adopted a more comprehensive law to overhaul the intermediate local authorities.

The Delrio Law focused on two main points. First, it transformed the territories of the ten most important Italian provinces (Rome, Milan, Naples, Turin, Genoa, Bologna, Florence, Venice, Bari, and Reggio Calabria) into metropolitan cities with special powers. On paper, metropolitan cities gained a different governance and more complex roles than the former provinces, such as general regional planning including communication facilities, service and infrastructure networks, public services organization of general interest, traffic, mobility, and economic development. Second, it reformed all the remaining provinces by reducing the representativeness of their councils and by depriving them of many functions, which were reallocated to municipalities and regions.

Even if it is not organized into homogeneous parts due to drafting issues, the law can be divided into two main sections. The first (paragraphs 5 to 50) concerns the organization, competences, and other rules regarding metropolitan cities, while the second (paragraphs 51 to 156) contains rules governing other local authorities, namely provinces, unifications (*unioni di comuni*), and mergers of municipalities (*fusioni di comuni*). The essential idea is that, with this novel system, local authorities will be organized according to the principles of 'subsidiarity', 'differentiation', and 'proportionality,' as set out in Article 1, paragraph 1, of the Law, as well as in Article 118 Const. According to these three principles, the local authority that is entrusted with an administrative function should be the one closest to the citizens, and only if it does not have the structure to carry out the service should the function be attributed to a higher territorial level (subsidiarity); the distribution must bear in mind the factual reality of territorial institutions and distinguish between institutions according to their capacity of government (differentiation); and lastly, an organization should be suited to ensuring the effective exercise of the competence (suitability).

A. The introduction of metropolitan cities

The first part of the Delrio Law defines the organization, competences, and principles guiding the activity of metropolitan cities. According to the law, from 1 January 2015, the territories of the provinces of Rome, Milan, Naples, Turin, Genoa, Bologna, Florence, Venice, and Bari were transformed into metropolitan cities. By August 2016, all the metropolitan cities considered by the Delrio Law had been instituted (Mobilio, 2017).

The Delrio Law strictly defines the number of metropolitan cities. Therefore, only the law has the power to institute a new metropolitan city, with a corresponding parliamentary change to the Delrio Law. For this reason, the State has been accused of having a centralized approach, also because local populations or municipalities cannot exercise the right of initiative to create a new metropolitan city.

Regarding the identification of metropolitan cities, the legislature seems to have followed an arbitrary criterion of choice, without referring to either clear spatial, demographic, or economic parameters. In particular, the selection has also been criticized as 'unreasonable,' since each area is very different (Salerno, 2014).

As a consequence, the metropolitan city absorbs all the municipalities, as well as the territories of the former provinces. Therefore, the Delrio Law tightens the borders of new metropolitan cities, impeding the easy change of the perimeter created by the law. The impracticality of an easy way to change their boundaries is considered a real obstacle to the promotion of local development and flexibility of the new institution. It would have been better for the legislature to modify the territory of metropolitan cities in accordance with the socio-economic features of territories—which are now different from a century ago when the provinces were instituted.

According to paragraph 44 of the law, the metropolitan cities retain all the fundamental powers that the Italian Constitution and legislation used to yield to the provinces, i.e. powers concerning the so-called wide-area (agriculture, environment, maintenance of school facilities, tourism, etc.). Innovatively, the Delrio Law sets out a list of six new competences: the adoption of a three-year strategic plan for the metropolitan territory; general urban planning; coordination and network of public services; local infrastructures; economic and social development; and promotion and coordination of Information and Communications Technology (ICT) infrastructures.

The national government has tried to correct this centralistic approach by granting metropolitan cities a certain margin of autonomy. Each metropolitan city has the power to adopt the 'Charter of Autonomy' (*statuto di autonomia*) and the possibility of integrating the rules of the Delrio Law regarding the organization of the new authority, the governance, the competences of the organs, and relations with the other municipalities of the area.

Moreover, the Delrio Law introduces important changes to governance arrangements for intermediate local government in Italy. Each metropolitan city has a mayor (*sindaco*), a council (*consiglio*), and a committee (*conferenza*), all tagged with the adjective 'metropolitan'.

The mayor of the metropolitan city is by law the mayor of the biggest city in that territory (e.g. the 'mayor of Florence' is also the 'metropolitan mayor of Florence'). The mayor has extensive powers, which are defined both in the Delrio Law and in every Charter of Autonomy – e.g. the duty to represent the metropolitan city and to control the administration.

The council has both the power to define the strategy of the metropolitan city and to prepare the Charter of Autonomy (*statuto*). The number of councillors varies according to the population of each metropolitan city (from 24 for the most populated to 14 for the least populated). Councillors are not directly elected by residents in the territory of the metropolitan city; they are elected from among the mayors and members of the local councils.

Exceptionally the Delrio Law allows the Charter of Autonomy (*statuto*) to opt for the direct election of the metropolitan mayor and council by residents. This possibility produces heavy consequences for the metropolitan city, like the duty of carving up the metropolitan territory into multiple boroughs with a wide margin of autonomy. Only the Charters of Autonomy of Milan, Rome, and Naples opted for this kind of election.

The committee is a residual board carrying out some of the functions once wielded by the provincial council – e.g. the capacity to adopt the Charter of Autonomy (*statuto*) and to express guidelines to the benefit of the metropolitan council and mayor. For this reason, the committee is considerably weaker and carries little weight in the metropolitan structure of government. Members of the committee are automatically the mayors of each municipality in the territory of the metropolitan city.

B. The destiny of provinces

While awaiting the constitutional reform that should have been leading to the elimination of all references to the provinces from Article 114 onward in the Constitution, the Delrio Law lays down a new regulation for all the other provinces that are not transformed into metropolitan cities. As we know, the constitutional reform has been blocked by a popular referendum held in December 2016.

According to the law, metropolitan cities and all the other provinces have similarities, but also many differences. As regards the similarities, the provinces have their own charter for integrating the rules of the Delrio Law. They also have a council (*consiglio provinciale*), a president (*presidente di provincia*), and an assembly (*assemblea dei sindaci*). The provincial councils are not elected from among the residents, but from among mayors and municipal councillors, as is the case with the metropolitan councils. The president of the province, unlike those of metropolitan cities, is a mayor of a municipality inside the province, freely elected by mayors and municipal councillors (paragraphs 58–60). The assemblies are composed of all the mayors of the municipalities in the territory of the province, as are the metropolitan committees.

On the other hand, the provinces lose many of the competences they had in the past, and so differ from metropolitan cities, which, on the contrary, gain many functions. In fact, the competences covered by the provinces now include only urban coordination, transport, and maintenance of schools (the situation is different in the regions with a special statute). Those functions that provinces exercised in the past have been transferred, from central government and regions, to the municipalities, and only if required to ensure unitary practice to the regions, pursuant to the principle of 'subsidiarity', 'differentiation', and 'suitability' (Article 118 Const.).

It must be noted that, in addition to reorganizing the provinces, the Delrio Law provides municipalities with the power to create 'unifications' and 'mergers' of municipalities to carry out specific administrative functions and deal with inefficiencies due to the small size of many of them.

C. The judgment of the Italian Constitutional Court over the Delrio Law

When Parliament approved the Delrio Law, it met with strong criticism. Commentators condemned, on the one hand, the lack of a clear relationship between metropolitan cities and the upper levels of government and, on the other, between the metropolitan cities and municipalities (Salerno and Fabrizzi, 2014; Mobilio, 2017). Another thorny issue concerned the destiny of the Province, whose constitutional fate was anticipated in the Delrio Law before the adoption of a constitutional amendment (Tubertini, 2016).

In a famous case, the Constitutional Court discussed the alleged unconstitutionality of several provisions of the Delrio Law. Four regions (Lombardy, Veneto, Campania, and Apulia) challenged 58 different paragraphs of the Delrio Law before the Court, as they were allegedly interfering with regional competences and were therefore violating the constitutional framework; this was with regard to Articles 1 (on popular sovereignty), 5 (on the principles of the Republic's unity and decentralization), 48 (on the right to vote), 114 (on authorities forming the Republic), 117 (on the distribution of legislative power to state and regions), and 133 (on modification of local boundaries) of the Constitution and Article 9 of the European Charter of Local Self-Government. The regions challenged almost every paragraph of the Delrio Law on metropolitan cities and, in particular, those parts relating to the institution and the replacement of the provinces, the metropolitan mayors, councils, and committees. The regions asserted that the Delrio Law tended to bend the meaning of the Constitution, shifting the balance of power between state and regional level.

The reasoning of the regions could be regarded as implying three different arguments on this problem.

First, they challenged the state legislative competence used to rule on the institution of metropolitan cities. The regions claimed that the law violated Article 117 of the Constitution, since it was not concerned with any of the subjects of exclusive legislative competence reserved to the national government.

Second, even though the State has not modified the boundaries of provinces by replacing the latter with metropolitan cities, the regions alleged the violation of the constitutional provisions on the modification of boundaries of local authorities.

Third, the regions challenged the democratic deficit which the provisions on metropolitan cities produced on local self-government. By also giving the office of metropolitan mayor to the mayor of the biggest city, and the entitlement to become members of the metropolitan committee only to the mayors, the Delrio Law is deemed in contrast with the tenets of local self-government, subsidiarity, democracy, as well as decentralization.

In March 2015 the Italian Constitutional Court upheld the Delrio Law (decision No. 50 of 2015). The Court ruled as groundless the various objections raised by the four regions challenging the provisions regarding the powers and elections of provinces and metropolitan cities. The decision was certainly one of the most significant judgments on local government in Italy in the last decade. It substantially endorsed the reform of second-tier authorities.

Despite the importance of every passage of this decision, only some aspects of it are worth commenting upon, also because the jurisdiction of the Court is limited to certain issues due to the characteristics of the Italian model of constitutional adjudication (Barsotti et al., 2016; Stone Sweet, 2012; Groppi, 2008).

The Italian Constitutional Court's ruling in the Delrio Law case is made up of two specific arguments.

First, the Court assumes the regulation of metropolitan cities as an area where the state is free to make laws in order to determine the basic organization, powers, and functions of these local authorities. In contrast, regions have no right to regulate this matter since they lack the competence to reform local autonomy. Against this background, the State acted under the provision of the separation of legislative powers set out in Article 117 of the Constitution. In this view, the ItCC neglected the thesis of the regions, which alleged they had the competence to regulate even 'the institution of metropolitan cities'. Commentators found a clear-cut example of the Court's changing attitude towards regionalism in this line of reasoning and, in particular, towards the regions' demands to regulate matters outside their legislative competences. Indeed, this judgment represents a good example of the Court's shift from regionally to centrally oriented decisions issued during a time of economic crisis (Groppi et al., 2013).

Second, the Court considers it necessary to endorse state efforts to reform local authorities, and, in particular, the introduction of metropolitan cities. The argument of the ItCC delves into the reason behind the reform of the second tier of local authorities that has been highlighted in this passage of the judgment: 'With this law' the Court affirms

> the legislature intended to make a significant and systematic reform of all public authorities forming the Republic (Article 114 of the Constitution) in order to simplify the character of local government, without arriving at the abolition of those established in the Constitution (cf. § 3.4.2 of the Conclusions on points of law).

The Italian Constitutional Court then alluded to two overlapping aspects of this law that we have already highlighted: (1) this law only anticipates a broad, forthcoming constitutional reform of those provisions governing local entities; (2) the complex nature of the provisions of the Delrio Law is excusable because it is the outcome of long and difficult political bargaining.

In this sense the argumentation of the Court reveals a hidden intent to ease both the transition from a more centrifugal to a more centripetal division of powers between the State and the regions, and the achievement of an independent constitutional role for metropolitan cities – with minimum interference from the regions. In addition, the ItCC refers to the pillars of this independence: European relevance, fiscal autonomy, and power of self-regulation (with regard to both functions and basic organization).

Based on this reasoning, the Court declines those issues on the boundaries and the structure of local government (mayor, council, and committee). State power to regulate metropolitan cities even overrides the international covenants that Italy has signed. Surprisingly, the ItCC invokes the lack of effectiveness of the European Charter of Local Self-Government in Italy in order to exclude both the infringement of this Charter (*statuto*) and the necessity for the direct election of metropolitan city members (Wienen and Dickson, 2017). For the Court, the expression 'freely elected' in Article 3 of the Charter (*statuto*) does not mean 'directly elected' since it asks only for the respect of democracy and representativeness in the choosing of local members.

Although a strict interpretation of the ruling leads to the consideration of the result of this decision as relevant only for determining the competence to regulate metropolitan cities, this judgment marks the end of the strong version of the regional state in Italy. To some extent, this would be an attack on the 2001 reform and the difficult implementation of subsidiarity, differentiation, and suitability set forth in Article 118 of the Constitution. We must admit that the reasoning and wording of this judgment could very well lead to this type of broad interpretation. The Court states in very general terms that the regulation of local authorities must be uniform for every city, no matter what its size, population, territory, etc. However, the Delrio Law has not covered everything because it allows the charter (*statuto*) of each metropolitan city to make some decisions in order to adapt the regulation to its specific conditions. Evidently, this 'margin of discretion' has been considered determinative for upholding the law.

D. The missing opportunities of the reform

If we consider the enforcement of the reform, the new provinces and metropolitan cities are not exactly what the Delrio Law promised they should be.

Institutionally speaking, some metropolitan cities (Firenze, Bologna, Genova) have innovatively interpreted the Law in their charters of autonomy, leveraging their powers to create a new institutional environment, to foster a strong collaboration with municipalities in the metropolitan area, and to create an 'experimental laboratory' for good administrative practices – mainly using those powers regarding ICT, strategic planning, and (smart) infrastructures.

Whereas there is another cluster of metropolitan cities (Milan, Rome, Naples, Venice, Turin, and Bari) that have interpreted the role of the new entity as continuity with the past provincial experience.

This difference has led Simoncini and Mobilio (2016) to carve out two models of metropolitan cities: on the one hand, those 'representative of local institutions,' which are created with the aim of offering coordination and support to the functions of their municipalities; on the other, those 'representative of the community,' i.e. the level of government of this community, which is a level of government similar to the municipal one, but with a wider area and capable of pursuing the development and direct implementation of supra-municipal policies.

Regarding provinces, the Law has been considered as an incomplete passage, since it was only a link in the chain that led to the Constitutional amendment of 2016. However, the failure of the constitutional referendum of 4 December 2016 stopped this process and put the provinces into a stalemate, while causing even more serious legal problems (Casamassima, 2018). Therefore, leaving only the largely incomplete and fragmentary design of the Delrio Law on the field, a brief reflection is required both on a political-institutional and on a purely structural and functional level.

Despite the differences, metropolitan cities as such seem unable to represent either the complexity of functional urban areas or the metropolitan areas as reformulated by the OECD. The new experience failed to take advantage of the debates, which during recent years have clearly shown how the new urban scale and forms deserve new governance and government solutions (Hirschl, 2020; Balducci et al., 2016).

On the one hand, the downgrading of the provinces made through the abolition of direct elections demonstrated the legislator's lack of trust in local communities, whose need of greater representativeness is indubitable. This could lead to the paradox of dire unrepresentativeness of municipalities other than the main city in national programmes, as has been clear during the negotiation of the National Operational Programme (NOP) 2014–2020 (Fedeli, 2017). In addition, without the completion of the Constitutional amendment, the essential structure of the Delrio Law seems to have undergone a singular 'heterogenesis of ends' (Agosta,

2018). The reform has not yielded the promised territorial simplification and has quickly led to a very unbalanced and inefficient system, while exponentially expanding administrative costs without a corresponding increase in the quality of essential services.

On the other hand, the reallocation of competences among municipal, regional, and state levels has not followed a linear path. Only a few regions have set out a real process of territorial reorganization of wide-scale functions with the aim of stepping up the level of services accessible to citizens and providing a real innovative answer to the general debate on the disconnection between the *città de iure* and the *città de facto* (Fedeli, 2017). Emilia-Romagna opted for a real multilevel governance with the distribution of programming competences to the region and provinces, and the management of services to the municipalities. Though the most important problem lies in the lack of funding. Despite the attribution of relevant competences, the allocation of resources has been less than adequate for the expenses (Crivello and Staricco, 2017).

IV. The comparative relevance of the Italian experience on metropolitan cities: a European overview

The Italian experience seems to exacerbate some problems already present in every country when we deal with the metropolitan level. It is still difficult to 'identify the city as an object' (Martinotti, 1999). This has strong implications for urban governance, for models of government, and for an understanding of their social impact (Arban, 2019). Another important problem of the Italian reform of local government lies in the contrast between administrative boundaries and their functional areas. The Delrio Law establishes automatically that each metropolitan city would cover the area of the province it replaced without considering the necessity to adjust the administrative perimeter to the functional area. The administrative boundaries of the former provinces were set in the past and never updated in accordance with the social, economic, and infrastructural changes occurring in the past two decades. Only the area of Bologna was set with these criteria, yet the other cities (such as Milan and Florence) have a perimeter with no reference to the real economic and social situation of the area.

This issue revives the recurrent argument of the existence of an institutional metropolitan 'path dependency' (Tomàs, 2020): forms of metropolitan governance are highly path-dependent on inherited institutional structures and even in embedded spatial configurations (Zimmermann and Getimis, 2017). It is impossible to revolutionize the administrative patterns of urban transformation, but only to make slight changes with the aim of establishing more equity, solidarity, competitiveness, efficiency, and rationality.

At metropolitan level, new waves of urbanization produce new demands for space (functional territory), while political and administrative units (institutional territory) lag behind citizens' needs (Lefèvre, 1998; Harvey, 1989) producing reforms at a different pace and form. This is the reason why in Europe there is a panoply of institutional forms of metropolitan governance while the necessities are the same. This great diversity is a result of the traditions and historical richness associated with the different countries and different systems of territorial government. In Italy, for example, one of the driving forces of local government reform has been the introduction of rationality into territorial organisation due to changes in the state expenditure for services and welfare, and due to changes in the state expenditure for services and welfare and to the exposure of territories to an ever-increasing global competition (Zimmermann and Feiertag, 2018).

Although Italy, Spain, France, Germany, and the UK have recently adopted legislation on metropolitan cities and large urban areas for analogous reasons (Zimmermann and Feiertag, 2018; Lorencka and Obrębska, 2018; Mobilio, 2017), they have carved out institutions only nominally similar (*Città metropolitane, Grandes Ciudades, Métropole, Europäische Metropolregionen*). The empirical world reveals an assemblage of multiple ideas about how a territory should be organized and governed. France, Spain, and Italy followed a top-down process due to their administrative structure, while the developments in Switzerland, Germany, and the UK followed a bottom-up approach (Fricke, 2020). Despite the difference, the six experiences are expressions of an ongoing process which has not yet ended.

If we look at the Italian case, we find that the State, while imposing metropolitan reforms and certain types of institutional models, is actually devolving austerity rather than empowering metropolitan cities. In this sense, the introduction of metropolitan cities marks the resurgence of state-level institutions. Five years after the entry into force of the Delrio Law it is clear that metropolitan cities are the weakest level of policy-making. Many authors are starting to question what capacity these institutions really have in terms of staff, finances, and coordinative power (Mobilio, 2017; Tubertini, 2019). Even in France the analysis of the two reforms of 2010 (LOI n° 2010–1563) and 2014 (LOI n° 2014–58) has ascertained that metropolitan regions are a 'weak' public authority. French metropolitan authorities remain public bodies for cooperation between municipalities depending on the transfer of competences and resources from other territorial authorities such as municipalities or regions (Fricke, 2020).

UK combined authorities are the effect of an intense collaboration between the central government and local authorities. The introduction of metropolitan authority is a response to a mix of policy issues: 'changing boundaries, employment and labour markets and the desire for functional geographies to aid competition in a global world', as well as a 'response to the UK and English devolution conundrum' (Shutt and Liddle, 2019a, b; Roberts, 2020). The Spanish law regulating local government establishes that Regions (*Comunidades Autónomas*) are responsible for creating, modifying, and abolishing metropolitan areas. In 2003, the *Large Cities Law on Measures for the Modernization of Local Government* (Ley No. 57/2003) aimed at modernizing the management council and the development of citizens' participation in large cities. However, this law does not address metropolitan problems.

Switzerland is a paramount example of a bottom-up process of metropolitan governance. The implementation of Swiss metropolitan cities basically follows the federal arrangement of this country, i.e. a horizontal and vertical cooperation between existing institutional entities, sometimes with the significant involvement of non-governmental actors (Kübler, 2004; Keuffer, 2020).

The situation is quite different in Germany, where metropolitan regions have developed a certain sense of 'mission' and 'express an interest in promoting their understanding of metropolitan cooperation and governance as a model on a European scale' (Lang and Török, 2017; Fricke, 2020). The German experience reveals an important truth about the relationship between the process of Europeanisation and the metropolitan question (Fürst, 2004). Despite the European dimension affecting the transition from traditional to new local government arrangements and the change in the decision-making process of regional and local authorities (Jones and Keating, 1995), the legislative framework of administrative reconfiguration does not depend directly on European policies. It is inappropriate to assume that in the EU an *acquis metropolitaine* is developing or that the metropolitan agenda is trying to transform soft law into binding regulations (Fricke, 2020).

Thus, there are four ways in which supranational changes have affected local government on a constitutional basis through the influence on domestic politics (Keating, 2008; Tatham, 2014; Keating et al., 2015). First, through the revitalization of the 'subsidiarity' principle (Martinico in this volume; Arban, 2015; Guastaferro, 2013). Second, by constitutionally transforming the way institutions cooperate and interact to constitute new forms of politics more devoted to help local governments and cities to socially and economically progress (multi-level governance) (Palermo and Wilson, 2014; Pernice, 2002). Third, by inducing Member States to introduce philosophies and working practices in a way that moves local authorities away from hierarchical and old forms of administration, towards more negotiated and participatory practices that blur the static view of administration and involve a wide range of interest groups (pluralism) (Simoncini, 2013; Goldsmith, 2002). Fourth, by transforming the funding criteria in a way that requires the institutionalisation of direct links between the institutions of local authorities and those of the EU – e.g. the relevance of cohesion policies and the use of structural funds (Bolgherini, 2014; Farole et al., 2011).

V. Concluding remarks

In today's Europe, local governance is increasingly being mobilised as a mechanism of economic development policy through which governments are attempting to boost national as well as local socio-economic assets. In Italy, after the constitutional amendment of 2001, a new phase of administrative reform occurred at metropolitan level during the 2010s. This process has been based on the conception of metropolitan territories as competitive areas, where global firms push for infrastructure and – more broadly – economic alliances. Despite the EU not having any competences in this field, Europeanization has promoted the institutionalization of metropolitan areas by defining the criteria for the allocation of cohesion or structural funds in association with a specific form of metropolitan governance.

In this context the case of Italy is a helpful example of what drives support for institutional change (equality, solidarity, competitiveness, efficiency, and rationality) and what limits it (such as path dependency, embedded spatial configurations, and boundaries). Through the Delrio Law, Italy has reasserted its power over local government eliminating the direct election of provincial executives and introducing the metropolitan city in the most populated regions. However, this reform has been hampered by the failure of the Constitutional Referendum held in December 2016.

The Italian top-down approach in regulating the functions and governance of metropolitan cities, based on government-driven regulation, seems, on the one hand, too strict, because metropolitan cities do not have the power to include in their territory new municipalities belonging to near provinces, and on the other hand, too weak, because in some domains the competences of metropolitan cities are smaller than those previously attributed to the provinces. We can conclude that in the Delrio Law there is only limited innovation. Even the implementation of the reform has failed to determine the creation of a new institution for the economic development of Italy. Thus, Italian style metropolitan cities remain too similar to the old provinces from which they derive.

Literature

Stefano Agosta, 'Il "risveglio" (dopo una lunga "anestesia") delle Province nella prospettiva di riordino del livello di area vasta' (2018) 46 (3) *Le Regioni* 413–452

Ugo M. Amoretti, 'Italy Decentralizes' (2002) 13 (2) *Journal of Democracy* 126–140

Erika Arban, 'Re-Centralizing Subsidiarity: Interpretations By The Italian Constitutional Court' (2015) *Regional & Federal Studies* 1–16

Erika Arban, 'Metropolitan Cities, Federalism and Socio-economic Challenges' (2019) Special issue of *I Diritti comparati* 226–251

Alessandro Balducci, Francesco Curci, and Valeria Fedeli, 'Una galleria di ritratti dell'Italia post-metropolitana' (2016) 76 *Territorio* 20–22

Vittoria Barsotti, P.G. Carozza, Marta Cartabia, and Andrea Simoncini, *Italian Constitutional Justice In Global Context* (Oxford University Press, 2016)

Giovanni Boggero, *Constitutional Principles of Local Self-Government in Europe* (Brill, 2018)

Silvia Bolgherini, 'Can Austerity Lead To Recentralisation? Italian Local Government During The Economic Crisis' (2014) 19 (2) *South European Society and Politics* 193–214

Sonia Bussu and Maria Tullia Galanti, 'Local Governments at the Time of the Crisis' (2015) 30 (1) *Italian Politics* 141–159

Simone Calzolaio, *Il Cammino Delle Materie Nello Stato Regionale* (Giappichelli, 2012)

Beniamino Caravita, 'Italy: Between the Hybrid State and Europe's Federalizing Process', in John Loughlin, John Kincaid, and Wilfried Swenden (eds.) *Routledge Handbook of Regionalism and Federalism Edited* (Routledge, 2013), 287–301

Paolo Carrozza, 'Per un diritto costituzionale delle autonomie locali' (2007) 12 *Rivista di diritto costituzionale* 219–267

Vincenzo Casamassima, 'Le Province nel flusso delle riforme degli enti locali. Questioni aperte e prospettive future dopo l'esito del referendum costituzionale del 2016' (2018) 4 *Rivista AIC* 512–575

Luca Castelli, 'The Territory of the Local Authorities in Italy: Characteristics, Dimensions, Transformations', in Stelio Mangiameli (ed.) *Federalism, Regionalism and Territory* (Proceedings of the conference, Rome – 2012 September 19–20–21) (Giuffrè, 2013) 357–389

Carlo Cattaneo, 'La Città Considerata Come Principio Ideale delle Istorie Italiane' (1858) 9 (42) *Il Crepuscolo*

Silvia Crivello and Luca Staricco, 'Institutionalizing Metropolitan cities in Italy. Success and limits of a centralistic, simplifying approach' (2017) 10 (2) *Urban Research & Practice* 228–238

Sergio Fabbrini, 'Intergovernmentalism and Its Limits Assessing the European Union's Answer to the Euro Crisis' (2013) 46 *Comparative Political Studies* 1003–1029

Giandomenico Falcon, 'Dieci anni dopo. Un bilancio della riforma del Titolo V' (2011) 39 (2-3) *Le Regioni* 241–250

Thomas Farole, Andrés Rodríguez-Pose, and Michael Storper, 'Cohesion policy in the European Union: growth, geography, institutions' (2011) 49 (5) *JCMS: Journal of Common Market Studies* 1089–1111

Valeria Fedeli, 'Metropolitan governance and metropolitan cities in Italy: Outdated solutions for processes of urban regionalisation?' (2017) 75 (3) *Raumforschung und Raumordnung | Spatial Research and Planning* 265–274

Carola Fricke, *European Dimension of Metropolitan Policies: Policy Learning and Reframing of Metropolitan Regions* (Springer, 2020)

Dietrich Fürst, 'Metropolitan Governance in Germany', in Hubert Heinelt and Daniel Kübler (eds.) *Metropolitan Governance in the 21st Century* (Routledge, 2004) 181–199

Michael Goldsmith, 'Central Control Over Local Government – A Western European Comparison' (2002) 28 (3) *Local Government Studies* 91–112

Boris Graizbord, 'Governance in Megacities in Federal Orders', in John Kincaid and Rupak Chattopadhyay (eds.) *Local Government in Federal Systems* (Viva Books, 2008) 71–92

Tania Groppi, 'The Italian Constitutional Court: Towards a Multilevel System of Constitutional Review' (2008) 3 *Journal Comparative Law* 100–117

Tania Groppi, Irene Spigno, and Nicola Vizioli, 'The Constitutional Consequences of the Financial Crisis in Italy', in Xenophon Contiades (ed.) *Constitutions in the Global Financial Crisis* (Ashgate, 2013) 89–113

Barbara Guastaferro, 'Reframing subsidiarity inquiry from an "EU value-added" to an "EU non-encroachment" test? Some insights from national parliaments' reasoned opinions', in Marta Cartabia, Nicola Lupo, and Andrea Simoncini (eds.) *Democracy and subsidiarity in the EU: national parliaments, regions and civil society in the decision-making process* (Il Mulino, 2013) 133–156

David Harvey, *The urban experience* (Blackwell, 1989)

Ran Hirschl, *City, State. Constitutionalism and the Megacity* (OUP, 2020)

James Barry Jones and Michael Keating (eds.) *The European Union and the Regions* (Oxford University Press, 1995)

Michael Keating, 'A Quarter Century of the Europe of the Regions' (2008) 18 (5) *Regional & Federal Studies* 629–635

Michael Keating, Liesbet Hooghe, and Michaël Tatham, 'Bypassing the Nation-state?', in Jeremy Richardson and Sonia Mazey (eds.), *European Union: Power and policy-making* (Routledge, 2015) 445–466

Nicolas Keuffer and Katia Horber-Papazian, 'The Bottom-up Approach: Essential to an Apprehension of Local Autonomy and Local Governance in the Case of Switzerland' (2020) 46 (2) *Local Government Studies* 306–325

Daniel Kübler, Fritz Sager, and Brigitte Schwab, 'Governing without Government: Metropolitan Governance in Switzerland', in Hubert Heinelt and Daniel Kübler (eds.) *Metropolitan Governance in the 21st Century* (Routledge, 2004) 181–199

Thilo Lang and Ibolya Török, 'Metropolitan region policies in the European Union: following national, European or neoliberal agendas?' (2017) 22 (1) *International Planning Studies* 1–13

Christian Lefèvre, 'Metropolitan government and governance in western countries: a critical review' (1998) 22 (1) *International journal of urban and regional research* 9–25

Erik Longo and Giuseppe Mobilio, 'Territorial government reforms at the time of financial crisis: the dawn of metropolitan cities in Italy' (2016) 26 (4) *Regional & Federal Studies* 509–530

Małgorzata Lorencka and Marta Obręebska, 'English Combined Authorities and Italian Metropolitan Cities: A Comparative Perspective' (2018) 18 (2) *Romanian Journal of Political Science* 119–148

Stelio Mangiameli, *Le Regioni Italiane tra Crisi Globale e Neocentralismo* (Giuffrè, 2013)

Lauro Martines, *Power and imagination: city-states in Renaissance Italy* (Johns Hopkins University Press, 1988)

Guido Martinotti (ed.), *La Dimensione Metropolitana* (Il Mulino, 1999)

Veith Mehde, 'Steering, Supporting, Enabling: The Role of Law in Local Government Reforms' (2006) 28 (2) *Law & Policy* 164–181

Giuseppe Mobilio, *Le Città metropolitane. Dimensione costituzionale e attuazione statutaria* (Giappichelli, 2017)

Francesco Palermo and Karl Kössler, *Comparative federalism: constitutional arrangements and case law* (Hart Publishing, 2017)

Francesco Palermo and Alex Wilson, 'The multi-level dynamics of state decentralization in Italy' (2014) 12 (4-5) *Comparative European Politics* 510–530

Ingolf Pernice, 'Multilevel constitutionalism in the European Union' (2002) 27 (5) *European law review* 511–529

Giuseppe Piperata, 'I poteri locali: da sistema autonomo a modello razionale e sostenibile?' (2012) 33 (3) *Le Istituzioni del federalismo* 503–522

Francesco Pizzetti, *La riforma degli enti territoriali, Città metropolitane, nuove Province e unioni di Comuni* (Giuffrè, 2015)

Robert D. Putnam, Robert Leonardi, and Raffaella Y. Nanetti, *Making Democracy Work: Civic Traditions in Modern Italy* (Princeton University Press, 1994)

Jane Roberts, 'The leadership of place and people in the new English combined authorities' (2020) *Local Government Studies* 1–20

Giulio Salerno, 'Sulla Soppressione-sostituzione delle Province in Corrispondenza all'Istituzione delle Città Metropolitane: Profili Applicativi e Dubbi di Costituzionalità' (2014) 15 (1) *Federalismi.it* 1–14

Giulio Salerno and Federica Fabrizzi, *La Riforma delle Autonomie Territoriali nella Legge Delrio* (Jovene, 2014)

John Shutt and Joyce Liddle, 'Are Combined Authorities in England strategic and fit for purpose?' (2019a) 34 (2) *Local Economy* 196–207

John Shutt and Joyce Liddle, *Combined Authorities in England. Moving beyond devolution: Developing strategic local government for a more sustainable future?* (SAGE, 2019b)

Andrea Simoncini, 'Beyond Representative Democracy: The Challenge of Participatory Democracy and the Boundless Galaxy of Civil Society', in Marta Cartabia, Nicola Lupo, and Andrea Simoncini (eds.), *Democracy and Subsidiarity in the EU. National Parliaments, Regions and Civil Society in the Decision-Making Process* (Il Mulino, 2013) 45–74

Andrea Simoncini and Giuseppe Mobilio, 'L'identità delle Città metropolitane attraverso i loro Statuti: sintomi di una sindrome "bipolare"?' (2016) 44 (4) *Le Regioni* 669–708

Alessandro Sterpa (ed.), *Il Nuovo Governo dell'area Vasta. Commento alla Legge 7 Aprile 2014, N. 56* (*Jovene*, 2014)

Alec Stone Sweet, 'Constitutional Courts', in Michel Rosenfeld and András Sajó (eds.) *The Oxford handbook of Comparative Constitutional Law* (Oxford University Press, 2012) 816–830

Wolfgang Streeck, 'A New Regime', in Desmond King and Patrick Le Galès (eds.), *Reconfiguring European States in Crisis* (Oxford University Press, 2017) 139–157

Michaël Tatham, 'Limited Institutional Change in an International Organization: the EU's shift away from "Federal Blindness"', (2014) 6 (1) *European Political Science Review* 21–45

Mariona Tomàs, 'Metropolitan revolution or metropolitan evolution? The (dis) continuities in metropolitan institutional reforms', in Karsten Zimmermann, Daniel Galland, and John Harrison (eds.) *Metropolitan regions, planning and governance* (Springer, 2020), 25–39

Claudia Tubertini, 'Le politiche di riordino territoriale locale: Province e Città metropolitane. Nuove dinamiche nei rapporti con le Regioni', in Franco Bassanini, Alberto Quadrio Curzio, Floriana Cerniglia, and Luciano Vandelli (eds.) *Territori e autonomia: un'analisi economico-giuridica* (Il Mulino, 2016) 69–94

Claudia Tubertini, 'Il punto sullo stato di attuazione delle Città Metropolitane' (2019) 1 *Giornale di diritto amministrativo* 44–52

Luciano Vandelli, *Città metropolitane, province, unioni e fusioni di comuni* (Maggioli Editore, 2014)

Jakob Wienen and Stewart Dickson, 'Local and Regional Democracy in Italy', Report of the Congress of Local and Regional Authorities CG33(2017)17 final, 18 October 2017

Daniel Ziblatt, *Structuring the State: the Formation of Italy and Germany and the Puzzle of Federalism* (Princeton University Press, 2006)

Karsten Zimmermann and Patricia Feiertag, 'Return of the metro-model?: Governance and planning in metropolitan regions under change. An international comparison of France, Italy and Germany' (2018) 61 *Papers: Regió Metropolitana de Barcelona: Territori, estratègies, planejament* 16–26

Karsten Zimmermann and Panagiotis Getimis, 'Rescaling of metropolitan governance and spatial planning in Europe: an introduction to the special issue' (2017) 75 (3) *Raumforschung und Raumordnung | Spatial Research and Planning* 203–209

10 Loyal cooperation

Systemic principle of Italy's regionalism?

Jens Woelk[1]

I. Introduction

The evolution of the principle of "loyal cooperation" (*principio di leale collaborazione*) directly reflects the different phases of Italian regionalism. In the beginning, it has provided, above all, an answer to the increasing difficulties of respecting a rigid system of strictly separated spheres of competences in the relations between State and Regions as originally outlined in the Italian Constitution. According to the case law of the Italian Constitutional Court (ItCC), the principle of loyal cooperation influences the whole system of relations between the State and the Regions and their respective competences. Its content ranges from reciprocal information obligations to consultation and expression of positions (*pareri*) to the realisation of agreements for specific action (*intese*) between the different levels of government. After the constitutional reform of 2001, the ItCC continued to make frequent reference to the principle.

This chapter presents the origins of the principle in the Italian regional system, before analysing its transformation after the constitutional reform of 2001. A main focus will be the case law of the ItCC which has developed and given concrete shape to the principle. Coordination and cooperation take place in intergovernmental relations, with the system of territorial conferences as the preferred institutional setting.[2] Without being structurally able to perform the role of a territorial second chamber, such as the Swiss State Council or the German Federal Council (albeit not a parliamentary body), the Standing Conference of State and Regions and the Autonomous Provinces of Bolzano and Trento (hereafter: Standing Conference) has actually become the very pivot in the system. It thus partially compensates the political deficit in these relations given the lack of a chamber of territorial representation in the Italian Parliament.

II. Origins of the loyal cooperation principle: from strict separation to "cooperative regionalism"

Linked to the peculiar design of the distribution of competences between State and Regions, the principle of loyal cooperation became fundamental for the evolution of the Italian regional system towards a "cooperative regionalism".

1 Professor in Comparative Public Law, University of Trento.
2 For an analysis of the institutional dimension and of the Italian Conference system, see Eleonora Ceccherini's chapter in this volume.

DOI: 10.4324/9781003104469-11

In its original version, Article 117 Const. listed all matters in which the Regions could legislate with concurrent powers (i.e. within a framework of principles adopted by the State legislator), thus leaving the general and residual powers with the State.[3] Both the State and the Regions were supposed to operate on different, separate, and parallel tracks. Powers in legislation (Article 117 Const.) were also to determine the administrative functions (Article 118 Const.). Before regional legislation could enter into force, it was subject to supervision by the central government.[4] These features of the original design of the competence system show the subordinated position of Italian Regions vis-à-vis the State.[5]

In its case law, the ItCC often used the term "spheres of competence", which evokes the idea of constitutionally clearly separated and determined functions between State and Regions, despite the fact that such clear and unequivocal attribution of powers was far from reality: already the option of delegating the implementation of ordinary State legislation to the regional legislator, as foreseen in the last paragraph of Article 117, leads to grey zones and greater complexity in reality.[6] Thus, constitutional doctrine was widely in favour of more flexibility in the action of the legislators at different levels, for overcoming a system considered too rigid (Gizzi, 1991, 296), and also the ItCC started to question the viability of a separated system (D'Atena, 1972, 2011ff.). After a first phase of decentralisation, in which the 15 ordinary Regions became effectively operational, characterized by a predominantly dual relationship of "separation and concurrence", a second phase in the relations between State and Regions followed, which was increasingly based upon "cooperation and coordinated action" (Baldassare, 1983, 43ff.). Questions regarding the conformity with the constitutional design were answered by the ItCC with reference to an unwritten constitutional principle of loyal cooperation. The wide acceptance of that principle as a complementary one, in turn led to the fundamental question of its limits, as a general expansion in every possible direction would have meant exactly the opposite of the original design and thus needed to be avoided (Costanzo, 1990, 2476).

While until the end of the 1980s there was not much conceptual clarity and distinction, in the early 1990s the ItCC began to define the principle for giving its content certainty and concrete shape (judgement 232/1991):

3 Apart from these concurrent powers, (only) the five special, autonomous Regions also have exclusive legislative powers according to the specific lists contained in the respective regional basic laws, the statutes of autonomy (which have the rank of constitutional laws, limited in their application to the respective and specific regional territory).

4 *Controllo preventivo*, see Article 127 Const., before it was abolished by the reform.

5 An important exception is the autonomous Regions, which do not only have exclusive legislative powers in some areas, but also special institutional channels and procedures in their relations with the State, which put both on equal footing, at least in formal terms. Reference is in particular to the joint commissions for the implementation of the autonomy statutes; see for instance (Palermo, 2008, 143–160) and (Woelk, 2008, 121–140).

6 While this did not change the competence order, as this is not possible without constitutional amendment, it opened the Regions new powers for regulation and thus questions the image of neatly distinguished and separated "spheres of competence".

> This principle influences all provisions and procedures for regulating the relations between regional and State competences (judgement. 153/1986), ranging from the compliance with 'mutual obligations of information' to the consultation or position statements (judgement. 153/1986) up to the realization of 'unanimously agreed action'.

Terminologically, the ItCC seems to equate "loyal cooperation" with "cooperation on equal footing",[7] while "coordination" is the preferred term used in order to highlight a "vertical cooperation" or participation; the latter is related to the numerous legislative, administrative, as well as financial instruments by which the central government can influence, orientate, or limit the activities of the Regions and local entities, such as setting objectives, guidelines, etc. (Carrozza, 1989, 479). It thus comes close to a hierarchical dimension, by contrast with a "horizontal" or "pluralistic model" of relations which presupposes equal standing of both sides, State and Regions.[8]

In numerous cases, the ItCC made reference to the principle of loyal cooperation for clarifying and coordinating the respective spheres of competence of State and Regions. Difficulties arose from the fact that State and Regions were responsible for different aspects of the same subject matter, e.g. the protection of the environment.[9] Despite the general strict separation of the respective spheres of competence, the necessity of a uniform regulation encompassing both spheres, without contradictions, may be recognized in exceptional cases.[10]

Additional space for State intervention in regional powers was opened by the interpretation of the limits of regional legislation (in Articles 117 and 127(4) and (5). Const.) as bases for the exercise of State powers, in the legislative and in the (corresponding) administrative sphere. In particular, through the so-called "function of guidance and coordination" (*funzione di indirizzo e coordinamento*), exercised by the central government. Similar to the "national interest" in the legislative sphere, over time it was transformed from a political instrument into a legal limit to be controlled by the ItCC.[11]

7 ItCC judgement 214/1988: "*cooperazione paritaria*".
8 In this sense, for instance, ItCC judgements 229/1989 and 53/1991.
9 In fact, the protection of the environment or the landscape is closely related to numerous subject matters listed as regional competences in Article 117 Const. (such as urban planning, tourism, hunting, fishery, agriculture, or forestry) which may easily contrast with State action implementing the constitutional objective of safeguarding "the landscape and the historical and artistic heritage of the Nation" (Article 9(2) Const.).
10 ItCC judgement 177/1988; before in judgements 66/1961, 40/1972, and 94/1985.
11 According to the case law of the ItCC, the Regions remained owners of their (new) powers but had to accept – for safeguarding 'national interests' – a State function justified by the 'requirements of unity', which allowed the State to influence and condition the exercise of regional powers. The ItCC underlined the parallelism between the legislative and the administrative spheres: 'requirements of unity' in the latter correspond to State legislation on principles in the former; see ItCC judgements 138/1972, 140/1972, and 181/1976; see (Barbera, 1973) and (Sciullo, 1993, 228–243).

However, the ItCC compensated the recognition of this transformation with reference to the principle of loyal cooperation which creates a connection between the actions of the State and the Regions in order to prevent unilateral intervention into the sphere of competence of the other side, respectively. Arguing with the "obviousness" and the "normalcy" of such cooperation,[12] the justification for the ItCC lies above all in the safeguards for the respective function of each level of territorial government rather than in a defence of its competences. This is confirmed by the result which is regularly the involvement of one level (mostly the Regions) into the decision-making process of the other. In fact, the determination of a comprehensive, overarching interest is mostly vested with the State level,[13] which has to guarantee regional participation in the decision, if specific regional interests are at stake. The reasonability of that decision is subject to control by the ItCC. The principle of loyal cooperation thus guarantees that legislative discretion is bound by the Constitution and lays the foundation for forms of regional participation in the decision-making process at State level.

In fact, the next step in the evolution of the ItCC's case law requires the State to respect the cooperation procedures established in legislation when exercising its powers. In case of strong interference with regional powers, specific forms of agreement (*intesa*) become the rule (ItCC judgement 180/1989; Costanzo, 1990, 2496). From the common objective (and the necessity of its effective realization) follows an obligation for the entities to search for an agreement (*dovere di previa intesa*) regarding the balance and compensation of the different interests involved (for instance, ItCC judgement 232/1991; see already Rimoli, 1988, 363ff.). Between bearers of heterogenous, but equally constitutionally protected interests, only cooperation in the form of an agreement allows for horizontal coordination respecting the procedural guarantees framed by the principle of loyal cooperation (*intesa forte*, ItCC judgements 351/1991 and 36/1992).

Thus, the focus shifts from regulation (and respect) of competences to the prevention of disturbances in the exercise of the respective functions (Costanzo, 1990, 2484). This safeguard of functions, guaranteed by the ordinary legislator through procedures providing coordinated links between the competences of the State and of the Regions, has characterized a series of decisions regarding the protection of the landscape (Anzon, 1986, 1039ff.).

However, these State powers, including those of substitution in case of regional inertia, do definitely not correspond any longer to the original design of separate and

12 Already in a very early judgement (49/1958), the ItCC used these expressions arguing in favour of cooperation where functions are divided but necessitate a uniform regulation within "a system of autonomies"; in the decided case, the State was exclusively competent for the sea, including the lagoons, while the Region Sardinia could regulate fishery activities.

13 For instance, in ItCC judgement 302/1988: fundamental issues in the regulation of matters relating to the protection of landscape are decided by the State legislator who exercises discretion in the balance between regional and State powers but needs to respect the "principle of a balanced competition and cooperation between the competences".

opposed spheres of competences, but see the implementation of the principle of loyal cooperation in practically all regional spheres of competencies. The respective case law has been criticized by some, as "[r]egions receive participation from one hand (as a substitute for) what has been taken from them before by the other, i.e. direct decision-making authority" (Anzon, 1986, 1039).

In 1994, the principle even justified specific financial obligations: "in the name of fundamental needs of national solidarity", the ItCC imposed stronger participation of autonomous Regions and Provinces in financing of the national Health Service, due to their favourable financial system (ItCC judgement 355/1994); however, neither a specific foundation nor the concrete content of this solidarity obligation has been given.

A further area of application of the principle is the implementation of EC/EU law, with an obligation for the Regions to implement European legislation correctly and in time, in order to save the State from responsibility for inertia vis-à-vis the European institutions. Loyal cooperation as guiding principle had already been invoked in ItCC judgement 39/1981. The supervisory function of State authorities (as those responsible at EC level) regarding the use of EC funds by regional authorities had to respect the principle (and the need for prior agreement) derived from it.

The principle of loyal cooperation is thus an expression of the balance (and tension) between respect of the unity of the Republic and the recognition and promotion of (territorial) autonomies, established by Article 5 Const. While the State function originates from the unity of the legal system, autonomy requires cooperative procedures, which include regional participation in the exercise of the State function. But the decision whether to introduce cooperative mechanisms required to overcome the limits and consequences of interlocking subject matters is regularly vested with the State; even in areas of regional competences the Regions do not have equal standing. For this reason, and because it underlines the supremacy of the State, the principle has been criticized as "pseudo-cooperation" (e.g. Bertolino, 2008, 39ff).

Loyal cooperation of State and Regions serves to overcome some cases of separation of competences in contrast with the exercise of the respective functions, but the ItCC recognized its importance for the whole area of relations between State and Regions. Its concrete implementation is set within the decision-making procedures at State level where regional participation in different forms is typically necessary before the adoption of legal provisions or other measures by the State. As a complementary principle, loyal cooperation guarantees a coordinated connection between the tasks and functions of different levels of government, in particular where it is necessary for reaching common goals prescribed by the Constitution.

However, the principle needs to be applied with caution and restraint, both due to its complementary character and due to the primacy of written constitutional provisions. Depending on the specific context and the facts, the ItCC has over time developed techniques for bridging contrasting positions through a kind of "cooperative proportionality" (examined by the Court in case of controversy); its self-restraint has often left the decision, when interlocking matters between State and Regions require cooperative measures, to the State legislator. This reflects the relatively weak position of the Regions vis-à-vis the State as well as the emphasis on guaranteeing the functioning of the whole system. In fact, the ItCC has identified Article 97 Const. and the necessity "to ensure the efficiency … of administration" as the constitutional foundation from which the principle of cooperation is derived (Martines/Ruggeri, 1997, 126).

III. Federal principles as a model? Comparative considerations

Constitutional Courts in different federal and regional systems have identified cooperation principles as inherent and related to the very nature of a composite, pluralistic system.[14] This view is shared by the ItCC which has derived the *leale collaborazione* from "the very nature of the system of constitutional autonomies".[15] Thus, a look at similar principles in federal systems and their ways of operation (Gaudreault-Debiens 2014, 23; Gamper 2010) may be of inspiration for the evolution of the Italian one.

In Austria, a rather centralised federal system, an unwritten, reciprocal duty of Federation and *Länder* is recognised, which obliges both levels to respect the sphere of competences of the other. As a prohibition of misuse or excessive use, it limits the exercise of own competences, if rules of other actors, adopted in conformity with the Constitution and the distribution of competences, would be contradicted or made impossible. However, not each form and degree of encroachment is covered, only serious obstacles to the other level's effective capacity to act. The principle of consideration (*Berücksichtigungsprinzip*) is considered a consequence from the peculiar Austrian competence system, which does not comprise any concurrent powers. Thus, the principle, confirmed by the Constitutional Court since 1984,[16] shall overcome rigidities resulting from the strict separation between the spheres of competences of Federation and *Länder* (Pernthaler, 1989, 59 and 63; Schäffer, 1985, 361; Woelk 1999, 309–312).

Also the Swiss Cantons are subject to a duty of neighbourly cooperation, and the need for mutual respect and cooperation (*Bundestreue*) had been underlined in legal doctrine and recognised as an unwritten principle or as constitutional principle deriving from the Rule of Law principle, Article 5.3 Federal Constitution (e.g. Kölz 1980, 169). In 1999, the Swiss Federal Court qualified it as a prohibition of

14 See for a brief comparison (Bifulco, 1995, 47), on Spain, Belgium, and Germany, as well as (Woelk, 1999, 308–322) on Austria, Belgium, Switzerland, and the European Union.

15 Already early on, in its ItCC judgement 49/1958; the fundamental and explicit recognition of the principle occurred in judgement 94/1984 (protection of the landscape as joint task of all entities and levels).

16 Austrian Constitutional Court, judgement VfSlg 10 292/1984. In this leading case, excessive emphasis and preference for hunting in State-legislation stood against recreational interests of population, e.g. hiking in the woods, guaranteed by the federal legislator. Despite the affirmation of the principle's mutual character, there seems to be a federal bias: only once, in 2007, a case has been decided against the Federation and in favour of the *Länder* (VfSlg 18.096/2007).

abuse of legal rights, specifically adapted to the federal context.[17] With the adoption of the new federal Constitution (2000), the unwritten principle was enshrined in great detail in the text (Section 2 "Cooperation between the Federation and the Cantons", Articles 44 to 49):

Article 44 Principles

1 The Federation and the Cantons support each other in the fulfilment of their responsibilities and work together.
2 They owe each other consideration and support. They grant each other administrative and judicial assistance.
3 Disputes between Cantons or between Cantons and the Federation are as far as possible resolved through negotiation or mediation.

Until the 1990's, the Belgian doctrine showed a critical attitude vis-à-vis any reception of the German principle due to the monarchical origins and the wide scope of application of the latter (Alen, Peeters, and Pas, 1994, 439ff.). However, a principle of "federal loyalty" had been recognized by the *Court d'Arbitrage*. In the wake of the fourth reform of the Belgian State, transforming it into a federal system, an obligation of mutual respect was introduced in the federal Constitution of 1994. The principle is, however, limited to conflicts of interest of political nature (Art. 143 § 1 Const.).[18]

In Germany, a complementary and subsidiary principle regulating the relations between the centre and the States (*Länder*), has been recognized as an unwritten constitutional principle since the imperial (con)federal system: *Bundestreue* or federal comity.[19] Its origins have been developed in the constitutional practice of the Weimar Republic (Smend, 1916/1968, 39) and later been taken over by the German Federal Constitutional Court (FCC or BVerfG). The German principle has been studied in Italy, with a view to serve as a model for reforming the Italian system (Anzon, 1995).

In a federal system, the Federation and the States together have an obligation to respect and effectively operate the constitutional order at all levels.[20] Positive constitutional provisions have priority in the examination of a controversy over an alleged violation of powers or rights, while recourse to the unwritten, wide, and undetermined principle of federal comity is only made in exceptional cases. In those cases, the principle shall serve the interests of the level of government which is unable to obtain the respect or realization of rights without the other. Thus, the

17 Swiss Federal Court, judgement BGE 125 II 152(*Rechtsmissbrauchsverbot*).
18 Belgian Federal Constitution (1994) – Article 143 [Prevention and Settling of Conflicts of Interest]:

(1) In the exercise of their respective responsibilities, the Federal Government, the Communities, the Regions, and the common Community Commission act in the interests of federal loyalty, in order to prevent conflicts of interest.

19 Bauer, Bundestreue, 1992; for an in-depth comparison between the German and the Italian principles Woelk, 1999.
20 Judgements BVerfGE 8, 139 and 12, 255.

principle serves at the same time the respect of competences and the safeguard of the functioning of the system. Only in few cases has an actual violation of the principle been found by the Federal Constitutional Court, which may be taken as an indicator for constructive and cooperative behaviour in the constitutional reality, within the system of "cooperative federalism". In the case law, three different obligations resulting from the principle can be distinguished: limits to the exercise of competencies, positive obligations to act, and procedural obligations.[21] However, due to its inherent (and necessary) flexibility, the principle is open to further evolution, with its concrete shape being determined by the constitutional judges in the individual case. The two cornerstones in its further evolution and concretization are its safeguarding function vis-à-vis the competencies and the functions of all actors in the federal system: all obligations to abstain from action or to engage in it can be developed with reference to these.

The comparison of the German principle with the Italian one shows a number of similarities regarding the operation, but also a clear difference in the emphasis on different degrees of procedural participation of the Regions (corresponding to the character of their interests involved), which shall be safeguarded by the principle of loyal cooperation (Anzon, 1995). The *Bundestreue* principle does not prescribe certain procedural solutions to be achieved through cooperation, but rather sets extreme limits to be observed in any case, balancing the guarantee of each level's functions with the protection of competencies. Stronger emphasis on the latter corresponds to the stronger constitutional position of the *Länder* in the German federal system. By contrast, in Italy a reasonable solution in the comprehensive, systemic interest, as a goal of the principle, is too often determined by the central government. There is a clear dominance of efficiency criteria over the guarantee of (regional) competencies which are limited to the regional territory.

The case law of the Italian Constitutional Court, in particular regarding the principle of loyal cooperation, has widely contributed to the evolution of the Italian system towards a form of "cooperative regionalism", characterized by a range of different "*raccordi*", i.e. institutional and procedural relations between State and Regions among which the "*intesa*" (agreement) with the State is central. Thus, cooperation serves the purpose of coordination as well as for compensating structural and institutional deficits in the participation of the Regions in the decisions at State level, at least in important areas regarding the impact on their own sphere of competence. With the unfolding and emancipation of the Italian regional system, cooperation procedures guaranteeing meaningful regional participation increasingly take the place of unilateral State-controlled mechanisms of supervision and substitution. Again, this is a structural difference compared to *Bundestreue*, corresponding to the lack of general, comprehensive federal supervision in the

21 In his seminal work on the principle, (Bauer, 1992, 332ff.) develops a different classification due to his derivation of the principle from the general *bona fides* principle (in its specific adaptation to the federal context): limitations of rights, creation of obligations, and additional rules for the treaty-law between Federation and *Länder*.

German federal system as well as to the strong participation of the Länder at federal level through their participation in the Federal Council (Article 50 Basic Law).

IV. The institutionalization of intergovernmental participation at central level

The principle of loyal cooperation paved the way for the institutional representation and regional involvement at central level. Established in 1988, the Standing Conference of State and Regions became the main interface in the intergovernmental relations between the State and the Regions, as well as the central institution for procedures of consultation and cooperation between the two levels of government.[22] The Standing Conference is composed of the presidents of all ordinary and special Regions (plus the Autonomous Provinces of Trento and Bolzano) and chaired by the central government: either by the President of the Council of Ministers or by the Minister for Regional Affairs. Therefore, it can neither be qualified as a true 'joint institution' (no equal standing), nor as a body of exclusive regional representation.[23] As an instrument for realizing the cooperation between State and Regions, its functions comprise information, consultation, and delivering positions and standpoints in all political issues of regional interest.[24] The Standing Conference has a permanent secretariat which includes detached civil servants from the single Regions.[25]

Regional participation in the exercise of the State "function of guidance and coordination" in the administrative sphere had been welcomed by the ItCC early on, but became the rule only with the so-called 'Bassanini reforms' (1997) which transferred administrative functions to the Regions involving them in fundamental decisions regarding their implementation. The involvement of the Standing Conference became mandatory "in all decision-making processes of regional, interregional and supraregional interest".[26] The Standing Conference needs to be consulted regarding all legislative proposals affecting the regional sphere of competences, but it is consulted in practice also regarding specific issues and delegations, by single ministries and before issuing governmental regulations. Often, consultation takes the form of an agreement. The political weight of the Standing Conference has much increased after the introduction of direct elections of the

22 See, for the establishment, composition, and evolution of the Standing Conference (Pizzetti, 2000, 473–494; Ruggiu, 2006; and Carpino, 2006, 13), as well as the analysis in Eleonora Ceccherini's chapter in this volume. In the present chapter, only those aspects are treated which are essential for the illustration of the institutional impact of the principle.

23 This is the purpose of the Conference of the Regions, which usually gathers the Presidents of the Regions and Autonomous Provinces before the meetings of the Standing Conference for finding a common regional position vis-à-vis the State (www.regioni.it).

24 Except foreign affairs, defence, and judicial affairs; Article 12 Law 400/1988 (on the organization of Presidency of the Council of Ministers).

25 Standing Conference of State and Regions and the Autonomous Provinces of Trento and Bolzano (www.statoregioni.it).

26 Article 9(1)(a) Law 59/1997 and Article 2(1) Legislative Decree D.Lgs. 281/1997.

Presidents of the Regions. A "conference system" has been created by establishing a parallel conference – State, cities and local bodies – for issues affecting municipalities, as well as a "Unified Conference", formed by joining both conferences, for issues of common interests. This evolution, which concentrates the functions of liaison and consultation within the Standing Conference, can be considered the beginning of an intergovernmental decision-making system (Ruggiu, 2000, 853–902).

V. The 2001 reform: a 'federalization' of Italy?

From 1999, a 'package' of three constitutional reforms aimed at transforming Italy into a federal(ised) system by considerably strengthening regional powers vis-à-vis the State.[27] Due to the political confrontation between centre-left parties (generally in favour of federalization as a means of modernization) and the centre-right bloc (with internal tensions between unitary post-fascist parties, such as the National Alliance, and at times secessionist movements, such as the Northern League) and a change of government just after the adoption of the reform, however, its implementation was extremely slow and dragged on for years with only poor results.

Based upon the notion of 'cooperative regionalism', the reform of Title V sought to balance the expansion of legislative and administrative powers of the Regions, with the obligation to exercise their autonomy in compliance with requirements of solidarity and financial equalisation between the different territories, acknowledging the State's role as guarantor of uniform minimum levels of benefits and services relating to civil and social rights throughout the national territory.

The evolution of the principle of loyal cooperation and its growing importance in the case law of the ItCC has led to its introduction into the Italian Constitution with the reform of 2001. However, the principle did not receive a central position, but is rather mentioned in a subordinate though practically important context. Indeed, the principle of loyal cooperation is enshrined in Article 120(2) Const. as a regulator in case of the exercise of coercive powers by the State vis-à-vis the Regions:

> The Government can act for bodies of the Regions, Metropolitan Cities, Provinces and Municipalities if the latter fail to comply with international rules or treaties or European Union legislation, or in the case of grave danger to public safety and security, or whenever such action is necessary to preserve legal or economic unity and in particular to guarantee the basic level of benefits relating to civil and social entitlements, regardless of the geographic boundaries within which local authorities operate. The law shall lay down

27 Constitutional Law 1/1999 targeted 'ordinary' Regions; Constitutional Law 2/2001 added some adaptations for the special Regions. Constitutional Law 3/2001 profoundly amended Title V of Part II of the Italian Constitution regulating the relations between State and Regions (Articles 114–133). See Erika Arbans's chapter in this volume for details.

procedures to ensure that substituted powers are exercised in compliance with the principles of subsidiarity and loyal cooperation.

Details of the procedure the government has to follow in order to proceed with substitution have been framed in Article 8 of Law 131/2003 (so-called 'La Loggia Law'). The ItCC has further clarified the coercive powers of substitution vis-à-vis the Regions and the regional powers vis-à-vis the local authorities, underlining the function of Article 120 as "final provision" (*norma di chiusura*) for the entire system which intends to protect some essential interests of national importance despite the new options for differentiation for territorial autonomies (Bertolino, 2008, 172).

However, the appearance of the principle in Article 120 Const. does not mean that it shall remain limited to this relatively narrow scope of application, as a restrictive interpretation might suggest; on the contrary, the principle remains of general character and continues to inform all provisions of Title V of the Constitution. This wide interpretation is based in particular on Article 5 Const. and on Article 114 Const. as amended (equating, at least on paper, the various entities constituting the Italian Republic).

Also, the elements contained in Article 119 Const., regarding financial autonomy, are closely linked to the subsidiarity principle as well as to the principle of loyal cooperation: again, the financial autonomy of the Regions must be reconciled with the protection of the constitutionally guaranteed, fundamental principles, such as substantive equality (Article 3(2) Const.), the individual rights and the fulfilment of the fundamental duties of political, economic, and social solidarity (Article 2 Const.). For these reasons, the State shall intervene through an equalization fund in favour of territories with minor fiscal capacity;[28] the principle of loyal cooperation necessarily plays a role also in this context, as well as in negotiations within the Standing Conference(s).

As the constitutional reform was limited to Title V of Part II of the Constitution, it did not create a chamber of regional representation; the Italian Parliament remained a symmetrical bicameral system. Not even the transitional solution was realized: Article 11 Constitutional Law 3/2001 foresees the participation of regional and local bodies in the respective parliamentary commissions on regional affairs, but the necessary parliamentary regulations have never been adopted (Bifulco, 2003, 211–218, and Bin, 2003, 211). Thus, the pivotal role of the Standing Conference remained unchanged.

VI. Case law of the Constitutional Court after the reform

The new competence order soon revealed a number of weaknesses of the amendments, starting from the wording and the rigidity of the subject matters, which led to interlocking competences which could not easily be assigned to or exercised by one or the other level of government. Thus, centralist tendencies have developed

28 For financial relations and equalization see Alice Valdesalici's chapter in this volume.

from the outset, both in the area of legislative powers as well as in terms of financial and political autonomy of the regions, with the central government reaffirming its irreplaceable role. Due to the lack of regional representation, Parliament did not function as a forum for balancing the roles in the new system, and the principle of loyal cooperation continued to remain confined to the intergovernmental relations and to a procedural role (Caridà 2018; Draghetti 2016).

This gave rise to an enormous increase in the controversies between the State and the Regions before the ItCC, which had the task to define the boundaries of the respective spheres of competence. Although the reformed Article 117(2) Const. assigns the central State only a limited exclusive legislative competence, the ItCC has made it clear that State powers may anyway extend into the area of regional competences embedded in Article 117(3) and (4) Const., in particular, where there is an overlap or where the subject matter is part of concurrent or residual regional powers (ItCC judgement 278/2010). Such a (re-)interpretation of the distribution of competences in favour of State legislation is all the more necessary the more the substantive legislative powers are intertwined between the two levels, and the more unitary interests must be safeguarded. Again, the protection of the environment serves as an example: it is part of the exclusive legislative powers of the State (Article 117(2)(*s*)), but according to the case law of the ItCC the protection of the environment is rather an objective and not a (pre)determined subject matter.[29] The realization of this objective is a task assigned to the State legislator, even in those areas which are constitutionally assigned to the Regions, such as public health system or construction sector (see Bifulco and Celotto, 2015).

The ItCC used its central role of arbiter to redesign the relations between legislative and administrative powers of State and Regions according to the concept of 'procedural subsidiarity': where unitary interests require a uniform exercise of administrative powers, for instance regarding the highway system or other principal infrastructures, the State is obliged not to consider the established distribution of competences, if State and Regions can reach an agreement (*intesa*), just as before the reform. This requirement, confirmed by in the ItCC judgement 303/2003,[30] necessarily leads to political negotiations between the central and regional governments in the Standing Conference. Over the last years, all major reforms were therefore subject to such negotiations about the delimitation of competences, financial resources, etc. (Repetto, 2020, 4).

However, the principle of loyal cooperation also requires the different levels of government to act elsewhere according to loyal cooperation (ItCC judgement 31/2006), i.e. to reach an agreement between different actors whenever administrative measures may infringe upon competence areas of other levels. In its case law on loyal cooperation, the ItCC has distinguished "weak" and "strong" forms of agreement, depending on whether a regional veto power on the matter is

29 ItCC judgements 536/2002 and 307/2003 now consolidated jurisprudence.

30 For an analysis of this landmark case (ItCC judgement 303/2003), see Giuseppe Martinico's chapter in this volume.

recognized or not (but the government can decide independently, if there is particular urgency or no agreement with the Conference within 30 days).[31] Other forms of participation, such as consultation or asking for a mandatory position may also be obligations prior to decision. In the absence of a systemic regulation, the specific form needs to be foreseen by the State legislator in each piece of legislation respectively. However, the central government always vests the power of ultimate decision, which can thus be different as long as the deviation is thoroughly motivated (D'Atena, 2018, 370; Carpani, 2007, 67ff.).

In areas where State measures interfere profoundly with regional subject matters, the procedure is only concluded if an agreement has effectively been reached (ItCC judgement 6/2004), which makes a joint decision necessary and puts State and Region on equal footing. However, to avoid blockade, the central government can adopt the measure it deems necessary, even if after intense negotiation no joint decision can be reached (e.g. ItCC judgements, 165/2011, 179/2012, 239/2013, and 7/2016). This presupposes that the procedures for reaching an agreement have been designed in a way to make an adequate development of the negotiations possible in order to overcome different positions (ItCC judgement 1/2016), e.g. through consultation procedures which include mechanisms for overcoming differences such as the reiteration of negotiations or specific instruments of mediation. Again, this does not question the role of the State's final – in case unilateral – and motivated decision.

In all the above cases, the principle of loyal cooperation remained limited to the area of administrative functions and the implementation of legislation (and to the forms of cooperation and participation established in that legislation); it did not apply to the legislative procedure itself (e.g. ItCC 6/2004). This changed with the judgement 251/2016, in which the ItCC clarified that the principle of loyal cooperation may also regard legislative powers, in particular those delegated to the government; in cases of their overlap with regional legislative powers, the government needs to strive for an agreement and may not insist on primacy of State powers (Repetto, 2020, 5; Amoroso, 2017, 473; Bifulco, 2017, 1; Marchetti, 2017, 1). In the judgement, some provisions of Law 124/2015 (so-called 'Legge Madia'), which delegated legislative powers for the reorganization of the public administration to the central government, had been declared unconstitutional for a violation of the principle of loyal cooperation. The parts concerned were those making the governmental decrees subject to mere regional positions instead of prior agreement within the Standing Conference. As legislative powers are delegated to the central government only, according to Article 76 Const., the agreement in question qualifies as a "weak" one (by contrast, a "strong" agreement would be subject to co-decision by the Conference). Other provisions of the same law, which required prior consultation (position of the Unified Conference) before the adoption of legislative decrees were considered as covered by State legislative powers. The different results appear in line with the general purpose of the principle, which is to guarantee the balancing of different interests. According to the

31 Art. 3 paras. 4 and 3 Legislative Decree (D.Lgs.) 281/1997.

ItCC, the aim of "reconciling the reasons for the unitary exercise of powers with the guarantee of the functions constitutionally attributed to the autonomies" cannot ignore the protection of the principle of uniformity on the national territory, which is to be guaranteed by the State. However, the inclusion of legislative powers in the scope of application of the principle of loyal cooperation does only apply to delegated legislation and not to Parliamentary legislation, as application to the latter would imply constitutional change.[32]

In sum, the ItCC took the opportunity to interrupt a previous trend, which saw it permanently involved in judging the merit on the extent of the interests involved in the contested acts. The emphasis on the "equal standing" of the levels of government that make up the Republic, the conceptual basis of the reform in 2001, and announced by Article 114 Const., provided a useful basis for the Court's argumentation to consider cooperative procedures as requisites that must be activated whenever the State wants to dictate rules on subject matters that do not fall entirely within its own constitutional competence sphere, but affect interests (and competences) entrusted to the Regions (Bin, 2007, 393). According to the ItCC, the negotiations and agreements constitute

> the principal way to concretise content and parameters of loyal cooperation which … also appears to be most coherent with the constitutional system of autonomy, since it follows a horizontal-collegial conception of reciprocal relations rather than a vertical-hierarchical vision of the same.
>
> (ItCC, judgement 31/2006)

VII. Perspectives and concluding remarks

In centralized states a strictly hierarchical organization and centralist orders guarantee the cohesion of the political and constitutional system. By contrast, in federal states a specific culture of solidarity and integration is needed in order to resolve the permanent conflicts between different levels of government. Besides specific provisions trying to capture a "federal spirit" (Burgess, 2012) in positive law, complementary unwritten principles of cooperation and conflict-settlement are still recognized in a number of federal (and regional) systems (Gamper, 2010, 157–170; Woelk, 1999, 309–326). A similar principle also applies in the supranational system of the European Union (Article 4(3) TEU; Klamert, 2014).

These principles cover aspects such as mutual consideration and respect, principles of efficient fulfilment of functions and duties, solidarity, etc. Their existence is explained by the typical relationship of mutual dependence and interdependence of federal/central and federated/sub-national entities, and the typical tension between unity of 'the system' and autonomy of its single parts. The respective allocation of competences and forms of supervision as well as participation explain

32 This limit has been confirmed by the Council of State (highest Administrative Court) in its Opinion 83/2017.

differences as well as the peculiar form of the principle in the single federal or regional system and its concrete shape in application.

In Italy, the principle of loyal cooperation has been mainly developed by the Constitutional Court. In a first phase, with the full unfolding of the regional system and the emancipation of the Regions, it was mainly applied as an unwritten, complementary principle to guarantee procedural safeguards in the form of regional consultation and participation, thus limiting and balancing central government's interferences in the (new) regional competence sphere. Based upon this case law, the principle has been constitutionalized in the reform of 2001, which gave Italian regions more powers and abolished supervision powers by the central government. The principle was now used as a counterweight for balancing the central government's powers of substitution (Article 120(2) Const.). Since then, it has been further developed by the Constitutional Court.

In occasion of the 50th anniversary of the first elections of the assemblies in the 'ordinary' Regions,[33] in August 2020, the Italian President of the Republic reminded that if "the establishment of a second, territorial Chamber" has not become a reality, it is also true that

> the already foreseen links between the regional and State levels of government remain in place. It is the system of conferences – State-Regions, State-City, Unified – that has proved its particularly important role, even during the health emergency countering the pandemic (…). The document presented by the Conference of Regions and Autonomous Provinces evokes the principle of loyal cooperation, explicitly referred to in Article 120 and repeatedly applied by the Constitutional Court. Alongside the coordination between the State and the Regions, which the intergovernmental conferences are able to ensure, a further important contribution of horizontal coordination is made by the Conference of the Regions.

The President expressly acknowledged the repeated calls and proposals made by the Conference of the Regions for a reorganization of the formal links between the State and territorial autonomies and underlined the "need to identify, with greater precision, forums and procedures through which the principle of loyal cooperation, the cornerstone of constitutional jurisprudence, can increasingly become the key principle of relations between the State, the Regions and local autonomies". For this reason, "further institutionalization and regulation of the 'Conference system' could increase the elements of articulation and connection between the national and regional levels", as the conferences are the forum of intergovernmental relations.

33 Speech by President of the Republic Sergio Mattarella on the occasion of the meeting with the Presidents of the Region, on the 50th anniversary of the establishment of the Regions with Ordinary Statute, Palazzo del Quirinale, 4 August 2020 (text of speech: https://www.quirinale.it/elementi/50028); the following quotes are from the same speech.

A "cultural change in the relations between the State and the Regions, which needs to be based on an upgrade of the forms of institutional cooperation", as advocated by the President of the Conference of Regions and in the above proposals,[34] would require a clear idea of the design of the system of territorial government and the purpose of each of its levels. In its evolution, Italy's regionalism seems continuously torn between a rock (unity, i.e. centralism) and a hard place (autonomy, i.e. differentiation) (Sterpa, 2015, and Woelk, 2014, 25–46): regionalism had been a very innovative idea in 1948, but it has been implemented with great delay and partially, then seen an emancipation of the Regions and a "federalisation" reform, which has been poorly implemented and in part been rolled back in practice; further, contradictory reform attempts followed in 2006 and 2016, both rejected in referendums. The most recent challenge is further differentiation by only some ordinary Regions according to Article 116 para. 3 Const.[35]

Thus, incremental improvement seems the only feasible way forward. An institutional upgrade of regional participation through the Parliamentary Commission for Regional Issues did not occur for two decades; it would be anyway a mere patch and not sufficient due to the limited areas of participation (Bin, 2016, 801). However, it also clearly points to the missing link in the whole system. The principle of loyal cooperation has been recognized and developed by the Italian Constitutional Court as a legal principle, with the limits described. For effectively penetrating the whole sphere of relations between the State and the Regions, however, cooperative regionalism needs a stronger political dimension in a political forum.

This is where the Italian reception of the German *Bundestreue* principle, which operates in a very different context, also finds its limits, despite obvious similarities between both cooperation principles in some fields. As regionalism may be considered "federalism's little brother", according to Peter Häberle (1994, 196), therefore the *leale collaborazione* may similarly be recognised as the *Bundestreue*'s "little sister" and be of inspiration for other regional systems.

Literature

André Alen, Patrick Peeters, and Wouter Pas, '"Bundestreue" im belgischen Verfassungsrecht' (1994) 42 *Jahrbuch des Öffentlichen Rechts – JöR* 439–505

Giovanni Amoroso, 'Legge di delega e principio di leale collaborazione tra Stato e regioni' (2017) *Foro italiano* 473

34 Declaration by President of the Conference of Regions, Stefano Bonaccini, in occasion of the 50th anniversary of Ordinary Regions, 4 August 2020 (summary: http://www.regioni.it/home/50-regioni-serve-collaborazione-istituzionale-2636/), and Conferenza Regioni e Province Autonome, Documento "Un Patto rinnovato tra le Regioni: le proposte per l'Italia", 4 August 2020: http://www.regioni.it/conferenze/data-20200804/

35 In 2018, three Regions – Veneto, Lombardy, and Emilia-Romagna – have reached preliminary agreements with the government (Cinsedo, 2019; Bertolino, Morelli, and Sobrino, 2020) as well as Francesco Palermo's chapter in this volume.

Adele Anzon, *La Bundestreue e il sistema federale tedesco: un modello per la riforma del regionalismo in Italia?* (Giuffrè, 1995)

Adele Anzon, 'Principio cooperativo e strumenti di raccordo' (1986) *Giurisprudenza costituzionale* 1039ff

Antonio Baldassare, 'Rapporti tra Regioni e Governo: i dilemmi del regionalismo' (1983) *Le Regioni* 43ff

Antonio Barbera, *Regioni e interesse nazionale* (Giuffrè, 1973)

Sergio Bartole, 'Intrecci di competenze, legislazione statale e ruolo della Conferenza Stato-Regioni' (2017) *Giurisprudenza costituzionale* 2801

Hartmut Bauer, *Die Bundestreue* (Mohr, 1992)

Cristina Bertolino, *Il principio di leale collaborazione nel policentrismo del sistema costituzionale italiano* (Giappichelli, 2008)

Cristina Bertolino, Alessandro Morelli, and Giorgio Sobrino (eds.), *Regionalismo differenziato e specialità regionale* (University of Turin, 2020) https://iris.unito.it/retrieve/handle/2318/1737860/608419/Volume_Bertolino-Morelli-Sobrino_Regionalismo%20differenziato_completo.pdf

Raffaele Bifulco, 'L'onda lunga della sentenza 251/2016 della Corte costituzionale' (2017) 3 *Federalismi* 1

Raffaele Bifulco, 'In attesa della seconda camera federale', in Tania Groppi and Marco Olivetti (eds.), *La Repubblica delle autonomie* (Giappichelli, 2nd ed., 2003) 211–218

Raffaele Bifulco and Alfonso Celotto (eds.), *Le materie dell'art. 117 Cost. nella giurisprudenza costituzionale dopo il 2001: analisi sistematica della giurisprudenza costituzionale sul riparto di competenze tra Stato e Regioni 2001–2014* (Editoriale Scientifica, 2015)

Roberto Bin, 'Dopo il referendum: puntare seriamente sulla leale collaborazione' (2016) 5–-6 *Le Regioni* 791–802http://www.robertobin.it/ARTICOLI/Dopo%20il%20referendum_Le%20Regioni.pdf

Roberto Bin, 'La "leale collaborazione" tra prassi e riforme' (2007) *Le Regioni* 393–397

Roberto Bin, 'I nodi irrisolti', in Sergio Bartole, Roberto Bin, Giandomenico Falcon, and Rosanna Tosi, *Diritto Regionale. Dopo le riforme* (Il Mulino, 2003) 191–241, at 211

Roberto Bin and Giandomenico Falcon, *Diritto regionale* (Il Mulino, 2018) 125

Stefano Bonaccini, Declaration by President of the Conference of Regions in occasion of the 50th anniversary of Ordinary Regions, 4 August2020. Summary: http://www.regioni.it/home/50-regioni-serve-collaborazione-istituzionale-2636/

Michael Burgess, *In Search of the Federal Spirit: New Comparative Empirical and Theoretical Perspectives* (Oxford University Press, 2012)

Paolo Caretti, 'Il sistema delle Conferenze e i suoi riflessi sulla forma di governo nazionale e regionale' (2000) *Le Regioni* 547

Rossana Caridà, *Leale collaborazione e sistema delle conferenze* (Cedam, 2018)

Guido Carpani, *La Conferenza Stato-regioni. Competenze e modalità di funzionamento dall'istituzione ad oggi* (Il Mulino, 2007) 67ff

Riccardo Carpino, 'Evoluzione del sistema delle Conferenze' (2006) 1 *Le istituzioni del federalismo* 13–63

Paolo Carrozza, 'Principio di collaborazione e sistema delle garanzie procedurali' (1989) *Le Regioni* 479

CINSEDO (Centro Studi Interregionale Studi e Documentazione), 'Autonomia differenziata' (2019) Dossier tecnico del Cinsedo n. 01 http://www.regioni.it/news/dossier/

Conferenza Regioni e Province Autonome, Documento 'Le Regioni italiane a 50 Anni dalle prime elezioni nel quadro dell'organizzazione pluralistica del sistema istituzionale.

Un Patto rinnovato tra le Regioni: le proposte per l'Italia', 4 August 2020 http://www.regioni.it/conferenze/data-20200804/

Angelo Costanzo, 'Modelli, principi e loro genesi' (1990) *Giurisprudenza costituzionale* 2476

Antonio D'Atena, *Diritto Regionale* (Giappichelli, 2018) 370

Antonio D'Atena, 'Osservazioni sulla ripartizione delle competenze tra Stato e regione' (1972) *Giurisprudenza costituzionale* 2011ff

Ilaria Draghetti, *La leale collaborazione tra i Poteri dello Stato: Il principio di leale collaborazione interorganica nell'ordinamento italiano e spagnolo.* (EAI edizioni accademiche Italiane, 2016)

Anna Gamper, 'On Loyalty and the Federal Constitution' (2010) 4 (2) *Vienna Journal on International Constitutional Law* 157–170

Jean-François Gaudreault-Desbiens, 'Cooperative Federalism in Search of a Normative Justification: Considering the Principle of Federal Loyalty' (2014) 23 *Constitutional Forum constitutionnel*

Elio Gizzi, *Manuale di diritto regionale* (Giuffrè, 1991) 296

Peter Häberle, *Europäische Rechtskultur* (Nomos, 1994)

Marcus Klamert, *The Principle of Loyalty in EU Law* (Oxford University Press, 2014)

Alfred Kölz, 'Bundestreue als Verfassungsprinzip' (1980) 81 *Schweizerisches Zentralblatt für Staats- und Verwaltungsrecht ZBl* 145–177

Gloria Marchetti, 'Le diverse declinazioni del principio di leale collaborazione nella delegazione legislativa elaborate dalla giurisprudenza costituzionale (alla luce della sent. n. 251 del 2016)' (2017) 2 *Rivista dell'Associazione Italiana dei Costituzionalisti* 1

Temistocle Martines and Antonio Ruggeri, *Lineamenti di diritto regionale* (Giuffrè, 1997) 126

Carlo Padula, 'Riflessioni (sparse) sulle autonomie territoriali, dopo la mancata riforma' (2016) *Le Regioni* 858

Francesco Palermo, 'Implementation and Amendment of the Autonomy Statute', in Jens Woelk, Francesco Palermo, and Josef Marko (eds.), *Tolerance through Law. Self-Governance and Group Rights in South Tyrol* (Martinus Nijhoff, 2008) 143–160

Peter Pernthaler, *Kompetenzverteilung in der Krise. Voraussetzungen und Grenzen der Kompetenzinterpretation in Österreich* (Braumüller, 1989)

Franco Pizzetti, 'La ricerca del giusto equilibrio tra uniformità e differenza: il problematico rapporto tra il progetto originario della costituzione del 1948 e il progetto ispiratore della riforma costituzionale del 2001' (2003) *Le Regioni* 599

Franco Pizzetti, 'Il Sistema delle conferenze e la forma di governo italiana' (2000) 3-4 *Le Regioni* 473–494

Giorgio Repetto, 'Das Mehrebenensystem im italienischen Regionalismus: Entwicklungslinien und offene Probleme', in H.-J. Blanke, S. Magiera, J.-C. Pielow, A. Weber (eds.), *Verfassungsentwicklungen im Vergleich. Italien 1947 – Deutschland 1949 – Spanien 1978* (Duncker & Humblot, 2021) 335–352 https://www.academia.edu/41906913/Das_Mehrebenensystem_im_italienischen_Regionalismus_Entwicklungslinien_und_offene_Probleme

Francesco Rimoli, 'Il principio di cooperazione fra Stato e Regioni nella giurisprudenza della Corte costituzionale: riflessioni su una prospettiva' (1988) 2 *Diritto e Società* 363ff

Giancarlo Rolla, 'L'evoluzione dello stato regionale in Italia: tra crisi del regionalismo omogeneo e aspirazioni a un'autonomia asimmetrica dei territori' (2019) *Le Regioni* 141

Ilenia Ruggiu, *Contro la Camera delle Regioni. Istituzioni e prassi della rappresentanza territoriale* (Jovene, 2006)

Ilenia Ruggiu, 'Conferenza Stato-Regioni: un istituto del federalismo "sommerso"' (2000) 3-4 *Le Regioni* 853–902

Rita Salerno, 'La "leale collaborazione" come principio cardine del sistema delle Conferenze', in *Presidenza del Consiglio dei Ministri*, Ufficio di Segreteria della Conferenza Stato-città ed autonomie locali, *Rapporto sulle attività* 2017–2018 93–100 http://www.conferenzastatocitta.it/media/1303/rapporto-sulle-attivita-2017-2018-conferenza-stato-citta-ed-autonomie-locali_per_sito.pdf

Heinz Schäffer, 'Kompetenzverteilung und Rücksichtnahmepflicht im Bundesstaat' (1985), *Zeitschrift für Wirtschaftsrecht – ZfW* 357–361

Girolamo Sciullo, 'Indirizzo e coordinamento' (1993) 7 *Digesto delle Discipline Pubblicistiche* 228–243

Rudolf Smend, *Ungeschriebenes Verfassungsrecht im monarchischen Bundesstaat* (Duncker & Humblot, 1916/1968)

Alessandro Sterpa, *Il pendolo e la livella. Il 'federalismo all'italiana' e le riforme* (Giappichelli, 2015)

Jens Woelk, 'Italy's Odyssey between Federalism and Regionalism (2001)', in Gudrun M. Grabher and Ursula Mathis-Moser (eds.), *Regionalism(s). A Variety of Perspectives from Europe and the Americas*, Schriftenreihe IFÖ - Institut für Föderalismus, vol. 119 (New Academic Press, 2014) 25–46

Jens Woelk, 'What it Means to be Special in Relations with the Central State: Institutions and Procedures', in Jens Woelk, Francesco Palermo, and Josef Marko (eds.), *Tolerance through Law. Self-Governance and Group Rights in South Tyrol* (Martinus Nijhoff, 2008) 121–142

Jens Woelk, *Konfliktregelung und Kooperation im italienischen und deutschen Verfassungsrecht. „Leale collaborazione" und Bundestreue im Vergleich* (Nomos, 1999)

11 Federalism, regionalism, and the principle of subsidiarity

Giuseppe Martinico[1]

1 Introduction

What is subsidiarity in Italian constitutional law? This Chapter explores the mutation that the principle of subsidiarity – enshrined in Article 118 of the Italian Constitution (It. Const.) – has experimented with in the national constitutional system over the last 20 years.

Subsidiarity could be regarded as an example of a principle that was originally alien to the Italian Constitution and was introduced under the pressure of European Union (EU) law. As defined in the *Oxford English Dictionary*, subsidiarity signifies 'that a central authority should have a subsidiary function, performing only those tasks which cannot be performed effectively at a more immediate or local level'.[2] This implies both a constitutional preference for the exercise of a competence by the periphery and a 'constitutional restraint on the exercise of those competences granted to the centre' (Schütze [a], 2009, 246).

The principle has been defined by the case law of the of the Italian Constitutional Court (ItCC). Indeed, soon after the entry into force of the constitutional reform, ItCC partly reshaped this principle, as we will see when analysing judgement 303/2003.

This Chapter is divided into two parts: first, I will make some theoretical considerations about the concept of subsidiarity in constitutional theory; and second, I will deal with the relevant case law of the ItCC.

My claim is that over the years, the principle of subsidiarity has, to a certain extent, lost its conceptual autonomy. The procedural understanding of this principle given by the ItCC has somehow reduced subsidiarity to a sort of ancillary instrument and has given loyal cooperation a primary role. Since loyal cooperation is treated in the chapter authored by Woelk, I will limit my considerations to subsidiarity as understood in a narrow sense. At the same time, subsidiarity has sometimes been reduced to adequacy and has thus worked as federal proportionality. For instance, there are very few cases in which one can still see a sort of

1 Professor in Comparative Public Law, Scuola Superiore Sant'Anna, Pisa. Many thanks to Erika Arban, Giacomo Delledonne, Francesco Palermo, and Giorgio Repetto for their help and comments.

2 Entry 'Subsidiarity' https://www.lexico.com/definition/subsidiarity.

DOI: 10.4324/9781003104469-12

conceptual autonomy of subsidiarity from loyal cooperation. I am referring to the cases concerning the constitutional autonomy of municipalities. For the sake of clarity, it is necessary to recall that in Italian constitutional law, we make a distinction between horizontal and vertical subsidiarity.[3] Horizontal subsidiarity refers to the relationship between public power and civil society and aims at involving citizens in activities that are of 'general interest'. Vertical subsidiarity instead has to do with the relationship between the State and the other territorial actors comprising the Republic according to the wording of Article 114 It. Const.[4] Both horizontal (also called social) and vertical subsidiarity are recalled by Article 118 It. Const. For the purpose of this Chapter, I shall mainly refer to its vertical dimension, which is crucial in order to understand the development of Italian federalism.[5]

2 The origin of the concept: different contexts, but similar concerns

EU law has undoubtedly represented a source of inspiration for the codification of the principle of subsidiarity in Italy[6], although the concept, especially in its horizontal dimension, can be found much earlier and, in particular, in the social doctrine of the Church, namely in some encyclicals such as *Rerum Novarum* and *Quadragesimo Anno* respectively issued by Pope Leo XIII on 15 May 1891 and Pope Pius XI on 15 May 1931.[7]

In its vertical dimension, the subsidiarity principle has also been a main feature of German federalism as we will see later in this Chapter.

3 'While "vertical" subsidiarity concerns the distribution of powers among different layers of the public sphere, "horizontal" subsidiarity relates to the sharing of competences and initiatives between public and private actors. In the "horizontal" sense, subsidiarity could be conceived like a sort of "division of labour" between public sector and civil society (person, family, non-profit organization, market)' (Colombo, 2008, 182).

4 Article 114 It. Const: 'The Republic is composed of the Municipalities, the Provinces, the Metropolitan Cities, the Regions and the State. Municipalities, provinces, metropolitan cities and Regions are autonomous entities having their own statutes [*statuti*], powers and functions in accordance with the principles laid down in the Constitution. Rome is the capital of the Republic. Its status is regulated by State Law'.

5 This does not mean the case law on its horizontal dimension is not interesting per se. On the contrary, some very interesting judgments concerning horizontal subsidiarity have recently been delivered. See Italian Constitutional Court, judgement 131/2020. On this, see Rossi, 2020; Gori, 2020. However, I not going to deal with this case law in this piece.

6 Something similar happened in Poland where subsidiarity is recalled by the Preamble of the Constitution, which is 'based on respect for freedom and justice, cooperation between the public powers, social dialogue as well as on the principle of subsidiarity in the strengthening the powers of citizens and their communities'. However, as Arban clarifies, in Poland the horizontal dimension of subsidiarity has so far been prevalent (Arban, 2015, 137).

7 Rerum Novarum (1891), available at: http://www.vatican.va/content/leo-xiii/en/encyclicals/documents/hf_l-xiii_enc_15051891_rerum-novarum.html; Quadragesimo anno (1931), available at: http://www.vatican.va/content/pius-xi/en/encyclicals/documents/hf_p-xi_enc_19310515_quadragesimo-anno.html.

The literature on subsidiarity is massive (Estella, 2002; Syrpis, 2004; Davies [b], 2006, 63; Fasone, 2013), especially with regard to EU law. Indeed, it is possible to argue that one of the goals of the Lisbon Treaty was to strengthen the principle, and this has been done by clarifying the competences of the EU and by introducing some political safeguards capable of ensuring its – so to say – physiological functioning. The subsidiarity principle, on the one hand, needs an arrangement of competences that at least tend towards a clear sharing of tasks and, on the other hand, presupposes an 'integrated' system like, for example, that of a federal arrangement of a cooperative type (Schütze [a], 2009). As a matter of fact, the principle, as regulated in Article 5(3) of the Treaty of European Union (TEU), refers to a relationship between two institutional actors (a lower actor, the 'regional and local level', and a higher actor, the 'central level') sharing the same power. The exercise of this power is preferentially given to the subject that is closer to the citizens (i.e., the regional or local level). Scholars usually label this as the negative side of subsidiarity since it implies the duty of non-intervention by the centre. At the same time, this principle allows for the possibility for the centre to replace the 'peripherical actor' if the same power can be exercised in a better or more efficient way by the 'higher' subject (the Union). Against this background, subsidiarity works as an elevator (Bin, 2002, 365) with regard to certain fungible acts that can be exercised by two institutional subjects, and the centripetal substitution and exercise of this power can be caused only by an objective impossibility to 'sufficiently' carry out the requested action for the peripherical actor. In other words,

> [v]ertical subsidiarity implies that action (usually, legislative action) should be taken, whenever possible, at the lowest appropriate level of government at which a given objective can be achieved, with the central authority simply playing a "subsidiary" role, performing only tasks that cannot be better completed at local level.
>
> (Arban, 2015, 130)

Another important fact is that such an impossibility to carry out the functions must be temporal. The subsidiarity principle actually works as a criterion for shifting, although not in a definitive way, the level that is supposed to intervene (Massa Pinto, 2003). Because of its constitutional relevance, it also serves as an element of flexibility in the system (Bin, 2002).

This would explain why, within the Community context, subsidiarity operated as a 'method of policy centralisation' (Davies [a], 2006) in the absence of a formal catalogue of competences rather than as a validating factor for decentred realities. Subsidiarity and competence are nevertheless not in a relationship of identity: the principle of subsidiarity is not intended so much for an *a priori* formal allocation of competences but rather for an *a posteriori* legitimation of the exercise of competences beyond those formally attributed (Massa Pinto, 2003).

Subsidiarity should in principle be based on a clear separation of competences but has *de facto* operated everywhere as a possible factor of flexibilisation of the exercise of power. This is the case in a context such as Germany, thanks to Article 72(2) of the Basic Law, which reads:

> The Federation shall have the right to legislate on matters falling within items 4, 7, 11, 13, 15, 19a, 20, 22, 25 and 26 of paragraph (1) of Article 74 [ambits of concurrent legislative powers], if and to the extent that the establishment of equivalent living conditions throughout the federal territory or the maintenance of legal or economic unity renders federal regulation necessary in the national interest.

Even in Germany, despite the constitutional reforms to make subsidiarity justiciable (Taylor, 2006, 119), concerns about its political nature have not been missing (Taylor, 2009). The German case is interesting, however, because it seems to confine subsidiarity within the realm of concurrent legislative powers. Here a terminological caveat is necessary. Italian constitutional law, in this area, the State and the Regions co-legislate. While it is for the State to set out the fundamental principles in so-called 'framework laws' (*legge-quadro*), each Region is free to implement the national framework through more detailed provisions. The Italian model of 'shared competence' is evidently different from the German system of *konkurrierende Gesetzgebung* (Anzon, 2003). When the German federal State and its *Länder* share a competence, the *Land* 'shall have power to legislate so long as and to the extent that the Federation has not exercised its legislative power by enacting a law'.[8] According to the Italian model, by contrast, the activities of the two actors are conceived of as 'complementary'. This is a fundamental distinction that should be considered when comparing the operativity of subsidiarity in Germany and Italy, especially with regard to the expansion of the concept by the ItCC beyond the field of shared competences.[9]

In the EU case, subsidiarity originally revealed its ambiguity because the Treaties defined competences in a finalistic manner in the pre-Lisbon phase given the absence of clear lists of competences. This is the reason that its introduction was described by Toth as 'totally alien' to the EU since it 'contradicts the logic, structure and wording of the founding treaties and the jurisprudence of the European Court of Justice' (Toth, 1993, 1079).

Subsidiarity is a very ambiguous concept, and confirmation of such an ambiguity may also be found in European law.

At an economic level, 'the principle of subsidiarity means that the production of public goods should be attributed to the level of government that has jurisdiction over the area in which that good is public' (Padoa Schioppa, 1995, 155). The

8 Art 72 German Basic Law.

9 Switzerland will not be treated in this Chapter, but it represents another example of constitutionalisation of subsidiarity, see Article 5a Swiss Constitution: 'The principle of subsidiarity must be observed in the allocation and performance of state tasks'. This norm seems to refer to both vertical and horizontal subsidiarity.

subsidiarity principle seems to be limited to its 'negative' aspect: the preference conferred upon the subjects closest to the citizen.

The EU case is interesting for at least three reasons: 1. it confirms the relevance of subsidiarity in cooperative federalisms; 2. it confirms the predominant procedural understanding of subsidiarity; and 3. it also confirms the proximity between subsidiarity and proportionality.

Concerning the first point, in his comparison between American and German federalisms, Schütze stressed the importance in both these experiences of the transition from dual to cooperative federalism, a transition characterised by the decline of constitutional and legislative exclusivity (which constitutes the premise of dual federalism). However, there is an important distinction between these two experiences: 'What is striking about the transition from dual to cooperative federalism in the European legal order is that—unlike its American counterpart—this development has been "constitutionalised"'(Schütze [a], 2009, 9). How has Europe constitutionalised such a development? According to Schütze, the answer can be found in the constitutionalisation of the subsidiarity principle and in the recognition of complementary competences. Borrowing the language from American comparative law scholars, namely, the concept of the 'political safeguard' of federalism used in 1954 by Wechsler (Wechsler, 1954), both concepts can be defined as the 'political safeguards' of the EU's federalism.

Concerning the second point, the matter for discussion remains the high level of political discretion which would characterise the application of such a principle because of the political nature of the control base and the difficult verification of the efficiency and context of the action.[10] This reading has been confirmed by the case law of the CJEU, which has traditionally avoided dealing head-on with the issue. Scholars have noticed some progress in this field, but the approach of the CJEU has remained quite hesitant (Öberg [a], 2017). The most telling example of this trend is an old case – *United Kingdom v. Council*[11] – in which *de facto* the subsidiarity control was seen as a kind of *extrema ratio* exploitable solely in the case of manifest error or misuse of power.

Finally, even in this instance, the EU law case is telling of a broader phenomenon with regard to the relationship between competence and subsidiarity.

This leads us back to the third point: in EU law, subsidiarity has mainly been understood as 'federal proportionality':

> The Court, and much of the academic literature, makes a distinction between "whether" the Community should exercise its competence and "how" it does it. The former is conceptualised as subsidiarity the latter is viewed as proportionality. This distinction is misleading. Subsidiarity must be understood in terms of federal proportionality. Why? There are two reasons – one theoretical and one conceptual. Theoretically, a subsidiarity principle that concentrates on

10 On the dangerous technocratic potential of subsidiarity, see Scaccia, 2009, 107.
11 CJEU, C-84/94 United Kingdom v. Council, ECR, 1996 I-5755.

> the "whether" of Community action operates within a philosophy of dual federalism. It is based on the either-or logic in which certain objectives should not involve the European Community or the Member States at all. By excluding the Community from the scene, subsidiarity *sensu stricto* protects a sphere in which the Member States can exclusively exercise their competences. And by insisting that certain objectives are "Community objectives" as they can only be achieved by the Community, the Court equally constructs a sphere in which only the European Union can operate.
>
> But more importantly: on a conceptual level, it is impossible to reduce subsidiarity to "whether" the Community should exercise one of its competences.
>
> (Schütze [b], 2009, 532)

In spite of the developments introduced by the Lisbon Treaty, the CJEU has not yet shown that it is ready to exercise a strong judicial review. This ambiguous relationship between competence and subsidiarity and the difficulty to make subsidiarity actually justiciable are issues that are also present in the Italian system, as we will see.

3 Italian subsidiarity at work: The role of the Italian Constitutional Court in judgement 303/2003

Having recalled the theoretical notion of subsidiarity, it is interesting to see that the principle was also slipped into the Italian Constitution. The principle of subsidiarity is enshrined in Article 118 of the Constitution:

> Administrative functions are attributed to the Municipalities, unless they are attributed to the provinces, metropolitan cities and Regions or to the State, pursuant to the principles of subsidiarity, differentiation and proportionality, to ensure their uniform implementation.
>
> Municipalities, provinces and metropolitan cities carry out administrative functions of their own as well as the functions assigned to them by State or by regional legislation, according to their respective competences.
>
> State legislation shall provide for co-ordinated action between the State and the Regions in the subject matters as per Article 117, paragraph two, letters b) and h), and also provide for agreements and co-ordinated action in the field of cultural heritage preservation.
>
> The State, Regions, metropolitan cities, provinces and municipalities shall promote the autonomous initiatives of citizens, both as individuals and as members of associations, relating to activities of general interest, on the basis of the principle of subsidiarity.

However, subsidiarity in Italian constitutional law did not come out of the blue in 2001, as this principle had been one of the pillars of some important legislative reforms about the decentralisation and simplification of the public administrations, the so-called 'Bassanini laws' (laws 59/1997, 127/1997, /191/1998, and 50/1999), named for the former Minister, Professor Franco Bassanini.

Germs of subsidiarity can be found even in the 1948 constitutional text, for instance, looking at Articles 4 and 5.[12] Authors have also found the track of subsidiarity in the preparatory works of the Constituent Assembly with regard to Article 2.[13] Indeed, Article 118 has been seen as 'as an elaboration of Article 5, where it mandates that the Italian Republic "implements the fullest measure of administrative decentralisation in those services which depend on the State"' (Arban 2015, 134).

Municipalities had a crucial role in the scheme designed by Article 118. This does not come as a surprise since Italy has a long municipal tradition. The origins of the Italian municipalities (*comuni*) can be traced back to the Middle Ages. In that era, the *comuni* were emblematic of the urban revolt against the feudal system.[14] Further evidence of Italy's long municipal tradition is provided by the fact that the National Association of Italian Municipalities was set up as early as 1901. To be sure, Italian municipalities have passed through different phases during their history. Most notably, their autonomy was largely affected by fascist centralism. Today, however, municipalities represent Italy's basic administrative subunit.[15] Some of the instruments provided by the Italian constitutional system for the reconciliation of regional autonomy and the principle of the unity of the Italian Republic[16] find their origin in the legislation on municipal autonomy. The best example thereof is the State's substitution or replacement power.[17]

In judgement 303/2003, the Italian Constitutional Court used the subsidiarity principle as a Trojan horse to reshape the distribution of competences codified in the Constitution. The Court expanded the original scope of application of the

12 Article 4 It. Const: 'The Republic recognises the right of all citizens to work and promotes those conditions which render this right effective. Every citizen has the duty, according to personal potential and individual choice, to perform an activity or a function that contributes to the material or spiritual progress of society'.

Article 5 It. Const: 'The Republic is one and indivisible. It recognises and promotes local autonomies and implements the fullest measure of administrative decentralisation in those services which depend on the State. The Republic adapts the principles and methods of its legislation to the requirements of autonomy and decentralisation'.

13 Article 2 It. Const: 'The Republic recognises and guarantees the inviolable rights of the person, both as an individual and in the social groups where human personality is expressed. The Republic expects that the fundamental duties of political, economic and social solidarity be fulfilled'. See also Armanno, 2010, 38 commenting upon the important contribution given by Giuseppe Dossetti.

14 See, e.g., Ascheri, 2006. Of course, those *comuni* cannot, in terms of functions, be compared to the current municipalities.

15 Art 118 It. Const: 'with the new art. 118(1), the legislator preferred to reserve all administrative functions to the level of government closest to the citizens, unless there is a prevailing common interest, and regardless of how legislative competences are allotted' (Arban, 2015, 135).

16 Art 5 It. Const ('The Republic, one and indivisible, recognises and promotes local autonomy').

17 Sometimes also called 'subsidiary power' or *potere sostitutivo*.

subsidiarity principle by inventing a mechanism analogous to the idea of 'national interest' which was present in the wording of the old Title V of the Constitution but was discarded in the 2001 reform.

To understand this judgement, it is necessary to briefly recall the division of powers that characterised the post-2001 system in Italy. According to the principle of conferred powers, the State and the Regions can only act within the limits of the competences conferred upon them by the Constitution to attain the objectives set out in the fundamental charter. In Italian constitutional law, there are three types of competences (D'Atena, 2003). The first type includes competences exclusive to the State. These competences are listed in Article 117(2) of the Italian Constitution. The second category consists of shared competences, which are also expressly enumerated in the Constitution (art 117(3)). Third, Article 117(4) of the Italian Constitution proclaims that the Regions have legislative powers in all subject matter areas that are not expressly covered by State legislation, that is, that are not included in the lists of powers laid down in Article 117. These regional powers should be understood as *exclusive* to the Regions.

The most important novelty of the 2001 Italian constitutional reform was the transformation of the Regions into 'residual legislators'. This could be seen as a sort of Copernican revolution. At least on paper, it looks as if the Regions have been vested with considerable autonomy. In reality, however, a very different picture seems to emerge. This is due to some judgments of the Italian Constitutional Court as well as to the so-called 'transversal matters' or clauses that allow the State to intervene in different areas (Carrozza, 2003; Benelli, 2007). An example of such a transversal matter is the legislation on the 'determination of the basic level of benefits relating to civil and social entitlements to be guaranteed throughout the national territory'. This kind of legislation can obviously serve as a Trojan horse leading to the centralisation of powers. When deciding case n. 303/2003, the Italian Constitutional Court fixed a set of conditions under which a derogation to the allocation of competences designed by the Constitution could be possible. The derogation should be:

> proportionate to the public interest that justifies the exercise of regional functions by the state, it must not be unreasonable in light of strict constitutional scrutiny, and, finally, the derogation should be the result of an agreement with the region.
>
> (Groppi and Scattone, 2004, 135)

Against this background, the ItCC insisted on the reasons which allow for a derogation of the system of competence when some unitary interests are at stake, even going beyond the areas of exclusive competence of the State.[18]

This judgement has been a milestone. First, the Court reintroduced a concept similar to that of national interest that had disappeared from the constitutional text in 2001. Second, subsidiarity is seen as an element of flexibilisation like those

18 Italian Constitutional Court judgment 303/2003. My own translation.

present in Article 72 of the German Basic Law. Third, the ItCC reshaped Italian regionalism with regard to the administrative functions in the name of the principle of legality. As stated by Groppi and Scattone:

> Under the principle of legality (a pillar of the rule of law), functions that are exercised at the national level according to the principle of subsidiarity must be organised and regulated by national law. In this way, one may derogate from the allocation of legislative competences contained in article 117 of the Constitution.
>
> (Groppi and Scattone, 2004, 135)

Judgement 303/2003 has also given a procedural understanding of subsidiarity by emphasising the importance of loyal cooperation (Mainardis, 2011, 476).[19] In order to have the principle of subsidiarity respected, it is necessary that the principle of loyal cooperation is respected as well. Thus, there are three requirements for the activation of the principle of subsidiarity:

> [F]irst, for a national law to legitimately attract administrative functions to the centre, there shall be a need for a unitary discipline. Also, while the law shall regulate such functions, it shall limit the regulation to what is necessary to achieve the ultimate goal. Finally, the adopted law shall guarantee the participation of the levels of government involved (i.e. central and peripheral) through a variety of cooperation mechanisms.
>
> (Arban, 2015, 137)

In other words, for the Italian Constitutional Court, the relationship between subsidiarity and loyal cooperation is that the former requires loyal cooperation ('leale collaborazione', Agosta, 2008) between the territorial actors, concerted practices, and bodies and, finally, a system of agreements between the institutional actors. This is in line with the pluralist flavour that subsidiarity has, at least in theory (Scaccia, 2009, 3).

The existence of an agreement between the institutional actors becomes an essential element for the review of the potential violation of the subsidiarity principle in the mind of the ItCC. What kind of agreements are they? Since this judgement, the ItCC has been struggling with ambiguous case law that has distinguished between different types of agreements. Scholars speak of weak agreements ('intese deboli') if after every attempt to reach agreement within a given period, the State may take the final decision, provided that it is adequately justified with regard to the circumstances which made it impossible to reach a consensus, and the reasons of national interest which led to the unilateral adoption of the act. On the contrary, strong agreements ('intese forti') are characterised by the fact that the failure to reach an agreement constitutes an insuperable obstacle to the conclusion of the procedure. This distinction was not new in the case law of

19 See, for instance, Corte costituzionale judgement 79/2011 and more recently Corte costituzionale judgment 246/2020.

the ItCC, but it was regained in the case law on subsidiarity and loyal cooperation.[20] Subsidiarity seems to have a cooperative nature which finds its arena in the system of the conferences (see Woelk and Ceccherini in this volume). What the ItCC did in judgement 303/2003 was to identity a possible negotiating path to be followed by the relevant institutional actors. However, there are also judgments in which the reference to the collaborative form disappears, as is the case of judgement 423/2004.[21]

As suggested by the commentators (Candido, 2016), the subsequent case law has made this distinction between strong and weak agreement unclear.[22] This explains the chemistry between loyal cooperation and subsidiarity that has characterised the constitutional case law over the years (see Woelk in this volume). This judgement also gave a new boost to the system of conferences existing in Italy, a jurisdiction characterised by the absence of a proper Chamber of the Regions (Ruggiu, 2006). As Mainardis suggested in judgement 303: 'The constitutional judge expressly states its intention not to verify, in concrete terms, the national importance or strategic importance of the planned interventions letting the appreciation be made in contradictory between State and Regions' (Mainardis, 2011, 463).

This kind of approach has *de facto* made subsidiarity a concept ancillary to that of loyal cooperation, jeopardising in this way its conceptual autonomy.

4 The subsequent case law

The subsequent case law has progressively eroded the original design of judgement 303.

The system designed by judgement 303/2003 was almost immediately readjusted and then put in crisis by the subsequent jurisprudence. In judgement 6/2004[23] the ItCC introduced an element of difference from what is codified in Article 72 of the German Basic Law by clarifying that the attraction in subsidiarity can also be used in the field of exclusive competences of the Region.[24] On that occasion, the ItCC again stressed the importance of necessity, adequacy and proportionality in the review of the State's intervention. However, rather than reviewing the necessity of the state intervention, the ItCC focused on declaring the unconstitutionality of those laws that did not provide for the regional involvement[25] or that did not provide for it in an adequate manner.[26] In particular,

20 For instance, Corte costituzionale judgment 233/ 2004 and judgment 31/2006. On this, see Capunzo, 2006; Mainardis, 2011, 474.
21 Corte costituzionale judgement 423/2004.
22 For instance, Corte costituzionale judgment 1/2016.
23 Corte costituzionale judgement 6/2004.
24 There was an attempt to rationalise judgment 303/2003 with judgement 270/2005, which recalls judgment 6/2004 by taking a different path. On this, see Scaccia, 2009, 87.
25 See Corte costituzionale judgments 242/2005, 285/2005, 383/2005.
26 Corte costituzionale judgment 285/2005. Vanoni, 2009, 68.

> with decision 383/2005, the ItCC explains that the agreement between the State and Regions shall be bilateral, thus excluding the possibility of a decision taken on one side only (usually, the State's), so that the two actors (State and Regions) shall have an equal position in the deal. Efforts shall be made so that this type of "strong agreement" is reached.
>
> (Arban, 2015, 137)

Another element which has partly contributed to transforming subsidiarity is that the case law by which the ItCC has extended the operability of subsidiarity to state non-legislative powers,[27] while originally the case law of the ItCC focused on legislative subsidiarity – and made it a factor of 'legislative unification' (Scaccia, 2009, 75). Another ambit in which the case law of the ItCC has developed is that of the State's substitution or replacement power.[28]

The lack of conceptual autonomy of subsidiarity in the constitutional jurisprudence can also be found in those judgments in which the control on subsidiarity was carried out as if it were control on proportionality. Evidence of this chemistry between proportionality and subsidiarity can be found in judgement 215/2010.[29] Provided with a polysemous nature, the success of proportionality in comparative law has been connected to 'the shift from a culture of authority to a culture of justification' (Cohen-Eliya and Porat, 2011, 466).

Administrative lawyers tend to distinguish between reasonableness and proportionality because the latter would control only the suitability of the administrative measure (Galetta, 1998, 14) and because

> unlike the reasonableness test, the very idea of proportionality is able by itself to shift judicial review from the control of the legality of administrative measures to their opportunity; that is, from a legitimacy control to a control of the merit.
>
> (Martinico and Simoncini, 2017)

In a nutshell, one of the main features of the proportionality test in the case law of the Italian Constitutional Court is that it tends to conflate proportionality and

27 Corte costituzionale, judgments 151/2005, 285/2005, 213/2006, 214/2006, 63/2008, 168/2008, 76/2009. On these developments, see Di Cosimo, 2009.

28 Corte costituzionale judgments 43 and 69/2004. For an overview of the debate, see Mainardis, 2007; Buffoni, 2007.

29 Corte costituzionale judgment 215/2010. Proportionality is commonly understood as a general principle of law in many national jurisdictions, and it has also over the years been accepted and used by international and supranational courts. Comparative lawyers have defined proportionality as 'a requirement for justification' (Cohen-Eliya and Porat, 2011, 474). In its simplest version, proportionality refers to the fact that the acts of a legal entity (for instance, the State) 'must be a rational and reasonable exercise of means towards achieving a permissible goal, without unduly encroaching on protected rights' (Crawford, 2011, 533). The genesis of proportionality is rooted in Prussian law as a test articulated in three steps (suitability, necessity and narrow proportionality). Born in the *Polizeirecht,* it has become a very trendy concept and a widespread tool.

reasonableness. Even in this case, one can detect a *terminological uncertainty* ('incertezza terminologica') (Cartabia, 2013). As Cartabia pointed out, there has been 'a promiscuous use of terms like rationality, reasonableness and proportionality, but also adequacy, consistency, not arbitrariness, relevance and many others, as they were synonymous' (Cartabia, 2013).[30] An emblematic example of this is given by decision 2/1999 whereby the Court argued that: '[T]he automatism of the disciplinary sanction is unreasonable, contrasting with the principle of proportionality, which is at the basis of the rationality which shapes the principle of equality.'[31] When comparing the 'toolbox' of the Italian Constitutional Court with that of other Supreme or Constitutional judges, one must make clear that the case law of the *Corte Costituzionale* does not really distinguish between the proportionality and reasonableness tests. The Court made this explicit in judgement 220/1995 by defining proportionality (there named 'principio di proporzione') as a 'direct expression of the general canon of reasonableness'.[32] This terminological ambiguity is confirmed by judgement 303/2003 itself in which the ItCC refers to both reasonableness and proportionality. Over the years, the reasonableness test has changed its nature in the case law of the Italian Constitutional Court (Paladin, 1994, 163) and today works as a pillar in the case law of the Constitutional Court combined with all the other principles of the Italian Constitution. Reasonableness has acquired a 'pervasive character' (Cartabia, 2013) in the case law of the *Corte costituzionale* because of that, being invoked by the Court when balancing fundamental rights and interests. In this way, the Court makes clear that the fundamental rights are not absolute in the sense that they limit each other and have to coexist.

These considerations lead us to the tricky relationship between proportionality and subsidiarity that in theory principles with a different scope of action but in actuality is hard to distinguish (Armanno, 2010, 19, 68; Moscarini, 2003, 80). Commenting upon this case law, Mainardis (2011) concluded that 'it is the principle of adequacy which is the true foundation of state intervention and, at the same time, the yardstick against which the Court scrutinises legislative measures' This reduces subsidiarity to 'a mere verbal formula' (Mainardis 2011, 491). Are there any areas in which subsidiarity and loyal cooperation can be decoupled? Interesting insights come from the constitutional case law concerning municipal autonomy.[33] Especially in judgement 179/2019, the principle of subsidiarity has been used as a shield to protect the 'constitutional core of municipal autonomy' (Gorlani, 2020) against a regional law. In the words of the ItCC, the principle of vertical subsidiarity

30 In Italian: 'Nella giurisprudenza costituzionale italiana si nota un uso promiscuo di termini come razionalità, ragionevolezza, proporzionalità, ma anche adeguatezza, coerenza, congruenza, non arbitrarietà, pertinenza e molti altri, quasi si trattasse di sinonimi', my own translation.

31 Corte costituzionale, judgement 2/1999, available at: www.cortecostituzionale.it.

32 Corte costituzionale, judgement 220/1995, available at: www.cortecostituzionale.it.

33 Corte costituzionale, judgements 119/ 2020 and 179/2020. Repetto, 2020.

> leads this Court to assess, in the context of a function recognised as fundamental within the meaning of Article 117(2)(p) of the Italian Constitution, how much the regional law removes from municipal autonomy and how much of it remains, in the name of what supra-municipal interests it implements this removal, what procedural compensation it provides for and for what period of time it provides for it.[34]

On this basis, the ItCC reviewed the regional law to verify its proportionality. This judgement confirms the importance of adequacy and proportionality in the cases involving the justiciability of the subsidiarity principle.

5 Final remarks

In this Chapter, I looked at the transfiguration of subsidiarity, whose codification has been one of the most important novelties introduced by the constitutional reform dated 2001.

As we saw, subsidiarity was not entirely new to the Italian legal system: it was somehow implicit in some constitutional provisions and, above all, it had been the pillar of some important administrative reforms passed at the end of the 1990s. As elsewhere, subsidiarity reveals its ambiguity. As the ItCC recognised in judgement 303/2003, it has both a static and dynamic aspect:

> the former relates to the allocation of administrative functions to municipalities as per Article 118(1), while the "dynamic" dimension pertains to the possibility of identifying an element of flexibility in it, thus allowing the satisfaction of unitary (or national) interests.
>
> (Arban, 2015, 136)

Judgement 303/2003 reshaped the constitutional reform passed in 2001 by betting its fortune on subsidiarity seen as an essential element of flexibility and dynamism. At the same time, it brought back to life the concept of national interest and tied subsidiarity to loyal cooperation, understanding it as a sort of procedural protocol. Many of the promises made in that judgement were not later kept. Subsidiarity went beyond shared competences and extended to non-legislative interventions, and the uncertain distinction between strong and weak agreements made subsidiarity more and more evanescent. This has also introduced inconsistencies in the case law of the ItCC. Make no mistake: the ItCC tried to make subsidiarity work in a system in which there is no proper federal second chamber, and the attempt to crystallise the material ambits of separated legislative interventions failed. The promises made in judgement 303/2003 were also not fulfilled because of these factors.

In conclusion, it is possible to trace these considerations back to some broader comparative remarks.

As we saw, according to the CJEU, since the control on subsidiarity touches the sensitive field of the legislative discretion, this reveals the 'political' nature of this test. Keeping this in mind, one can understand the rationale behind the introduction of

34 Corte costituzionale judgement 179/2020. My own translation.

the Early Warning System (EWS). This case law explains why in the last few years all attempts to reform the principle of subsidiarity have attempted to emphasise the procedural side of such a control, entrusting a crucial role to the national legislatures, as the provisions included in the (defunct) Constitutional Treaty and in the Lisbon Treaty demonstrate. The only way to limit legislative discretion seems to be to impose procedural guarantees such as those contained in the Protocol on the application of the principles of subsidiarity and proportionality. Moreover, a similar procedural shift can be found even in the case law of the CJEU (Öberg [b], 2017).

As a result, the EWM (Granat, 2018; Russo, 2020), as a form of political monitoring, was provided in that Protocol. This idea confirms the deference shown by the CJEU towards the legislatures; since subsidiarity involves political control, the best option is to entrust its control to the political/legislative competitors of the European Parliament and Council: the national parliaments, tasked with the mission of watchdog of subsidiarity. This idea relies on the view that the primary democratic organs in Europe are the national parliaments but, as the German Constitutional Court pointed out in its *Lissabon Urteil*,[35] sometimes the national parliaments underestimate this role, giving up competences or not fully understanding the importance of their role.

In this respect the Lisbon Treaty offers some important elements in this field: the codification of a list of competences (although it is not a hard list) and that of the principle of sincere cooperation in Article 4(3) TEU. Subsidiarity and competence are two distinct yet strongly related concepts and, in this respect, a detailed distribution of powers in the configuration of the Union might be useful for the CJEU, since it might help the latter to implement the constitutional nature of the subsidiarity principle under lesser political pressure.

In conclusion, it is possible to identify similarities and differences between the Italian and the EU legal contexts.

Whereas the Court of Justice of the EU traditionally avoids engaging in debates concerning subsidiarity, the Italian Constitutional Court has tried to use subsidiarity to reshape Italian regionalism. Due to the crisis of competences (Carrozza, 2003), the separation of labour enshrined in the Constitution acquires a tendential character (Scaccia, 2009, 175). The paradigm of separation has been overcome but the original design endorsed by the ItCC in judgement 303/2003 has been abandoned (Mainardis, 2011, 486; Repetto, 2020). Different but still interesting trends can be detected in Germany where the national Constitutional Court tried to give subsidiarity teeth, especially between 1994 and 2005 before the constitutional reform dated 2006, which has *de facto* limited the scope of application of subsidiarity by reducing the number of subjects in which *konkurrierende Gesetzgebung* can be triggered (Scaccia, 2009, 35).

The ItCC has tried to give a concrete legal status to the principle of subsidiarity (Armanno, 2010, 280), while the CJEU has always avoided entering this burning terrain and more recently has understood proportionality as a call for transparency.

35 Lisbon Case, BVerfG, 2 BvE 2/08 from 30 June 2009, available at: http://www.bundesverfassungsgericht.de/entscheidungen/es20090630_2bve000208.html.

Both of these strategies have contributed to the difficult justiciability of the principle and its procedural understanding, which has given the principle of loyal cooperation centrality, at least in Italy. Scholars have written of a strong proceduralisation that has led to an evident depoliticisation in the control of subsidiarity (e.g., Scaccia 2009, 129). In conclusion, almost everywhere in Europe, subsidiarity has remained a Cinderella principle because of its evanescent nature and of its difficult justiciability.

Literature

Stefano Agosta, *La leale collaborazione tra Stato e Regioni* (Giuffrè, 2008)

Adele Anzon, 'La delimitazione delle competenze dell'Unione Europea' (2003) 9 *Diritto pubblico* 787

Erika Arban, 'Re-centralising subsidiarity: Interpretations by the Italian Constitutional Court' (2015) 25 *Regional and Federal Studies* 129

Marco Armanno, *Il principio costituzionale di sussidiarietà. Premesse teoriche. Modelli operativi. Esperienza dell'Unione Europea* (Giappichelli, 2010)

Mario Ascheri, *La città-Stato* (Il Mulino, 2006)

Filippo Benelli, *La 'smaterializzazione delle materie'. Problemi teorici ed applicativi del nuovo Titolo V della Costituzione* (Giuffrè, 2007)

Roberto Bin, 'La funzione amministrativa nel nuovo titolo V della Costituzione' (2002) 30 *Le Regioni* 365

Laura Buffoni, *La metamorfosi della funzione di controllo nella Repubblica delle Autonomie. Saggio critico sull'art. 120, comma II, della Costituzione* (Giappichelli, 2007)

Alessandro Candido, 'La leale collaborazione tra intese deboli e forti: una contrapposizione sbiadita (Osservazione a Corte cost. 14 gennaio 2016 n. 1)' (2016) 61 *Giurisprudenza costituzionale* 15

Raffaello Capunzo, 'Le intese fra Stato e Regioni come specificazione del principio di leale collaborazione. La giurisprudenza della Corte costituzionale dalla sentenza n. 303/2003 alla sentenza n. 31/2006' (2006) *Innovazione e Diritto*, http://www.innovazionediritto.unina.it/archivionumeri/0604/capunzo.html

Paolo Carrozza, 'Le "materie": uso delle tecniche di enumerazione materiale delle competenze e modelli di riferimento del "regionalismo di esecuzione" previsto dal nuovo Titolo V della Costituzione', in Giuseppe Franco Ferrari and Giampaolo Parodi (eds.), *La revisione costituzionale del titolo V tra nuovo regionalismo e federalismo. Problemi applicativi e linee evolutive* (Cedam, 2003), 69

Marta Cartabia, 'I principi di ragionevolezza e proporzionalità nella giurisprudenza costituzionale italiana', Trilateral colloquium, Palazzo della Consulta, Rome, 24–26 October 2013. www.cortecostituzionale.it/documenti/convegni_seminari/RI_Cartabia_Roma 2013.pdf

Moshe Cohen-Eliya and Iddo Porat, 'Proportionality and the Culture of Justification' (2011) 59 *American Journal of Comparative Law* 463

Alessandro Colombo, 'The "Lombardy Model": Subsidiarity-informed Regional Governance' (2008) 42 *Social Policy & Administration* 177

Emily Crawford, 'Proportionality' in Rüdiger Wolfrum (ed), *The Max Planck Encyclopedias of International Law* [*MPIL*] (Oxford University Press, 2011) 533

Antonio D'Atena, 'Materie legislative e tipologia delle competenze' (2003) 23 *Quaderni costituzionali* 15

Gareth Davies [a], 'Subsidiarity as a Method of Policy Centralisation' (2006), http://papers.ssrn.com/sol3/papers.cfm?abstract_id=921454

Gareth Davies [b], 'Subsidiarity: the wrong idea, in the wrong place, at the wrong time' (2006) 43 *Common Market Law Review* 63

Giovanni Di Cosimo, 'Trasfigurazione della chiamata in sussidiarietà' (2009) *Regioni* 20

Antonio Estella, *The EU Principle of Subsidiarity and Its Critique* (Oxford University Press, 2002)

Cristina Fasone, 'Competing Concepts of Subsidiarity in the Early Warning Mechanism' (2013), https://papers.ssrn.com/sol3/papers.cfm?abstract_id=2243503

Diana Urania Galetta, *Principio di proporzionalità e sindacato giurisdizionale nel diritto amministrativo* (Giuffrè, 1998)

Luca Gori, 'La "saga" della sussidiarietà orizzontale. La tortuosa vicenda dei rapporti fra Terzo settore e P.A.' (2020), https://www.federalismi.it/ApplOpenFilePDF.cfm?artid=43410&dpath=document&dfile=12052020212907.pdf&content=La%2B%27saga%27%2Bdella%2Bsussidiariet%C3%A0%2Borizzontale%2B%2D%2Bstato%2B%2D%2Bdottrina%2B%2D%2B

Mario Gorlani, 'Il nucleo intangibile dell'autonomia costituzionale dei Comuni' (2020), http://www.forumcostituzionale.it/wordpress/?p=13772

Katarzyna Granat, *The Principle of Subsidiarity and its Enforcement in the EU Legal Order The Role of National Parliaments in the Early Warning System* (Hart, 2018)

Tania Groppi and Nicoletta Scattone, 'Italy: The Subsidiarity Principle' (2006) 4 *International Journal of Constitutional Law* 131

Cesare Mainardis, *Poteri sostitutivi statali e autonomia amministrativa regionale* (Giuffrè, 2007)

Cesare Mainardis, 'Chiamata in sussidiarietà e strumenti di raccordo nei rapporti Stato-Regioni' (2011) 39 *Le Regioni* 463

Giuseppe Martinico and Marta Simoncini, 'An Italian Perspective on the Principle of Proportionality', in Stefan Vogenauer and Stephen Weatherill (eds.), *General Principles of Law European and Comparative Perspectives* (Hart, 2017) 221

Ilenia Massa Pinto, *Il principio di sussidiarietà. Profili storici e costituzionali* (Jovene, 2003)

Anna Moscarini, *Competenza e sussidiarietà nel sistema delle fonti* (Cedam, 2003)

Jacob Öberg [a], 'Subsidiarity as a Limit to the Exercise of EU Competences' (2017) 36 *Yearbook of European Law* 391

Jacob Öberg [b], 'The Rise of the Procedural Paradigm: Judicial Review of EU Legislation in Vertical Competence Disputes' (2017) 13 *European Constitutional Law Review* 248

Tommaso Padoa Schioppa, 'Economic Federalism and the European Union', in Karen Knop, Sylvia Ostry, Richard Simeon, and Katherine Swinton (eds), *Rethinking Federalism: Citizens, Markets and Governments in a Changing World* (University of British Columbia Press, 1995) 154

Livio Paladin, 'Esiste un "principio di ragionevolezza" nella giurisprudenza costituzionale?' in Corte costituzionale (ed.), *Il principio di ragionevolezza nella giurisprudenza della Corte costituzionale. Riferimenti comparatistici* (Giuffré, 1994) 163

Giorgio Repetto, 'Das Mehrebenensystem im italienischen Regionalismus: Entwicklungslinien und offene Probleme' (2020), https://www.academia.edu/41906913/Das_Mehrebenensystem_im_italienischen_Regionalismus_Entwicklungslinien_und_offene_Probleme

Emanuele Rossi, 'Il fondamento del Terzo settore è nella Costituzione. Prime osservazioni sulla sentenza n. 131 del 2020 della Corte costituzionale' (2020), http://www.forumcostituzionale.it/wordpress/wp-content/uploads/2020/07/07-Rossi-FQC-3-20.pdf

Ilenia Ruggiu, *Contro la Camera delle Regioni. Istituzioni e prassi della rappresentanza Territoriale* (Jovene, 2006)

Anna Margherita Russo, 'I "Parlamenti regionali" nel Multilayered Parliamentary system europeo: le relazioni interparlamentari attraverso la "lente" del principio di sussidiarietà' (2020) 45 *DPCE Online* 2837

Gino Scaccia, *Sussidiarietà istituzionale e poteri statali di unificazione* (ESI, 2009)

Robert Schütze [a], *From Dual to Cooperative Federalism: The Changing Structure of European Law* (Oxford University Press, 2009)

Robert Schütze [b], 'Subsidiarity after Lisbon: reinforcing the safeguards of federalism?' (2009) 68 *Cambridge Law Journal* 525

Phil Syrpis, 'In Defence of Subsidiarity' (2004) 24 *Oxford Journal of Legal Studies* 323

Greg Taylor, 'Germany: The subsidiarity Principle' (2006) 4 *International Journal of Constitutional Law* 115

Greg Taylor, 'Germany: A slow death for subsidiarity?' (2009) 7 *International Journal of Constitutional Law* 139

Akos Toth, 'The Principle of Subsidiarity in the Maastricht Treaty' (1993) 29 *Common Market Law Review* 1079

Luca Pietro Vanoni, *Federalismo, regionalismo e sussidiarietà: forme di limitazione al potere centrale* (Giappichelli, 2009)

Herbert Wechsler, 'The Political Safeguards of Federalism: The Role of the States in the Composition and Selection of the National Government' (1954) 54 *Columbia Law Review* 543

Concluding remarks

Regionalism: Italian lessons offered to complex states seeking legitimate and effective governance while being reluctant to federalism

Eva Maria Belser[1]

I. The beginnings of Italian regionalism: balancing between opposite aspirations

In 2001, the Italian constitution was significantly amended in order to redesign the relations between the central, the regional, and the local tiers of government. The aim of the reform was to introduce a new mode of cooperation between the centre and the peripheries of the Italian state, to better accommodate unity in diversity, to encourage institutional innovation, and to improve good governance. The reform affected all political entities, municipalities, metropolitan cities, provinces, regions, and the centre, but its main focus lay on the regions, which were to become strong centres of political, legislative, administrative, and financial power.

The idea of regions operating as crucial intermediate entities between the central and the local tiers of government had been a controversial and much-disputed ingredient of Italian statehood since its beginning. Given the fabulous geographic, political, cultural, linguistic, economic, and social diversity of the peninsula and its islands, a full-blown unitary state appeared as an unrealistic plan, even to those who would have preferred to have one. When Italy united, the centralistic nation-state was the model of the time and federalism still a new and rare model of state organisation. While some Italians enthusiastically praised the federal idea as well suited for the diversity of the country, others sturdily rejected it, mostly out of fear for a still fragile Italy with no Italian identity to call its own. The *Statuto Albertino*, the constitution of the Kingdom of Piedmont since 1848, extended to the whole peninsula in 1861, imposed a unitary model, but was largely disregarded and did not silence the claims for regionalism. Those rather amplified when the country was, more than once in its history, tasked with integrating provinces which formerly belonged to the Austrian-Hungarian Empire. Giving a role to the regions appeared as the only possible compromise between those imagining a legislative and administrative unity and those wanting to preserve the great variety of traditions and aspirations. Thus, a new model of dealing with diversity in unity which was neither unitary nor federal had to be found. And it was: regionalism.

1 Professor of Constitutional Law and Co-Director of the Institute of Federalism at the University of Fribourg, Switzerland.

DOI: 10.4324/9781003104469-13

Regionalism as ingrained in the republican constitution of 1948 was the outcome of a long struggle about the right balance between centripetalism and centrifugalism. The unique model first proposed by Gaspare Ambrosini constituted an exceptional system blending both unitary and federal elements. Regionalism was not an Italian invention – the short-lived Spanish Constitution of 1931 had experimented with autonomous communities before. But it was in Italy where the "third way" of giving regions a role oscillating between a genuinely autonomous federal and an administrative unit, came to stay. It was also in Italy where the term "regional state" was coined and from where it started to travel to many other parts of the world where it raised the interest of countries, such as Belgium, Spain, the United Kingdom, Poland, South Africa, Kenya, Sri Lanka, and many other countries characterised by great diversity and – at least at first – a deep reluctancy towards federalism.

The 1948 constitution endowing regions with legislative and administrative powers was drafted by a directly elected Constituent Assembly hoping to silence separatist claims and to replace an obsolete administrative system and an inert bureaucracy. The Assembly produced a supreme law, not a *foedus* resulting from negotiations between different territories, peoples – or regions – of the country. The regional state, composed of 15 ordinary and 5 special regions, was based on decentralisation and asymmetric autonomy. As often, asymmetry had already been a matter of fact, geography, demography, politics, culture, and economy, before it became a matter of law. The ordinary regions of Italy were either historic entities which had constituted independent states before unification or new units designed to serve the purpose of the new regional state. The special regions, in contrast, had never been fully integrated in the united Italy. They were either islands (Sicily and Sardinia) or bordering areas with linguistic minorities (Aosta Valley, Trentino-Alto Adige, Friuli Venezia Giulia). They all enjoyed some level of autonomy and were hungry for more – the potential secessionist trouble-makers thus had to be appeased to save the country from exhausting turmoil. As it is often the case in federations, regionalism was the compromise acceptable to most Italians, not their vision or dream.

The making of the compromise was eased by foreign intervention as Italy was confronted with international obligations resulting from peace treaties and imposing special treatment to special regions. Much sooner than most other countries, Italy thus had to realise that the treatment of (bordering) regions and their populations was not a purely internal matter to which the rule of non-interference applied. A large number of interventions by kin- or neighbour states or the international community has since spread this insight to other parts of the world. One of the many lessons Italy has to offer in this regard is that international interferences when transposed into transparent international obligations are not necessarily illegitimate or harmful to the country but can facilitate the making – and prevent the breaking – of a power-sharing arrangement. The Paris Peace Treaty of 1946 imposed obligations aiming at the protection of the German-speaking minority in South Tyrol – the *raison d'être* of regionalism. It is here in the northernmost region that the heart of Italian regionalism beats.

Another important innovation of the Italian constitution of 1948 was the establishment of a judicial system of constitutional adjudication. As in Austria and Spain, both innovations, regionalism and judicial adjudication by a specialised court, were triggered by the desire to end authoritarian government. On the one hand, autonomous regions should serve as territorial counterpowers checking and balancing the centre; on the other hand, a constitutional court should strengthen the rule of law and serve as a counter-majoritarian mechanism protecting rights and freedoms. Born out of the same anti-authoritarian atmosphere of post-war Italy, regionalism and judicial review are profoundly interlinked. Entrenching regional autonomy and sharing power between the centre and the periphery needs a neutral umpire adjudicating conflicts between the various actors of the same state. In the absence of such an umpire, it is unlikely that the more powerful centre and the national majority it represents stick to a deal of power-sharing. Power, after all, has a natural tendency to increase and concentrate, not to spread and be given up.

II. The reform of 2001: passing a stage on the difficult path towards regional emancipation

Despite the new post-war arrangements, however, a strong centralist thrust prevailed. Path-dependency and political reluctance prevented the new trends from rapidly changing the institutional and political landscape, and neither the constitution nor the judiciary were able to transform the centripetal culture. Like in many other countries confronted with the tremendous task of rebuilding a dramatically devastated and disunited country, centralism was considered the better and more efficient approach – by those in power at least. Here again, Italy offers an important lesson: the fact that power-sharing is accepted, entrenched in the constitution, and welcomed as the only or best way to solve long-standing conflicts or governance failures, does not mean that it is later put in practice. While the Italian national parliament stalled the implementation of the constitution, the Constitutional Court curtailed regional powers by interpreting them narrowly and by referring to the national-interest clause. In addition – and because of that – the regional legislatures remained institutionally and politically weak. Italy was still characterised by a centralist spirit, and regional and local forms of government could only develop timidly.

With the exception of the special regions, the idea of regionalism had to await the 1970s to finally be invigorated by national legislation as part of a broader political deal. Even then, the political culture of centralism left its mark. When direct elections started to be held in all the regions, regional party competition reflected national strategies and mostly copied the features of the national party system, sharing its instability. Outside of the Northern special regions, where ethno-regionalist parties continued to play an important role, the main function of regional elections was to serve as a testing ground for potential national coalitions. Consequently, national leaders subordinated regional campaigns to national strategies, even at the price of losing regional elections. In 1995, a new regional electoral system introducing the direct election of regional presidents and replacing proportional election by a first-past-the-post system, was supposed to stabilise the regions politically and to invigorate power-sharing. However, the centralised party system did not easily make room for regional politics.

Even though centrifugalism had always been a characteristic of the Italian constitutional edifice, it had difficulties to determine its features in practice. A fertile soil for change was only created at the end of the millennium when the economic, social, and cultural situation changed, the traditional political parties weakened, the European concept of subsidiarity left its marks, and regional sentiments in the north vigorously resurged. Numerous decentralising modifications paved the way to the reform of 2001. After a period of constitutional stalemate, a first constitutional breakthrough was achieved in 1999 when the 15 ordinary regions were given the power to adopt their own statutes, to define their form of government, and to make their institutional arrangements. The reform of 2001, following this path, was supposed to blow real substance into regionalism and to narrow the institutional and financial gap between the special and the ordinary regions. Italy was to become a more symmetric system with regionalism spreading to the entire country.

The fascinating reform was put together quickly and without much conviction by a centre-left coalition attempting to appease the rising power of the Lega Nord (a party later dropping "the North" in order to become a national party). It brought numerous changes: new actors, such as metropolitan cities, the entrenchment of the subsidiarity principle, the possibility for ordinary regions to increase autonomy by negotiation, a detailed list of exclusive national and shared competences, a new allocation of residual powers to the regional level, and the abrogation of the overbroad national interest principle. To mark the equal rank of national and regional legislation, regional laws were no longer to be submitted to an *ex ante* control; instead, regional and national laws – almost alike – were to be challenged by constitutional review. In addition, the fiscal capacities of regions were to be strengthened.

Numerous Italian observers as well as outsiders considered the reform as a far-reaching first step to the federalisation of Italy. For a short time, the Italian state was qualified as quasi-federal, federalising, or almost federal. But soon it became clear that the Italian parliament, now in the hands of a centre-right coalition, was not too eager to implement the reform, and that the Constitutional Court was not able or not willing to enforce the new constitutional arrangements. Thus, the high expectations raised by the reform were rapidly disappointed and the "federal" departure delayed once more. The obvious difference between the constitutional system and its practice curbed the enthusiasm for federal reforms, and regionalism, as a third genus – neither federal nor unitary – once again came to the floor as the only viable compromise. But for many reasons, even the "little sibling" of federalism (as Peter Häberle once labelled regionalism) did not succeed in pushing back centralist traditions.

First, the constitutional powers of the regions did not hold what they seemed to promise. The constitutional practice soon revealed that regions were not granted a great margin of manoeuvre. While it is true that the Constitutional Court abstained from striking down impugned provisions in a number of cases, it was not very open to institutional diversity and tended to reduce the supreme norms of the regions to mere political or cultural statements. As the scope and legal relevance of the statutes of ordinary Italian regions are thus limited, they are far from constituting or resembling constitutions. They are also subject to broad homogeneity requirements – and end up being very similar.

The direct and non-simultaneous election of regional presidents, however, stabilised regional executives, and helped the national and regional party dynamics to differ. Interestingly, Italian party regionalism is not characterised by new parties establishing themselves but by traditional parties maintaining their power in the regions while losing it at the centre. Due to a majoritarian system which even includes a majority bonus, the regional party system has been more merciful with traditional parties and hardly touched by the rise of new populist parties occupying the national scene. Regional presidents and mayors increasingly take an independent approach towards the central party line, are often at odds with the party leadership in Rome, and have been able to carve out some room of manoeuvre and to strengthen self-rule. Their self-confident stance offers the best hope for the regionalisation of the party system and the further development of the Italian regional state.

The strengthening of regional presidents has come at the price of weakening regional assemblies meant to be the harbour of regional representation. The new regionalism *in statu nascendi* surely took a blow when the Constitutional Court in 2002 prevented regional councils to identify as parliaments. The councils were to have significant legislative power – even the power to adopt a regional statute establishing a regional form of government – but were prevented from viewing themselves as representatives of a regional constituency. While it makes sense to see the parliament in Rome as the sole place of national representation, it is far from self-evident that regional councils cannot be the place of regional representation. It is true that the decreasing power of subnational parliaments is a phenomenon which is not unique to Italy. Most parliaments are currently struggling to determine the political fate of a political entity and to oversee and direct the executive more and more deeply involved in intergovernmental relations. But denying the label of being a parliament surely does not help.

What about the reshaping of financial relations the 2001 reform aimed at? The old financial system suffered from two major shortcomings. On the one hand, it was based on central state transfers and the heavy strings attached to them crushed regional autonomy. On the other hand, the transfers were based on former spending, compensated inefficiency, and gave no incentive to save up. The aim of the finance reform was thus to reduce the large fiscal gap and to inject efficiency and democratic control into the system by prompting a better match between those who decide, those who benefit, and those who pay. At the same time, the reform had to ensure an equalisation system effective enough to prevent the socio-economic cleavage between the northern and southern parts of the country from deepening.

Such broad principles of fiscal equivalence and equalisation can be found in most federal systems but are implemented in few. Italy is no outlier in this regard.

For many years, the reformed financial constitution has remained on paper. When parliament in 2009 finally adopted a law, it was a framework law delegating the matter to the executive which took it up only hesitantly. As a result, no dramatic change has taken place. The tax system remains mostly centralised, and autonomous regional taxes are still the exception. The most relevant reforms occurred in the field of fiscal discipline. But when the parliament constitutionalised the principle of balanced budget as imposed by the EU fiscal compact, EU driven austerity measures further curtailed the financial margin of autonomy of regions, even of the special regions.

The interdependence of financial and institutional aspects partially explains the current stalemate. While finances can fuel institutional improvements, they can also block them. Autonomous regional resources are necessary to bring regional autonomy to life. It is, however, hard to conceive a profound change of the financial regime without the regions taking part in the decision-making. The fact that the centre it not willing to give up its dirigiste approach, especially in financial matters, openly or implicitly monopolising the debate about power-sharing, thus perpetuates a deficient system and acerbates the asymmetry of Italian regionalism.

Even though the reform aimed at narrowing the gap between special and ordinary regions, Italy for the time being remains a country characterised by deep *de facto* inequality between the regions, and by exceptional *de iure* inequality. Asymmetry affects most elements of governance, constitutional status, rank of statutes, legislative and administrative powers, institutions, intergovernmental relations, and financial regimes. Each special region thereby is special in its own way and evolves differently. All attempts to open regionalism to all regions, to reduce asymmetries, and to broaden the experiment of the third way to all Italy brought only very partial and unstable success. Although several regions, some encouraged by unequivocal political mandates provided by popular referenda, started negotiations to become "less ordinary", the discussions ended up in a cul-de-sac. As money matters, the project of differentiated regionalism seems doomed to be frozen as long as the implementation of the financial relations reform is deficient. Even if ordinary regions should manage to complete the negotiations making them close to special – and even if all regions were to become special so that specialty became the new ordinariness – a fundamental asymmetry would remain: the original status of special regions is entrenched and irrevocable, while a newly achieved differentiated status would always be devolved and susceptible of being revoked unilaterally by the national legislature.

III. The Constitutional Court: adjudicating a vague regional system

Another reason preventing the reform from fully fulfilling its promises is the attitude of the Constitutional Court. The case law of the Court soon contributed to attenuate the clear separation of competences and to widen the field of concurrency. The duty of the state to implement EU directives and regulations and to defend Italy's performance in Brussels and Luxembourg was crucial for this evolution. The state was allowed to interfere with regional affairs in case of non-compliance with EU law, before involvement in other regional matters was tolerated. Matters of compliance with overriding law hence became more and more intermingled with matters of competence – and the state ensured compliance not merely by monitoring, supervising, and imposing but by substituting itself for the regions. This tendency of supervisory and substitutional powers might be linked to the absence of an explicit supremacy clause in the Italian constitution. Instead of imposing overriding law, the Italian Constitutional Court postulates concurrency to empower the state to enforce its external obligations internally, thereby limiting exclusive regional competences almost to extinction.

Given the numerous challenges linked to implementing an ambiguous constitutional reform when the inertia of parliament and government must be tackled, the question of the role of the judiciary must be raised more generally. The reform of 2001 aimed at strengthening the position of the regions before the Constitutional Court and to transform the umpire in a powerful actor able to operate as a neutral arbiter between the tiers of government. The Italian parliament was no longer competent to review regional laws on substantive grounds. The change implied the acceptance of the fundamental idea that regional laws do not require the implicit or explicit approval of the majority represented in the national parliament and thus can differ from what the majority believes to be the right way forward. Such change requires trust – that the region will make proper use of its autonomy, that the centre will accept regional decisions even when it disagrees, and that both will submit to the judgement of the judiciary in case of conflict. Without such a clear departure from majoritarianism, regionalism and diversity cannot flourish. Until the reform, the Italian Constitutional Court had mostly been seen as guarantor of fundamental rights; with the new millennium it more and more decidedly – and at the price of being overwhelmed by cases – took the role of guarantor of competences as well.

Was the Constitutional Court up to the challenging task of umpiring a flawed multitier system based on an unclear wording of the constitutional provisions dividing power between the state and the regions? Was it the right actor to deal with the unfinished implementation of legislative, administrative, and fiscal power-sharing? Was it strong and independent enough to constrain spoilers of power-sharing? One of the many lessons Italy has to offer to other power-sharing systems is that the role of a constitutional court is overstrained when it is mandated to interpret a hastily drafted constitution with numerous semantic flaws, to implement a reluctantly drafted legislative, executive, and fiscal reform and, in addition to all that, to compensate for the notorious lack of an effective institutional representation of regional interests at the state level. Channelling conflicts about self-rule and the consequences of the insufficient shared rule into judicial litigation runs the double risk of drowning the court in hundreds of cases and of judicialising political trade-offs and politicising the judiciary. There is no doubt that some constitutional courts manage to sort out constitutional ambiguity and to fulfil the challenging function of making sense of open and broad constitutional norms and to adapt them to new circumstances, moods, and aspirations. But courts need inherent stability and a conducive environment to operate as a crucial turntable of power. An environment is conducive to judicially led power-sharing when courts are anchored in an overall spirit of subsidiarity and compromise, and in a political culture of respecting actors of different tiers as partners cooperating face to face and on equal footing. And when both tiers of government are equally guided by the constitution and the democratic will of their constituencies. If such an atmosphere is missing, constitutional courts struggle to fulfil their mission. They cannot – on top of their constitutional role – compensate for insufficient institutional cooperation between the state and the regions and blow a "regional" spirit into actors preferring to inhale and live off central air.

Hence, it does not come as a surprise that principaliter review as done by the Italian Constitutional Court since 2001 has been broadly criticised for its trend to instrumentalisation. It is inherent to power-sharing systems that subnational units are more likely to challenge national legislation when they are controlled by opposition parties. A fully nonpartisan use of constitutional review can only be expected when the regional branches of national parties enjoy as much autonomy from the central party as the regions from the state. This condition is rarely fulfilled. Hence, the capacity of constitutional courts to fulfil their role as guarantor of the power-sharing system often depends on regions falling into the hands of the opposition. However, constitutional courts cannot play their role when they are perceived as mainly occupied by solving political quarrels in the disguise of a constitutional conflict.

The Italian Constitutional Court strongly relied on the principle of loyal cooperation to deal with constitutional unclarity, and to sort out hitches of the system. However, this principle limited the powers of the regions. The Court soon started to apply the (later partially codified) principle of loyal cooperation to infringe on clearly defined regional competences and to broaden the spheres of national influence. What is particularly interesting about the Italian case is that the Court then gave the principle yet another crucial meaning. When it opened the door to centralising intervention, it simultaneously compensated the regions for the loss of powers suffered. The principle of loyal cooperation, rapidly becoming the cornerstone of state-regions relations, was operationalised by the Court to strengthen shared rule where self-rule was compromised. When interfering in regional matters, the state legislature must ensure appropriate regional participation in the decision-making process and abstain from unliteral action.

IV. Regional participation: opening the door to negotiations

Notoriously, the Italian constitution does not provide for formal consultation of regions and cooperation processes. The Senate was not designed to fulfil such role and all attempts to transform it into a territorial chamber failed. Remarkably, the Constitutional Court succeeded in introducing regional participation "through the backdoor" of loyal cooperation. This is a significant judicial innovation. Apex courts typically tinker around the division of powers between the different tiers (and tend to be more favourable to subnational units when their participation at the centre is weak) but rarely get involved with the sharing of power. It is rather unique that a court paves the way for the institutional involvement of subnational units at the centre. According to Italian case law, the non-observance of a strong regional involvement in state law-making processes can lead to the invalidation of the impugned law – as if (explicit) constitutional participation processes had been violated. Just like in many other federal systems, shrinking regional room for manoeuvre is thus – at least in part – compensated by enlarged participation and cooperation duties.

Seeing the parliamentary structure of Italy, the participation of regions has always been organised outside of parliament, the permanent conference of the State and the regions playing an increasingly dominant role. In keeping with the principle of loyal cooperation, regional governments must be involved in state decisions. If no agreement can be reached, the suggestions of the regions must be considered, and reasons must be given when the state deviates from views expressed and agreements made – these are minimum requirements validating the state's unilateral decisions. While it is true that the central government is still vested with the power of ultimate decision – even when agreement is required and each region is given a veto right – all major reforms were subject to negotiations and agreed by the two tiers of government.

Regional participation and the necessity to find a vertical agreement are particularly crucial in Italy, as the combination of the principle of loyal cooperation with a centralising reading of the principle of subsidiarity profoundly challenges the constitutional power-sharing arrangement. In most multitier systems, having embraced the principle of subsidiarity, the focus lies on the negative or scaling-down side: competences are constructed bottom-up and the higher level of government only intervenes when the lower, closer to the citizens, is not able to fulfil a task. The main function of subsidiarity then is to serve as a break to centralisation, injecting self-restraint into the centre and self-confidence into the units. However, there is also a positive or scaling-up side to subsidiarity: the centre then attracts powers the lower units can no longer fulfil – or not to the satisfaction of the centre. When authorities apply this form of power attraction, subsidiarity operates as an instrument of – and justification for – centralisation. When the principle of subsidiarity allows for the upward shifting of constitutional competences of the regions to the centre, the very idea of power-sharing – and constitutionalism – is at stake. Subsidiarity then turns out to be a Trojan horse reshaping the competences entrenched in the constitution. The fact that such in- or extra-constitutional upward shifting of competences requires the approval of regions only partially serves as a consolation to the invaded Trojan population – as it is only their leaders negotiating with the Greeks and agreeing on new arrangements.

In most federal systems, second chambers only very partially fulfil their role of representing territorial interests. They do, however, serve as a parliamentary countermajoritarian device thereby relieving the courts. Replacing them by intergovernmental bodies necessarily shifts power from parliaments to executives, transfers public parliamentary debates into more secretive bargain-making, and affects the overall system of checks and balances. Such is particularly the case when state and regional executives acting jointly can agree to disregard the supreme law and the distribution of competences it provides for.

As the layer cake with its watertight competence departments has long ago given way to the dynamic marble cake and even more complicated bakery products, most significant government activities require combined efforts of both the centre and the subnational units. Hence, it does not come as a surprise that the relevance, density, and frequency of intergovernmental relations are increasing in all federal systems. This is also true for systems with fully-fledged territorial second chambers, be they senatorial or ambassadorial. The subnational autonomy is shrinking in almost all federal systems as national and international standards and directives increasingly frame regional decision-making. Hence, voicing regional and local concerns at national and international levels becomes an increasingly important factor of good governance: government failures are inevitable when the entities implementing policies are not involved in their making. In most federal systems, just like in Italy, the necessity of more and deeper information exchange and cooperation has given rise to a system of conferences in which the executives come together to debate, and more and more frequently, to decide. The bodies and procedures aim at giving regions a collective voice in national decision-making and allow for input and feedback loops. Such cooperative regionalism is crucial but comes at the price of strengthening the executives and reducing the role of parliaments. The Italian State-Regions Conference stands not alone with its competence to initiate legislation, and to give its view on budget laws: just as other intergovernmental bodies, it evolved from an advisory body to a forum where governments of different tiers co-determine national policies. The effects on democracy and transparency are far from ideal. When competences are blurred, so are accountabilities. However, collective action also affects diversity. An overwhelming need or obligation to cooperate horizontally and to coordinate vertically risks crushing the space of diversity. Systems of executive conferences often require subnational units to speak with one voice, despite their diversity of views and priorities, and thus limit the potential of representing different regional standpoints.

The question therefore emerges whether regions should be allowed to raise their own individual voice and to talk separately to the state. Here, the Italian experiences are particularly inspiring. The principle of bilateral negotiation and cooperation brings the necessary flexibility to the system, ensures the equality of the parties, and safeguards their diversity. For each special region of Italy, a joint body with an equal number of representatives from both sides is in charge of clarifying and amending powers and finances. While guaranteeing parity, such bilateralism, however, also augments imparity between the ordinary and the special regions as well as the differences between the five special regions – as they all make their separate deals with the centre, the outcome depends on *de facto* powers, imparity hence increases over time. Such accommodation of special regions limits democracy, in particular the democratic control of the executive. As the outcome of bilateral negotiations overrides ordinary laws, parliament has no means to raise its voice. Regional bilateralism also affects the rule of law as the Constitutional Court is reluctant to strike down implementing decrees. By presuming that the approval of both sides ensures the constitutionality of an agreement, the Court applies the old rule "*qui dit contractuel, dit juste*" and permits consensus to trump constitutionalism.

Bilateralism thus has an unexpected effect: it allows the governments of two tiers, if they manage to reach consensus, to substantially change the basic laws made to constrain their powers.

V. Adding levels of government: from a dyadic to a multilevel system?

The 2001 reform failed to reach the goal of narrowing the gap between the special and the ordinary regions. How did it affect the municipalities located in special or ordinary regions? Like other federal or devolved systems, Italy struggles to evolve from a dyadic regime to a triadic or multiple arrangement. The old federations typically considered the local level a creature of the subnational units and turned its back on it. Similarly, old international organisations were blind to the internal organisation of their members and operated dyadically between the international and national level. More recently, federal systems have turned their attention to local governments, adopted national strategies and laws to guarantee their autonomy and to empower cities in particular to function as hubs of innovation. Similarly, international organisations have opened the black box of member states' internal organisations and reached out to lower tiers.

The EU integration process differs diametrically from the regionalisation process in member states. While the first aims at bringing into being an ever closer union and tends to centralise policies, the regionalisation focuses on opposite objectives. While the two processes are different, they inform each other in various ways. Borders are increasingly permeable, and ideas, concepts, and trends, as well as hesitations and reluctances, leak from one level to another. Regions have rebelled against European intrusion into their spheres of competences, but have also been constructed or strengthened under the economic influence of European financial flows. Despite a move from EU blindness to a concept of a Europe of regions, the European architecture has not developed into a full-fledged multitier system in which subnational units are fully recognised actors. It is true that regions are no longer mere containers of economic development policies and have been able to carve out some constitutional space. However, as the member states determine how and when to consult their subnational partners and to transmit or filter their ideas, concerns, and warnings, regions still struggle to turn into political actors in their own right. The states rather continue to function as doorkeepers. Unfortunately, most member states are not very eager to speak with more than one voice, and the EU, preferring the single voice to the chorus, seems to consider regional involvement more as a burden than as a crucial contribution to the union.

Has Italy been more successful in transitioning from a dyadic to a multilevel system? At first sight, the reform of 2001 was ground breaking for the local tier. Local governments and metropolitan areas received a constitutional guarantee and were endowed with more autonomy. However, the strong momentum for the local authorities was not sustainable. The national legislature was in no rush to fulfil the constitutional promises and curbed the enthusiasm for local powers. Just as for the autonomy of the regions, a reversal trend soon occurred knocking back the pendulum of decentralisation. In reaction to an enormous amount of litigation, the Constitutional Court soon undertook it to rewrite the division of legislative and administrative powers. As in relation to the regions, the Court rarely used the principle of subsidiarity to bring government closer to the people and to contain the centralising zeal of the state, but – quite the opposite – instrumentalised it to allocate competences to the higher level.

As in many federal systems, the national interest in the local tier creates the risk of turning the power-sharing arrangement into an hourglass system. Subnational units then fear to be wiped out between a dirigiste centre and empowered local governments. The Italian Constitutional Court did little to reassure the regions but made it clear that the state was free to make laws on the powers and functions of local authorities, irrespective of the regions' development plans for their urban centres.

As often, economic constraints played a crucial role in curbing devolutionary fervour. When the outbreak of the financial crisis marked the beginning of an anti-regional backlash, the parliament and the Constitutional Court interpreted national principles more extensively, and curtailed regional and local autonomy in financial and other matters. Regions and local governments, however, are suffocated when austerity measures are devolved instead of powers and resources. Italy thus seems to confirm the widespread concern that power-sharing is a fair-weather model which cannot take a blow.

There is ample evidence that constitutional power-sharing arrangements – even when guaranteed by an independent judiciary – have a hard time to be implemented. Successes are often slow and unstable. The progresses one government achieves are often undone by the next. Periods of enthusiasms for decentralisation are often short-lived, and when their time is over, centralist fervours return with new force. There always seem to be countless motives to question, delay, and thwart power-sharing – democracy, equality, efficiency, austerity, urgency being amongst the most popular. Yet the very same motives also speak in favour of decentralisation. Power-sharing deepens democracy, improves accountability, mediates tensions, and allows fast and tailor-made reactions. But these beliefs, while regularly convincing constitution-makers, seem to be extremely volatile. They find it hard to take root in centralist grounds. This is why so many authors and experts refer to the federal spirit or culture of autonomy and partnership without which power-sharing cannot flourish – no matter what the constitution says. In Italy, as in many federal systems, this spirit is not only absent at the centre, but often seems to lack in the regions as well. Constitutional arrangements alone are clearly not sufficient to achieve deep transformations. In Italy, as in many other parts of the world, the never-ending season of institutional reforms or attempts thereof, seem unable to herald a new spring or summer.

The Italian experiences with regionalism are so rich that they cannot possibly be summarised. It is not even clear what regionalism is and what distinguishes it from unitary and federal systems. What is the distinctiveness of regionalism? Can it be situated in a continuum between the two or is it a third model of its own?

Given the trials and tribulations of Italian regionalism, there cannot be an easy answer. It seems clear that any attempt to provide an answer must consider asymmetry as a characterising element of the system. Italy has the longest and deepest experience with asymmetry and applies different rules to almost everything. But when we look for subnational autonomy serving the aim of diversity, what do we find? The ordinary regions have not succeeded in discarding their role as subordinate bodies with limited autonomy. Competences and resources have only very reluctantly been given to them, and few ordinary regions have developed a sustained enthusiasm for using them, innovating and going their own way. The two main islands, Sicily and Sardinia, currently enjoy a degree of autonomy which resembles much more the one of ordinary than of special regions. At the end, the only truly special regions are the two small alpine areas, Trentino-South Tyrol and Aosta Valley, inhabited by sizeable minority groups.

Regionalism *all'italiana* in fact is a peculiar, unique, and inspiring power-sharing system. It is made of a rather unitary state divided into regions, characterised by impressive *de facto* diversity and far-reaching legal homogeneity, and two truly special regions. The "normal" regions of Italy are subordinate to the centre and depend on it. Like in unitary states, they struggle to become more than administrative units fulfilling the plans of the state by spending its money. In contrast, the two special regions in the North confront the central government on terms of equality. The joint committees, which are quasi-legislative bodies (and at times quasi-constitution-making bodies) follow procedures resembling international relations. Decisions require consensus, an agreement or a *foedus* between the parties. Hence, when it comes to the making of shared rule, the status of the two northern regions is stronger than the one of most subunits in federations. In the sphere of bilateralism, these regions have veto powers. They can oppose any change and do not risk to be overruled by other regions or subjugated by the centre. In many regards, the two northern regions have the status of member states of Italy – the state allows their right to internal self-determination and cannot deprive them of their powers without their consent. In sum, Italian (special) regionalism in the North does not only reach deeply into the federal toolbox, but adds important confederal elements. The lessons Italy has to offer in this regard are most important: regionalism *all'italiana* can offer real guarantees to special regions. These guarantees can be strong and effective enough to compensate, at least in part, for a lack of trust. Federalism as we know it cannot operate without a federal spirit. This is particularly true for multinational federations characterised by a dominant nation and one or several smaller groups risking to end up as permanent losers – even when there are second chambers and qualified majority requirements. What guarantee does an individual unit have when it is different in culture, language, religion or ethnicity from the other units? Why should numerically small groups like the Tamils in Sri Lanka or the Kurds in Iraq or in Syria build trust in a system when any agreement, even a constitutional one, can be revised or broken by the majority? As long as such a group has no veto rights, no constitutional provision, and no second chamber, no court can truly make it feel safe in the long run. It is the concept of bilateralism, the touch of confederalism, which can add the glue necessary for distrustful partners to cooperate peacefully and efficiently. In this regard, regionalism is not the little sister or brother of federalism, as which it is often seen. It rather stands on a par and has a lot to offer – to unitary and federal states!

Index